He Was
FIRE
AND ICE

He had three wives—yet he conducted one-night stands wherever he went, sometimes hiring three prostitutes for a session.

What he spent on custom-made shorts was more than most of his employees earned in a year—yet he screamed if they discarded pencils longer than stubs.

His tyranny led to heart attacks and crack-ups among the people who worked for him, yet he endowed charities and hospitals with an open hand.

He was so lonely he summoned subordinates as company in the middle of the night, yet he dropped his wife after ten years of marriage without a word of goodbye.

He was an undisputed leader in the business world, yet he hungered for a kind of recognition that was always just beyond his grasp.

He was Charles Revson—the man who
built the Revlon Empire—
and this is his
UNAUTHORIZED BIOGRAPHY

About The Author

ANDREW TOBIAS, a graduate of Harvard College and Harvard Business School, writes for *New York* Magazine. *Business Week* called his last book, *The Funny Money Game*, "highly entertaining—no, outrageously funny."

FIRE AND ICE

The Story of Charles Revson—
the Man Who Built
the Revlon Empire

by Andrew Tobias

WARNER BOOKS

A Warner Communications Company

Library of Congress Catalog Card Number: 76-6124

ISBN 0-446-82409-7

A portion of this book originally appeared in *New York* magazine.

This Warner Books Edition is published by
arrangement with William Morrow and Company, Inc.

Cover design by Gene Light

Cover art by Tom Hall

Warner Books, Inc., 75 Rockefeller Plaza, New York, N.Y. 10019

 A Warner Communications Company

Printed in the United States of America

Not associated with Warner Press, Inc. of Anderson, Indiana

First Printing: August, 1977

10 9 8 7 6 5 4 3 2 1

for my parents

Acknowledgments

I could not thank all the people who took time to help me prepare this unauthorized biography—and not all would want their names to appear. Let me thank at least these:

The late Charles Revson himself, for agreeing to cooperate with what he knew would be at best not a totally flattering portrait, and for allowing me three magnificently pampered days on his yacht;

His younger brother, Martin; his former wife, Ancky (and her husband, Ben Johnson); and his sons, John Charles and Charles, Jr.;

Former Revlon employees, particularly Sid Stricker, Bill Mandel, Walter Ronner, and the late Kay Daly; Joe Anderer, Barbara Britton, Bea Castle, Howard Cohen, Dan Cone, Charles Diker, Lillian Dunn, Joe Famularo, Sheldon Feinberg, Sidney Fread, Andrew Furlane, Andre Goutal, Suzanne Grayson, Norman Greif, Ruth Harvey, Robert Hoffman, David Horner, Jerry Juliber, Robert Kamerschen, Charles Lachman, Warren Leslie, Ray Myers, Jack Price, Burt Reibel, Dan Rodgers, Dr. Harvey Sadow, Mike Sager, Joel Schumacher, Dorothy Silverman, Eli Tarplin, Sy Wassyng, and Michael Wyler;

Current Revlon employees, particularly Joe Liebman, Irving Botwin, Stan Kohlenberg, Jay Bennett, Dave Kreloff, Paul Woolard, and Sol Levine; Bob Armstrong, Victor Barnett, Irving Bottner, Gail Boucher, Dr. Earl Brauer, Sandy Buchsbaum, Harry Doyle, George Feld, George Hastell, Sam Kalish, Jerry Levitan, Mickey Soroko, Marty Stevens, Irving Sunkin, Larry Wechsler, and John Williford;

And others not directly employed by Revlon, particularly Carl Erbe, Iris Gallin, Harry Meresman, Max

Samberg, and Jack and Lorraine Friedman; A. C. Bailey, Hazel Bishop, Earl Blackwell, Gertrude Brier, Antonio Branco, Ben Colarossi, Mildred Custin, Barbara Dorn, Barbara Feldon, Bill Fine, William Fioravanti, Dr. Bernard Herzog, Jules Holden, Lauren Hutton, Louise Keller, Dorian Leigh, Stuart Levin, Manchester High School, Lucio Martella, Aileen Mehle, Norman Norman, Suzy Parker, Henry Rice, Eugenia Sheppard, Elsa Sieff, Ray Spector, Erica Spellman, Dr. Alfred Steiner, Selma Stetzer, Dr. Joseph Stovin, the marvelous Mr. Wu, Dan Wynn, and Jerome Zipkin.

I taped one, two, or three interviews with most of these people, and the transcripts of those interviews run to around a million words. Special thanks, therefore, to Rosemary DeTore for transcribing all those tapes, for helping with the library research, for typing the manuscript, and for offering numerous insightful comments.

Special thanks also to James Brady, Marie Brenner, Nora Ephron, Joni Evans, Richard Fischoff, Gael Greene, Carol Hill, Sterling Lord, Patrick O'Higgins, Ed Rosner, Liz Smith, and Bill Stern, for their stories, contacts, advice, enthusiasm, and support.

And to Clay Felker and Sheldon Zalaznick, of *New York* Magazine, for their patience with a project that took much longer than planned.

Indebted though I am to all those named above, the responsibility for the material in this book is not theirs but my own.

New York City
February 1, 1976

Contents

FIRE
AND ICE

(I)

New York on $5,000 a Day

Well, he certainly was an original.
—Lauren Hutton

It is the fall of 1972. Charles Revson is on the phone with the assistant manager of Campbell's funeral parlor, trying to arrange for the burial of Norman Norell, namesake of a major Revlon perfume. He is used to dealing with the manager at Campbell's, not the assistant manager, but the manager has stepped out. "This is Charles Revson," he says. "Do you know who I am?" The man apologizes. "Charles Revson, Charles Revson—don't you know who I am?" Sorry. "Where's your boss?" He stepped out.

Revson tries another tack: "Mr. Norman Norell. Do you know who *he* is?" He doesn't know Norell, either. "Norman Norell! You don't know who Norman Norell is?" He is supposed to be making funeral arrangements, but he hasn't been able to make contact with this man. He says, "You don't know Revson, you don't know

13

Norell. *You live in New York?"* The man says something about the suburbs.

Charles's inclination is to hang up and wait for the man's boss to return, but he still has to make the funeral arrangements. He says: "Norman Norell. He's a leading name in fashion, if you don't know him. He's just died at Lenox Hill Hospital and I want to make arrangements. Go over and get him. I don't know what he is." By which Charles means religion. Norman *Levinson* was his real name, from Noblesville, Indiana.* He was half Jewish, half something else. "I don't know what he is," Charles says, "so I don't know what the service is going to be. How big is that chapel of yours?" The man says it seats however many people, and Charles says, "No, it doesn't." He's arguing with the guy. "Oh, it has a balcony? You have to *tell* me that when you talk to me. How big is your air-conditioning unit? It's going to be very hot there." The man says it's whatever it is, and Charles says, "I don't know if that's enough, couple of thousand people going to be there . . ." The man reassures Charles that they've had plenty of people there and the system has been adequate. So Charles says, "Well, I don't know yet if we're going to have it at your place, but you go pick him up and fix him up and we'll see. I'll be down in a little while to pick the box. My name is Charles Revson— don't you know who I am? Well, when I get there make sure the other guy's there." Click.

The point is that there certainly were people who didn't know who Charles Revson was. (No, *Peter* was the race car driver who was killed . . . Charles's *nephew*, not his son.) On the other hand, Charles Revson was not the sort of person whom, once you had met him, you would easily forget. "I know that man," a waitress at the Sands in Las Vegas said as she refused to allow his party at her table. "I can't deal with him."

Shortly after noon on a Sunday in August 1975, with only a nurse in attendance, Charles Revson himself died. He left:

* Designers Halston, Bill Blass, and Ken Scott also grew up in Indiana.

14

One cosmetics and pharmaceuticals empire—Revlon, Inc.

Three ex-wives—including one whose name he couldn't remember, one on whom he had cheated like a cardsharp, and one—Lyn—on whom he walked out days after giving her $30,000 in a tin can for their tenth anniversary (she wore everything he hated to the funeral).

One brother—with whom he had feuded bitterly for thirteen years.

Two sons and two stepsons—all working for their father, none entrusted with the execution of his estate or the direction of his charitable foundation.

One granddaughter—on whom he was able to lavish the affection he denied everyone else.

Hundreds of shell-shocked, verbally assaulted, overworked, overpaid, and in some cases wiretapped executives.

Scores of intimate one-night acquaintances.

And, withal, a great many more admirers than is commonly thought.

He left, too, an estate valued at barely $100 million. It would have been more had he not been given to spending money on a par with men five and ten times as wealthy. Raised in a cold-water flat in Manchester, New Hampshire, he had fought his way up to a standard of living that was New York on $5,000 a day. Literally.

His mahogany-paneled living room was by no means the world's largest, but it was ample (26' by 36'), particularly when you appreciate that it was the living room not in his triplex penthouse but on his triplex yacht. (The first element in gracious New York City life-style, as any New Yorker knows, is a place to get away from New York.) Air-conditioned so vigorously as to require electric blankets on every bed, the *Ultima II* was 257 feet long—a full New York City block; slept fifteen guests; and employed a year-round, full-time, uniformed staff of thirty-one—nine officers and twenty-two crew. It was powered by the equivalent of ten Cadillacs and a Toyota. Its propellor blades measured eight feet from tip to tip. A thirty-foot air-conditioned launch, a twenty-four-foot speedboat, and a little motorboat sat on one corner of the deck like bicycles on the back of a Lincoln. Sixteen bathrooms, twenty-two touch-tone telephone extensions . . . a walk-in freezer for the several hundred pounds of specially-cut meat flown down from New York before each cruise (A typical shopping list telexed from Puerto Rico to New York. sixty pounds of chateaubriand, twenty pounds of corned beef, twenty pounds of brisket, forty-eight pounds of hamburger, 168 chickens and sixty ducks.) Without taking into account its adjoining study and enormous dressing room, the Revson stateroom occupied 391 square feet—more than twice the size of the master stateroom on the presidential yacht *Sequoia*. Six other *Ultima II* staterooms were not much less grand. After Onassis's *Christina* and Niarchos's *Atlantis* Revson's was the largest private yacht in the world. (Too large. its captain pointed out, to dock in most yacht basins.)

Revson bought the *Ultima II* in the summer of 1967 from D K. Ludwig, the secretive billionaire shipbuilder, and then went about a major overhaul and total redecoration. The Burma teak decking alone. hand laid in Naples, cost $125,000 Also three new electric generators; two new evaporators (to desalinate 10,000 tons of water a day) rada with a fifty-mile range forty-eight sterling silver place settings from England forty-eight gold-plated setting from France two movie projector for nightly movies engraved gold lettered Cartier stationery with the blue, green and white "R" flag flowing in the wind, at $1.75 or so for each sheet and envelope (about what it costs to manufacture a 750-page telephone book), fine wood paneled walls . . .

Ask for a typewriter at the Mayflower Hotel in Washington and the front desk will not even be able to arrange to have one rented to you Ask for it aboard the *Ultima II* and the response was. simply, "Will you require carbon paper sir? Sniffle imperceptibly at lunch and Kleenex would be waiting by your deck chair when you went to take the afternoon sun You wish pizza? Sweet and sour pork? Lobster Newburg? Filet mignon? Fresh-squeezed juice in your Dom Perignon? Chief steward Wu would positively *run* to bring what you desired. And

16

not out of fear, either, but pride. He would watch you take your first cup of coffee and, if it met with your pleasure, deliver every cup that followed precisely that way.

The *Ultima II* cost $3.5 million to buy and refurbish, perhaps a fourth what it would cost to reproduce today. The maintenance and crew, the transoceanic phone bills, the Gucci Bingo prizes, the fuel ($20,000 for a tank of gas), the steaks, the buckets of golf balls whacked off the bridge by 1975 expenses were averaging $1,800 a day. Add in the cost of tying up $3.5 million, plus depreciation and the ship cost Revson, personally, better than $3,000 a day. Four days out of five no one used it.

Little wonder that after his death potential buyers were not besieging the estate with offers. Henry Ford looked and decided it was too rich. The Arabs, by and large, are not yachtsmen. There is Adnan Khashoggi, of course, but at the time of Revson's death he already owned one yacht— Revson's old one, in fact—and had another under construction. (A Milanese minerals magnate was all set to buy it, then backed out the day before the closing. A Dutch-based petrochemicals potentate, Samuel Johannoff, bought it instead. He paid in the neighborhood of $2 million.)

Yacht aside, there were scores of $650 suits and $1,000 tuxedos, dozens of pairs of $300 shoes. I came, I saw, and I counted. Each custom-made Jule Holden button-down shirt cost $42 (there were ninety-eight at his apartment), each pair of pajamas, also custom-made, was $68 (his last order was for a dozen pairs), each pair of custom-made undershorts, $26.50. (I didn't count his shorts but one executive tells of having had to transport an order of sixty pairs from Switzerland.) These plus eighty-six monogrammed handkerchiefs, ninety-five pairs of black socks, etc., were stored in glass-fronted drawers he designed to be able to tell at a glance what was where. And the custom-made drawers were just a small part of a custom-made cooperative apartment that easily qualified as one of New York's most expensive. It was sold after his death—in a terribly depressed real-estate market—to the Shah of Iran's twin sister for $1.4 million. But even at that it represented no capital gain. He had purchased the Park Avenue triplex from the estate of Helena Rubinstein for a mere $390,000 in 1967, but spent thirty months and $3 million gutting it and redoing it to his gold-everything taste.* It had been an extremely open, airy, cluttered, eclectic apartment. His first step, characteristically, was to seal shut all the windows and provide a controlled, artificially-lighted, air-conditioned environment. Fans ran at all times, blowing warm or cool air; the electric bill alone approached $100 a day. Maintenance charges came to another $200. And that did not include the eight live-in servants or odds and ends like food.

If anything, the apartment was too large. The board-room-like dining room seemed embarrassingly empty with fewer than twenty-four guests, so most dinners were served in the library. The third-floor marble-and-mirror ballroom (which had been Madame's picture gallery) and its adjoining industrial-sized kitchen cost $750,000 to do up, but were used not even once. Oilman Leon Hess, whose company's 1974 profits dwarfed Revlon's, manages to get by with half a floor in the same building.

Unlike many chief executives, Revson charged off none of his apartment or his yacht to the business (and deducted only 15 percent of the yacht in figuring his taxes). And then you had the country estate at Premium Point; the $200-a-day Waldorf Towers suite (formerly Herbert Hoover's) he camped in while the Rubinstein apartment was being made over; the masseur, the medical bills, the phone bills, the florist's bills, the $50,000 fifteen-minute gambling losses, the million-dollar U.J.A. pledges, the chartered jets . . . plus Lyn's chauffeur, Lyn's $3,000 dresses ("I'm sure he was in favor of them," his brother Martin says, "but not five at a clip"), Lyn's jewelry, Lyn's pinball machines, Lyn's daisy chain of $100 bills, Lyn's lunches at Lutece . . . there was no way Charles could

* When Madame Rubinstein had herself first tried to rent the apartment, she was turned down for being Jewish. So she bought the whole building. When she died, an attorney purchased it from her estate and turned it into a co-op. It was from him, actually, that Revson bought the apartment.

make ends meet on his $1,650,000 annual salary-plus-dividends. He had occasionally to sell a few of his million-plus shares of Revlon stock.

"It was a pleasure to go shopping with him," his second wife, Ancky, recalls wistfully, "because he bought everything in sight. Anything that looked good on you you could have. That was fabulous."

He enjoyed realizing fantasies. Paying three women to service him simultaneously . . . standing at the helm of his own floating castle . . . placing a $5,000 chip on a single number at roulette. As a boy, he had taken baths in a tub that doubled as a washbasin. It would be filled part way from the tap—cold water—and then pot after pot of hot water, heated on the stove, would be dumped in until there was enough of the lukewarm mixture to bathe in. At 625 Park Avenue, in a resplendent bathroom easily large enough for a chic little cocktail party, he made sure he had the fastest draw of any marble tub in town. Special water tanks were installed on the roof to step up the flow.

A Revson secretary who lived "in constant fear" from 1968 to 1971, by which time the man had mellowed a good deal, put together a handbook for her successor. It ran 108 pages and included instructions on flowers. ("If Mr. Revson is invited out, always include $150 for flowers as his gift to the hostess"); on every detail of office decorum ("Check that Kleenex boxes are at least half full . . . Curio shelf should be dusted. Mr. Revson is concerned about the items on this shelf . . ."); and on the daily nap ("It is the responsibility of the second secretary to prepare his sofa for rest . . . The sofa pad is to be kept in the bathroom closet on a hanger with clips"). The manual specified that the Revson bathroom be checked hourly, and that there always be "two glasses, his brush and three combs" out on the sink. Only twice in the previous year, the author noted, had Revson deviated from Geisha-brand tuna salad at lunch in the office (when he opted for a well-done hamburger); but for the occasional sorties out to the plant the secretary was to order a "double, double corned beef on rye, very lean with no fat, with mustard, wrapped in tinfoil. Also ask for a very old pickle . . ." An elaborate telephone procedure included the information that all Revson's phones have "a cut-off switch. The moment Mr. Revson picks up on any wire, you cannot hear the party on the other end." One frequent caller, the manual advised, was Lyn Revson. "He always takes her calls no matter who he is with or where he is." Still, "Mr. Revson is fully entitled to his privacy. Therefore, any caller, including Mr. Revson's immediate family, should never be informed concerning Mr. Revson's whereabouts or who he is meeting with."

Revson liked this manual and handed its author five $100 bills on her last day at work.

(II)

Separating Truth from Legend

We had just come from someone's funeral. I forget whose it was, but he was lauded and eulogized—and he was a prick. When we got back and were having tea, Charles said: "When I go, I don't want any of that bullshit. I want the good and I want the bad."
—Evan W. Mandel,
former Revlon executive vice president

No one who grows up in a tenement, starts a business in the middle of the Depression, and ultimately builds a half-billion-dollar global corporation, is ordinary, or even "normal." Charles Revson least of all. His business style was so abrasive, his personal style so eccentric, and his success so stunning, that he became something of a legend not just "in his own time" but, indeed, midway through his career.

In forty-three years he built one of the 300 largest industrial enterprises in the United States, and one of the 200 most profitable. He managed to do this not by capitalizing on a single great invention—which is easy once you have the invention. Nor by acquiring the ongoing enterprises of others and merging them into his own, as were built so many of our largest corporations, from General Motors and United Airlines to Gulf & Western and ITT. He was granted no monopoly, he was no bootlegger-turned-legit, he struck no oil—he didn't even have friends in high places.

Instead, Revson built Revlon product by product, shade promotion by shade promotion, country by country, year by year. Most men would have sold out and retired by the time the first $10-million plateau had been reached. The kind of entrepreneur who can take a company from nothing up to $10 million in sales is often not suited, either by temperament or training, to take it the next step, or the next or the next. But Revson, like very few other entrepreneurs, took his company all the way to the top. He sold the first bottle of nail enamel personally, and he was deeply involved with the selling of the half-billionth bottle. He wasn't just nominally in charge, after a while, checking in from the golf course to see how his young dynamos were doing. *He* was the dynamo, and he was running the place. To the day illness forced him to stop, he was the chief executive officer of the company—and, for all intents and purposes, the chief operating officer, the creative director, the marketing director and, for that matter, the *board* of directors.

This is not to say that he was a creative genius or an executive superman. He was not. You could even make the case that after a certain point his company would have been better off without him. But he did have a deeply probing, agile mind, incredible dedication and tenacity, a genius for color, an eye for detail, and an instinctive marketing sense. He also had the rare capacity, at least in part, to broaden himself and his horizons as the company grew. The extent to which he was *not* able to do this was, largely, what made for his peculiarities and for the Byzantine way in which he ran his company.

Revson's handpicked successor, Michel Bergerac, will not be a legend, because he is just the kind of highly accomplished multinational business executive you would expect to find at the head of a company like Revlon. But put into the same spot a Charles Revson, whose father was a cigar-roller in Manchester, New Hampshire (Bergerac's father was an executive in Europe), who never got further than high school (Bergerac collected graduate degrees in Paris and Los Angeles), and who never even worked for any other large company to see how it was done (Bergerac was executive vice president of $11-billion ITT), and you have the stuff of quite a story. Not to mention massive insecurities, two hushed-up "heart attacks," and a nervous stomach.

In the annals of American business, Revson has to be compared not with Helena Rubinstein and Elizabeth Arden, though those comparisons are themselves fascinating, but with staggering egomaniacs like Walt Disney or even the original Henry Ford. *Big*-time sons of bitches. He entered a fledgling, highly unprofessional industry of one-man shows (one-woman shows, really) and, more than anyone else, was responsible for building it into a $5-billion industry. While his social impact was obviously not as great, nor as practical, as that of Henry Ford, he nonetheless changed the appearance of women throughout the world—both in how they looked to others and how they looked to themselves. He injected a little excitement into what Martin Revson, borrowing from Thoreau, liked to call the "quiet desperation" of the average housewife's daily life.

The irony is that he held women in such contempt. And that he himself, the beauty-maker, was so unbeautiful.

The paradox is that, for all the warts, many of the people who knew him well—women particularly, but men, too—fell in love with him. Literally, or as a sort of father figure.

It would be easy to paint Revson only as a bullying egomaniac who would scratch his crotch or stand up and break wind in the middle of a meeting. In fairness, one tries to understand *why* a man as concerned with his image and dignity, and as afraid of being embarrassed, would do such things. He *was* the terror of Madison Avenue, but it's not enough to say that he would degrade

23

his subordinates or that he was often hopelessly inarticulate. The question is, why? What was he trying to say?

The problem with legends-in-their-own-time is that it is sometimes difficult to tell where truth leaves off and legend begins. Truth, at least as much as beauty, is in the eye of the beholder. Or "the beholden," as Charles used to say.

"There are so many myths built up around this man," his friend and executive assistant, Irving Botwin, told me, "such as, to be perfectly frank with you, that he's tough, he's a prick. He's not. He finds it tough to fire somebody. He's the softest-hearted and most compassionate guy in the world."

Like any man, and perhaps more than most, Revson had different sides, different moods, acted differently with different people, and changed somewhat over the years. (Botwin saw him at his best . . . and subsequent to our several interviews was left $250,000 in Revson's will, one of only two nonrelatives who got a thing.) It's hard enough, then, to pin down the "real" Charles Revson, as though all his actions could have been predicted by a simple formula. And it's made all the more difficult by having to see him through the eyes of others, who have their own axes to grind. Needless to say, one doesn't hear too many stories in which the narrator himself comes out the fool or the blackguard. More often, the narrator is the hero with the clever tongue who, alone, would stand up to Charles and set him straight.

Revson loyalists go to great lengths to laugh off as "myth" anything that might seem the least bit unbecoming. Beware, they say, of talking with people who have left the company and who ascribe their own lack of success to some failing in Charles. Meanwhile, people outside the company dismiss those within as a coterie of lackeys not worth talking to.

But to a larger extent than either group might have expected, the basic pictures that emerge from each are not so very dissimilar. The main difference is in point of view. Both groups agree, for example, that Charles frequently tore his executives apart (though the loyalists

24

deny he would bring grown men to tears). But the loyalists ascribe this to his desire to teach, while others ascribe it more to a need to bully and degrade. Both groups, with a few exceptions, concede the man's basic honesty. But the loyalists attribute this to pureness of heart, while some others see it as an inordinate fear of being caught doing something dishonest. One group sees him as having been generous; others concentrate their attention on the motives behind the generosity. And so on.

Certainly, though, apart from differences in point of view, stories abound which are simply untrue. One day, while Charles lay in intensive care at Columbia Presbyterian Hospital, an ex-Revlonite, George Abrams, who claims to have invented the chocolate chip cookie, was telling me that Revson was in fact on his yacht, cruising in the Caribbean with a helicopter hovering overhead, ready to fly patient and doctor to shore at a moment's notice. How did Abrams know this? He had "heard it from a good source."

So, to begin with, one must disregard almost any information that is not, in some way, at least, first-hand. But that by no means suffices to screen out the unicorns. A key Revlon executive told me that Lyn Revson had given him a tour of their Park Avenue apartment and had shown him their huge bed—which, he said, had been fitted out with special flaps to prevent Charles from falling out at night. Charles tossed and turned a lot, Lyn told him, and these flaps would automatically come up at two in the morning to form a sort of cradle, and recede at six. Lyn pressed a button on the wall that activated these flaps "before his very eyes," he said.

Now, it is true that Charles often had trouble sleeping that he had a huge bed; and that his apartment was customized almost beyond belief. But despite the fact that this story comes from a supposed eyewitness, who owed his six-figure income to Revson, it is, as near as I can tell, complete fantasy. "Why in the hell would he want to fall out of bed?" his former wife, Ancky, asked when asked if he ever did.

Yes, there was a button on the bed that would elevate the head-and-shoulders portion of the mattress up to a

TV-viewing angle. And, yes, there was a button concealed in the side of the bed that summoned the police, who would come dashing up to the apartment every time it was pressed accidentally. But—and I inspected this bed at some length—there were no automatic side flaps. Yet this man (and only this man) swears he saw them.

Similarly, when Revlon was moving into new offices at 666 Fifth Avenue, Charles did have the manufacturer of the boardroom chairs come to him for a "sitting," and did go through four different handmade models before he was satisfied. But he did *not* have them built so that all the directors, regardless of height, would end up at eye level—or, as the story is best told, with him one inch above the others.

(On the other hand, it *is* true that, presented with a series of valuable eighteenth-century Piranesi etchings for his approval, he said, "Shit, Sam, couldn't we get the artist back to put a little color in them?")

In verifying any story it helps to have *two* eyewitnesses. To be sure, even husband and wife, witnessing the same event side by side, will not remember it identically. Yet the fact that details don't check out does not alter the substance of the story:

"Richard and I were on vacation at the Dorado Beach Hotel in Puerto Rico in June of 1966," one such eyewitness told me, "and one night, in the plush gambling casino, Revson and Lyn arrived and asked to have a table roped off privately so that he could play blackjack on all six available hands. I remember the chips he chose were some odd color that I hadn't seen before—purple, I think—and which later turned out to be either seventy-five- or hundred-dollar chips (Richard and I, you understand, were working on one-dollar chips, as was most of the casino.) A crowd formed behind Revson (looking smashing—the most terrific suit and socks and shoes) and Lyn, who perched next to him like the straight man and looked up at him adoringly. He was gambling five or six of the purple chips on each hand, but was as calm and cool as could be, almost as if he didn't care. It was impossible to tell from his expression whether he was winning or losing—yet the climax, for me, came when

26

one of the groupies behind Revson, clad in her Dorado Beach finest, empathized to the degree that when he asked for a 'Hit me' on some draw, she gasped—'Oh, no, don't do it!' Revson, hearing her, turned around very slowly in his seat and glared at her. *Now here's the problem* [italics mine]: *I* remember him saying to her, 'Shut up, you cunt,' but *Richard* remembers him saying, 'Shut your fucking mouth, lady.' Whatever it was he did dare to say was so crude and shocking that the crowd recoiled in horror. Revson then turned to his table in disgust, picked up his chips, and walked out—as though to blame his loss of concentration on this terrible spectator. We didn't see him again, and I never discovered if he was staying at the hotel."

Unfortunately, there are no "White House tapes" to nail down with certainty just what Charles did do or say on a given occasion.* Nor can I vouch for any of the Revson stories at first-hand. But one thing did happen during an interview with Charles's brother, Martin, that I think sheds some light.

Martin's spacious Park Avenue office makes no pretense to magnificence, as Charles's did. There is no elaborate private washroom, for example, but rather a coat closet and a sink. Still, it is the office of a millionaire, a former Revlon executive vice president, and the chairman of a small cosmetics firm listed on the American Exchange. It is also the office of a proud, conservative man, who, though very likable and down-to-earth, is concerned with projecting a dignified image.

We had finished the interview and were both getting ready to leave, he to visit Charles in the hospital and I to go home. Martin went to the coat closet, donned his overcoat, donned his rubbers, pissed in the sink, and showed me out the door.

Now, I have two points to make. If I saw one Revson

---

* I did manage to come by the verbatim transcript (expletives deleted) of a rambling two-hour talk given to his marketing people in 1969—"the culmination of all my experience and I just didn't want it wasted"—from which a number of quotes throughout this book are taken.

piss in the sink in front of a virtual stranger—a reporter, no less—then I can believe that another Revson, known to be rather more crude and less personable, would do equally unorthodox things, or worse, when not under the gaze of the press. I was told, in fact, that Charles used to piss in the sink, too. But at the same time, this is just the kind of incident that is easily overblown. The fact is that Martin was quite discreet in what he did—he didn't stand back and arch, or anything—he was not out to demean anyone; he offended no one . . . and, oddly, it wasn't all that crude a thing to do. Not at all. It wasn't as if he had pissed on the carpet or out the window, which would have been an entirely different story. In other words, yes, most of the Revson stories that first-hand witnesses tell are probably true, if often embellished. But many of them, considered objectively, are less damning than they seem.

For example. One day Revlon was rehearsing a commercial that would be performed live in front of 50,000,-000 people a couple of hours later on *The $64,000 Question*. There was no one in the theater but the technical crew, the model, the agency people and the people from Revlon. Charles was in the control booth. As they were running through this commercial, Charles's voice boomed out through the empty theater. "GET RID OF THAT GIRL, SHE LOOKS TOO JEWISH!" ECHO, Echo, echo. And the model, naturally, burst into tears and went running off the stage with two hours to air time.

What no good storyteller will bother to point out, and neither of the eyewitnesses who told me the story did, is that Charles almost surely did not know that the mike in the control room was open or that anyone outside would hear him. Which, if so, makes his conduct (a) a good deal more believable and (b) a good deal less offensive.

Thus there were often unreported circumstances which retrieve the man from utter caricature. He *would* take his pulse during meetings, he *would* check the color of the phlegm in his handkerchief, and he *did* have an electrocardiogram taken daily when he traveled. But he had also had two mild "heart attacks" in his midforties, which

28

were kept very quiet. Knowing that, his hypochondria seems a little less outrageous. Likewise his bizarre eating habits.

There is the temptation to take sides. To say, with Victor Barnett, perhaps the least-liked executive at Revlon and the loyalest of the loyalists, that Charles Revson was "a truly great human being." Or to say with Josh Rothstein, former president of one of the companies Revson bought, and one of his most passionate detractors, that Revson was "the worst bastard who ever lived." Not surprisingly, the truth lies somewhere in between. Many spoke in terms of love/hate feelings. As one former Revson associate summarized: "He was not the most wonderful person around and certainly not the worst. At times, he had the worst characteristics a man can have in his need to diminish people. I think he is most interesting through his contradictions. He could do it all; he could make you want to die and he could make you want to live."

However his virtues and motives might be debated, and however murky the details surrounding certain of his affairs, the basic outline of Charles Haskell Revson's life is clear enough. He was born in Somerville, Massachusetts, outside Boston, on October 11, 1906. He grew up with his older brother, Joseph, and his younger brother, Martin, in Manchester, New Hampshire. There his father worked for the R. G. Sullivan Company, rolling the "724" cigar by hand, and his mother worked on and off as a saleswoman and supervisor at Nightingale's, a novelty and drygoods store. Both were Russian-born Jews. His mother, Jeanette Weiss Revson, was brought to America by her family while still an infant. His father, Samuel Morris Revson, emigrated in his early twenties to avoid conscription into the czarist army.

In Manchester the family lived in a six-unit tenement house on Conant Street. Their apartment faced the rear on the first floor. They had running cold water, a coal-burning stove for cooking and heat, and always plenty to eat. Oatmeal or Cream of Wheat with Dutch hot chocolate for breakfast, lamb chops or steak for dinner many nights, fish on Friday, and a roast of some kind on Sunday.

Almost everyone else on the west side of Manchester, the wrong side of the Merrimac River, was Gentile. Martin can remember only one other Jewish family. The Revsons kept largely to themselves. They virtually never entertained, virtually never went out to eat, attended no synagogue, and had no telephone. (Or radio or gramophone.)

Joseph, who in his own way was even stranger than Charles fell behind in school because of illness. Though sixteen months older, he and Charles were in the same class in elementary school (the Varney School) and throughout high school. Martin trailed four years behind. Charles and Joseph got along well and would often do their homework together, although physically and emotionally Charles and Martin seemed to come from one mold, and Joseph, from another. Joseph, red-haired and pasty-faced, was the aloof one, off in his own room; Charles and Martin, although further apart in age, palled around more and shared the same room—even, for a while, the same bed.

The boys walked to school, nearly two miles each way, on even the coldest New Hampshire winter mornings. Joseph, miraculously, graduated second in their class of 127 (a boy named Harry Litvinchook was first). The best explanation for Joseph's academic success would seem to have been his memory, his delight in detail, and his ability to learn by rote. Charles who was more outgoing than Joseph and whose intelligence was sharper and more intuitive, graduated third or fourth. The Manchester High yearbook listed Joe's hobby as "reciting" and Charles's as "argumentation." The parrot versus the fox.

Charles was "Slotkin, a tailor" in the senior class play, worked on the school magazine and the yearbook, and helped organize a school debating team. Classmate Louise De Nies, alias "Lulu" or "Weezie," remembered him as having been popular with the girls in the class (although she can't remember which ones), mischievous (though she can't remember just how) and, even then, sometimes

30

curt or cutting with his sense of humor. Joseph, she says, kept more to himself.

Henry De Nies, Weezie's cousin, recalls going with Charles to look for summer work, and standing outside a shoe store, Charles told him, "Look, I'm the better talker of the two of us, so let me go in and see what I can do." After a while he came out. "Well," he said, "it was pretty rough in there and they only would hire one of us and I got it." He spent the summer selling ladies' shoes.

Class president Rufus ("Ruff") King, who starred on the football and baseball teams and still lives up in Manchester, says that the Revson boys kept pretty much to themselves. They weren't on any of the school teams. He remembers that "Chick," as Charles was then called, was "a real peewee." He was still just sixteen when he graduated, and it was only afterward that he shot up several inches to his full five-foot-eight or so. He subscribed to Charles Atlas to build up his body, but never in his life weighed much more than 140 pounds.

The boys belonged to a gang (tame by today's standards) called the Squogs. "Squog" was short for the Pistaquog River, where the boys used to fish, swim, and skate. (A few miles farther up, and accessible by streetcar, was beautiful Lake Massabesic.) The Squogs played baseball with other neighborhood gangs and, to earn money for their gear, all had paper routes. Charles delivered both the morning and afternoon papers, although no one remembers his having been much of a baseball player. Martin was the jock in the family, but so little he was once knocked over by a right-field fly ball. He recalls going around to collect the money for his papers. "I can still smell the smell in the kitchens," he says. "You know, it was like a rathouse. It smelled terrible, between the smell of babies, etc. Not like in a regular kitchen, but in a hole. Like in a poor kitchen."

The Revsons lived in the same part of town, but they lived better and cleaner than most. They were a proud family. Charles's father, whom all three sons called "the Major" (none could remember why), was a five-foot-one, balding, distinguished-looking man, and an introvert. But proud, and forever talking about his family in Russia

31

who had been "purveyors of grain to the czarist government." (Just how successful his family really was is an open question.) A Litvak Jew, he took pride in the supposed superiority of the Litvaks over the Galicians. And while he obviously was not a great success the job he advanced to at R. G. Sullivan- packing the various shade of tobacco attractively- did require a modicum of artistry He didn't look like he belonged on the west side of the river people said; he looked more like a banker. When the family moved to Brooklyn in 1925 in the hope of bettering its financial situation he became a life insurance salesman But, being neither especially aggressive nor articulate nor personable he did not excel.

He was not a practical thinker He was, instead, an ill-equipped intellectual Martin remembers him as having been "very curious and interested in world affairs but not too sound in his conclusions One of his friends knew a couple of instructors at St Paul School in Concord, and it seemed to Martin that they always talked about "fascinating things they didn't want to have get around— and usually it was about socialism." Whether he was more a frustrated Russian aristocrat or a frustrated Socialist revolutionary, or just confused, the Major had no difficulty adapting to the luxuries his sons provided him later in life.

Charles's mother was the taller and more outgoing of his parents Many years younger more practical, more dynamic. A fair cook but not much interested in the house Where the Major led a secluded life always reading, her prime interests were on the outside. "I don't think there was a great marriage between my mother and father" Martin says She died of a strep throat in 1933. (Penicillin discovered in 1929, had not yet come into practical use.) It may have been from his mother that Charle inherited much of his drive the rest would have stemmed from a need he felt to supply the success his father's pride cried out for.

Upon graduating from Manchester Central High School in 1923 along with "Weezie De Nies "Dimples' Dexter, "Ruff' king "Spoofy' Reed "Red Revson, and the rest, "Chick' left Manchester for New York, where he went to work selling $16.75 dresses for a cousin's Pickwick Dress Company. With that, the family's hope that he would become a lawyer began to fade He was getting an education in women's fashion instead By the time he left Pickwick he had worked his way up to being a piece-goods buyer, a job he preferred because it gave him the opportunity to work with materials and colors. He supposedly became proficient in differentiating between shades of black which demands a sensitive eye.

The story goes that Charles was fired from Pickwick in 1930 for buying too much of a pattern he fell in love with. By the time it was apparent the pattern would sell out, he had already found himself other work. Supposedly, he went right into selling nail polish for a company called Elka in New Jersey. *Actually* he ran off to Chicago with Ida Tompkins, the daughter of a farmer from Pennsylvania and a show girl (according to sketchy accounts), and married her instead of the lovely girl at Pickwick he'd been expected to wed. His parents were heartbroken when they found out.

In Chicago he signed up with an outfit that sold sales-motivation materials Sales plans. The year 1930 was not the most auspicious time to start selling them, however, and for the next six or nine months he was in Chicago things were very bad. There were days when he had hardly anything to eat. He returned to New York with his wife but had no better luck selling the sales plans They soon separated Charles enjoyed confiding to intimates that it was because the girl's parents were sure he would never amount to anything.

Whoever Ida Tompkins was, she should have tried to stick it out a little longer as from here things started to go right for Charles He moved back in with his family, by then living at 173rd Street and Amsterdam Avenue, and began selling nail polish for a firm in New Jersey. Then with his brother Joseph and a man named Charles Lachman now described alternately as "the world's oldest living hippie and "the world's luckiest man," he formed Revlon The "l" was for Lachman who says they were first going to name the company Revlac, but it didn't sound good.

Revlon was born on March 1, 1932, when Charles Revson was still only twenty-five. Unfocused to this point, his life would be, for the next forty-three years, 100 percent Revlon.

(III)

The Obsession

In terms of marketing, you've got to have the will to
win. You've got to see the blood running down the street.
You've got to be able to take it. You've got to be able to
shove it. If you're not, you're nobody. You never will be.
You think you are? Fine. Love it. Go on—have happi-
ness, have love, have this, have everything. But as far
as marketing is concerned [which is what *really* counts]
—*nyenta*. Nothing.

—Charles Revson

Whatever else he was—nasty, crude, lonely, virile, brilliant, inarticulate, insecure, generous, honest, ruthless,
complicated—Charles Revson was a man of single-minded
persistence and drive, entirely dedicated to his business.
And a perfectionist. You could even say he was a fanatic,
in the same way Bobby Fischer is, or J. Edgar Hoover
was. Each lived exclusively for his own particular "business," and each knew his business better than anybody
else.

"To Charles, Revlon was not a business, it was a religion," explains Irving Botwin. And while, unlike Fischer and Hoover, Revson had enough sexual diversions to fill one of those FBI file cabinets, even these were carried on with a certain market researcher's detachment. Women were his business. And nothing distracted the man from his business. The day John Kennedy was shot, Charles was in a meeting in New Jersey at the offices of Evan-Picone, a sportswear company he had bought the year before. A secretary came into the conference room with the news. Revson looked up, got up, walked around the room, and then continued with the meeting. The secretary was instructed to keep them posted. What good would it do to listen to the radio or call off the meeting? Would that help Kennedy? Not everyone would have been able to concentrate on the spring fashion line after hearing such news, but Charles Revson could.

Nor was he one to sit around at home wallowing in the national tragedy. On the official day of mourning, when businesses were closed and families throughout America were sitting sadly around their television sets, Charles Revson was at Revlon headquarters presiding over a marketing meeting. There was too much work to be done to take the day off. Because no matter how large or profitable Revlon grew, it was always nothing compared to what it should be. Nothing was ever right. It was one continuous crisis (a state of affairs he fostered), which only he could straighten out. "Why am I the only one who thinks around here?" he would complain to his people, most of whom were killing themselves on his behalf.

On November 9, 1965, the evening of the great blackout, he was up at the lab—his great love—working with a group of people on the new men's line Revlon was introducing. (Braggi.) Bill Mandel, his top marketing man, was there; Norman Greif, the newly appointed head of the lab, was there; Sam Kalish, a miniature Revson who would later be sent out to terrorize the international division, was there; and several others. Charles was pontificating about how he wants the image and how he wants the look and how . . . and the lights begin to

36

flicker. And he is going on about the concept and the market . . . and they flicker again Suddenly the lights dim and go out altogether. Charles, people who were present swear, did not miss a beat. He simply went on talking in the dark.

In those days the company was selling little candles soaked with the Intimate fragrance. Someone groped around for a batch of them, and the meeting. which took on the look of a séance (but a considerably stronger smell) went on for a good forty-five minutes more, by candlelight, until Charles decided he was through. Fairly soon, of course, word filtered in from outside that this was no blown fuse, but rather a full-scale emergency. But Revson would have none of it. "That's Con Ed's problem." he snapped. "They don't worry about how we sell lipsticks." He felt he had important business to finish, and finish it he did.

(Later driving into Manhattan in Bill Mandel's car, as his chauffeur had been unable to make it up to the lab through the chaos, he turned his attention to the blackout—and, now that he was focusing on it, became thoroughly intrigued. The sensible thing would have been to drive *away* from the city the ten minutes or so to his home in New Rochelle. But he was not about to let this emergency push *him* around. He insisted on going into the city, snuffed traffic lights and lifeless elevators be damned. And when he stopped off first for his well-done greaseless steak at Billy Reed's Little Club, he would not accept the fact that an electric kitchen couldn't prepare a steak during a blackout. In great detail, he instructed Billy Reed on how to rig up a special burner of some sort . . . and he got his steak.)

The weekend in 1969 when the first astronauts were landing on the moon—certainly one of man's more dramatic achievements—Revson called Joseph Anderer at home. His call came about ten minutes before mankind, in the persons of Neil Armstrong and "Buzz" Aldrin, was to land. Anderer, an ex-marine flier, said, "Charles, I don't want to talk to you now. I want to watch them land." Being president of Revlon and on good terms with

Charles, he could talk to the chairman of the board that way.

"Oh," said Charles, not used to being rebuffed. "I didn't think that was the big thing. I thought it was when they got out and walked."

"Well, it's big enough for me, Charles," said Anderer. "If they get down safely, then we'll worry about their walking. Why don't we talk later in the day?"

Charles frequently called Anderer and others after midnight. "He didn't do it deliberately," says Anderer, who left Revlon at the end of his three-year contract to become president of a half-billion-dollar textile company. "He would just have something right then he wanted to get into and wouldn't be conscious of what time it was. Time meant nothing to him. Being best meant everything."

Revson was just too absorbed by his own world to pay much attention to the schedule of the world outside—and so close to the business he sometimes missed what was going on. There is the story, for example, that he once called a meeting of all his top people to discuss the problem of executive turnover. *Why couldn't Revlon keep its goddamn executives?* The meeting was called for six o'clock on the Friday of a July Fourth weekend; Charles walked in at eight o'clock; and he proceeded to tell the assembled that the *reason* they couldn't keep their goddamn executives was that they weren't *training* them properly.

He knew about national holidays and events like Christmas, of course. But for him holidays were interruptions in the urgent work to be done. He hated holidays and vacations and did his best to keep his people from taking them. As for Christmas, that was no holiday—it was the pivotal selling season and, always, the greatest crisis of all. More than once he called meetings late on December 24—because to him it was just December 24. There were the decorations at home and the chestful of silver dollars for his wife, Ancky, but these were secondary and in the heat of the business easily forgotten. One yuletide meeting was called to discuss how heavy the returns of unsold Christmas-promotion merchandise might be. The

38

bells of St. Patrick's down the street chimed eight . . .
nine . . . ten times. But he was oblivious.

To some extent, of course, Revson would feed his
voracious ego with such displays of power over his people.
But it wasn't that *they* had to stay late while *he* was
home decorating the tree. He was right there at the head
of the table with them. Which suggests, inasmuch as he
was highly competitive with his men, that such meetings
were also a way of testing their stamina and devotion
to the business against his own. Two tests he could never
lose. Then, too, he may simply have been trying to milk
every last ounce of effort out of them, as was his standard
procedure. Finally, he and at least a few of the other men
at such meetings must have taken some pleasure in the
self-sacrifice involved in working late on Christmas Eve.
By implication, it made their work seem that much more
urgent, that much more important.

Still, whatever other motives may have been involved,
Charles's basic obliviousness to time and complete absorption in his own empire were genuine. Like a sports addict
with the score tied in the last inning of the last game of
the World Series, he wondered how anyone could have
his radio tuned to anything else. And for Charles the
score was *always* tied, at best. He never felt secure enough
in his lead to sit back and relax a little; egotist though
he was, he did not think of himself as "a winner." He
was constantly, irrationally afraid he might lose . . .
which is to say, fail.

He made little effort to remember where business began
and left off. Asked to say a few words at a farewell party
at Raffles for one of his international executives—a man
with whose performance he was uncharacteristically
pleased—he turned it into a half-hour harangue of the
others present, chiding them for not performing as well.
This was hardly the occasion for such a lecture. "But
that was Charles," as those resigned to his behavior were
given to saying. He could almost never bring himself to
verbalize praise or thanks or affection. Such warm and
positive sentiments did not fit his tough, manly, street
fighter's self-image, or his generally negative outlook on
life. So that on those few occasions when he *did* say some-

39

thing nice, he generally accompanied it immediately with something cutting or sarcastic. People who were close to him understood this. They could usually tell when he was trying to express the warm feelings that, most of them say, he genuinely had.

He did not waste time going out to lunch or socializing over executive martinis in the middle of the day. Instead, he ate lunch at the office with one group or another of his executives. For years lunch was prepared in a private kitchen by Henri Gieb, formerly chef at "21." For Charles, it would typically consist of an extremely well-done, entirely dried-out hamburger patty, preceded by tomato juice, followed by Jell-O, accompanied by Fresca, and served by either the maid (Rosa) or the butler (James) on magnificent gold-plate tableware in Revson's private dining room.

These were always working lunches and they would sometimes run until four or five in the afternoon. All business. Charles had no patience for small talk. One day Pope Paul was in town and scheduled to pass right by Revson's office as lunch was underway. Charles excused himself to go into his adjoining sitting room for a minute or two, and while he was gone somebody says, "Isn't it great? We have perfect seats to see the Pope—a once-in-a-lifetime thing." And as he is rambling on about how the Pope has never set foot in America before, Charles comes back into the room. "What the hell are you guys talking about?" Charles asks testily (for him a standard entrance.) So somebody says, "We were talking about the Pope's visit." And Charles says, "What the hell for? We don't sell to the Vatican."

One may guess that when Charles said things like this he was only half serious, in the sense that he was conscious of the role he was playing. And, for that matter, he may have assumed the others were conscious of it, too. John Wayne *knows* he is being John Wayne when he is being John Wayne. But whether or not this was the case with Charles, two things are certain: First, he wasn't just trying to be funny. He almost never tried to be funny. Second, though he may in fact have understood perfectly well why his people were talking about the Pope, he didn't want them wasting their—which was really *his*—time with it. Is that what he was paying them so well to talk about? Besides which, Charles could be comfortable in a group of people only if he was dominating it. The Pope's visit was not a subject on which he was the authority, so he would want to belittle its importance and return to the game at which he was, in both senses of the word, master.

Why couldn't these guys concentrate? Christ, you leave them alone for three minutes and they're talking about the Pope. Well, Charles Revson could concentrate. Not just on the business in general, but on individual details, as well. He would home in on a nail enamel bottle and study it and study it long after everyone else in the room would have run out of things to study, and *nothing* would be more important than that bottle. Or that lipstick shade. Or that advertisement. Needless to say, he often drove less exacting people (which is to say, everybody) crazy.

At one lunch he took a phone call, and while he was yeah?-yeah?-ing into the phone, the other men at the table got onto a new topic of discussion. "The trouble with you guys," he said when he got off the phone, "is that you don't know how to concentrate on what you're doing. I'm going to tell you something. You know what that phone call was about? That was my broker, and he told me that I lost a million dollars just now. But it didn't bother me. I got right back into this conversation."

Granted, he had not gotten back into the conversation at all—he had switched it to the news from his broker. And granted, every time Revlon stock went up or down a point, he "made" or "lost" a million dollars—so it was hardly devastating news. But there was no disputing his ability to concentrate. He could spend an hour and a half going over one engraving proof trying to decide what color red the lipstick on the model's lips should be. "It happened all the time," says Norman B. Norman who, for a longer time than most, serviced the Revlon advertising account.

He could go through thirty drafts of an ad before he was satisfied. And then make a change at the last minute. In the early days he had an advertising director working for him named Helen Golby, whose fingernails were bitten and bloody from the experience. She came in to him one day with a mock-up of an ad that was really sensational. But Charles never commented on what was right. What was right could be left alone. He only saw what was wrong. And there was something in this ad, down in the corner somewhere, that didn't look right. So as Helen Golby held up this terrific ad for him to see, he zeroed in on the corner with his fingers and said, "That stinks!" And out she went in tears.

He could see subtleties in color, in particular, that few laymen could see and even fewer printers reproduce. On nothing did he so stickle as on color. There was a meeting of salesmen and distributors at a hotel in Asbury Park, New Jersey, in the forties at which he was to be the main speaker. Everyone was already seated when he arrived. The regional manager made a brief introduction, but Charles refused to speak. He was offended by the tablecloths. They clashed with the rest of the room. This was Revlon, a color-conscious company; he was Revson, the color genius; he owned the goddamn company and was paying the hotel for the goddamn meal . . . and he wouldn't start talking until the tablecloths were changed. It took at least half an hour for the waiters to find acceptable tablecloths, remove all the silverware, dishes, glasses, water pitchers and so forth, switch the tablecloths, and then put everything back again. Then, and only then, could the luncheon begin.

Charles was not being theatrical; he was being typical. He wanted things right.

He set up a full-scale laboratory and sophisticated quality controls long before anyone else in the industry had them; he recalled batches of products long before— thirty years before—product recalls and "consumerism" were invented. Revlon's Sheer Radiance, a recent example, was selling very well when Charles, having first approved it, began to have second thoughts. "It could be better," he said. Right in the middle of a promotion he made them empty every bottle in the house, wash them all, and refill them with an improved formula. Sheer Radiance was out of stock for three months; Revlon lost a small fortune. But he didn't care. He thought the product was a little too frosty, and that it had to be a bit oilier so that women could have more time to put it on their faces. ("Play time.") Any other company that had a product selling so well would either have left well enough alone or gradually changed the formula as new batches were prepared. Not Charles.

If you were a bank president or an advertising hotshot or a potential supplier, you couldn't get him on the phone. But if you were a woman with a Revlon lipstick that smeared, you got through to him like *that*. "The reason I talk to them," he used to say of such consumer calls, "is that they are the real boss."

To show some skeptical ad men how easy it could be for a stranger to get through to Charles Revson (years ago), a Revlon executive told them to have one of their secretaries give him a call. She happened to have a Revlon lipstick in her pocketbook—who didn't?—and she was told to say she had bought it at such and such a place in Brooklyn, and that it bleeds. It's too soft. She called Revson's office, with the others crowded around to hear, and in a minute he was on the line. "You got the lipstick with you?" he asked. She said she had. "Turn it around and there's a batch number. Give me the number." She gave it to him. "What kind of dress were you wearing with that lipstick?" She shouldn't wear *Fifth Avenue Red*, he told her, she should wear *Pink Lightning*. Or whatever. She got a nice lecture about what she should wear with what, her name was put on the list with the consumer relations department, and they sent her samples and questionnaires and everything else.

That batch of lipsticks may not have been recalled; but others were, on the basis of no more than a complaint or two from the field. A malicious competitor could have cost Revlon a fortune in recalls by planting complaints.

If Revson was in the company of a woman using a competitor's product, he had to know why. And in most cases he would replace it with a bunch of his own. When Ruth Harvey was first interviewed by Revson to become his secretary, Charles asked what kind of makeup she

43

was using and she admitted that, though hers was definitely "a Revlon family," this particular liquid makeup happened to be a competitor's. He told her he had this marvelous liquid makeup, called Touch & Glow, and she should wear such and such a color. He called down and got one for her and asked what she planned to do with the competitive makeup. "I guess I'll put it in the wastepaper basket," she said. "No, don't do that," said Revson, "the cleaning lady will get it. Put it down the drain."

Surely he was at least half-joking? Yes and no, says Ms. Harvey, who to this day reveres the man. "When he says something like that," she believes, "he is saying it with a certain amount of charm, but he is dead serious."

Charles would not joke about the business any more than Hoover would joke about the Bureau. The enemy, whether Communists or competition, was anathema.

Even his friends were all business. He had no "lifelong" friends as some people do. The only boys from Manchester with whom he kept in close contact were his brothers . . . and that was business. In fact, after Joseph (1955) and then Martin (1958) left, or were forced out of, Revlon, Charles froze them out of his consciousness altogether. He said barely a word to Joseph from 1955 until he died in 1971. And though Charles and Martin settled their differences around that time, for years they would pass each other in public places without so much as a nod of recognition.

The few close friends Charles did have over the years all worked for him in one way or another:

For many years, he and his wife Ancky would socialize with Harry and Helen Meresman. Meresman was Revson's accountant from Day One and remained his closest financial adviser.

Lester Herzog was Charles's closest friend from the late thirties to the early fifties. He and Charles shared a "bachelor's" pad on Central Park South (the quotation marks in recognition of the fact that Charles was not a bachelor). Lester worked for Revlon as one of Charles's key yes-men, despite his lack of any apparent talent. If brains were dynamite, one veteran explained, Lester

44

couldn't have blown his nose. But he was thoroughly devoted to Charles, and Charles was genuinely fond of him. Yet even Lester was pretty well forgotten when he married and could no longer spend his evenings out on the town. (I refer to the second time Lester got married. The first time, Charles was so displeased that he persuaded Lester to "get rid of her" within months.)

Lester Herzog's successor in this role, Bill Heller, was first brought in as Revlon's controller, and later became head of the fledgling international operation. Divorced, he was for some years Charles's closest companion. Another friendship that was born of the business.

From the late sixties until Charles's death in 1975, he was closest to Jack and Lorraine Friedman, both bright, charming people. There was less lackey-ism in this friendship than in the others, but Jack Friedman's company, Florasynth, was Revlon's chief supplier of essential oils for perfumes. Revlon was by far Florasynth's largest customer. The relationship between the two companies was so close that many people in the industry were under the mistaken impression that Revlon owned Florasynth. So Jack and Lorraine, in a sense, worked for Revlon, too.

Particularly in later years, Charles was too much consumed with Revlon to have any interest in or time for making friends outside the business. For the better part of his life, most of the people Charles knew worked for him. Which may have had something to do with his autocratic outlook. He did not feel comfortable outside his own environment, or with equally forceful, successful men or women whom he could not dominate. Nor were the corporation heads, financial men, political figures, and New York cultural people you might expect to find in the circle of the chairman of a leading fashion company beating down his doors to gain entry. He was not first on everyone's guest list, since before each appearance his wife or his secretary would call up once or twice to dictate his menu and to check that it would be cooked specifically as required. And woe to the hostess who was not prepared with the Dom Perignon. (Sometimes he brought his own.) One hostess recalls having him over among such distinguished guests as Gore Vidal and Judy Holliday. And while she cannot recall his taking much interest in them (or they in him), she vividly recalls him at her sumptuous, elegantly decorated buffet table, mixing some white, chalky Maalox-type liquid into a glass, right there on the table, to accompany his dinner. She recalls, too, that he passed judgment on each dish, unasked. "But that was Charles." True to his need to be in charge, he was a better host than he was a guest.

He belonged to Old Oaks Country Club in Purchase, New York. But he had no friends there. Whenever he came to the club to play golf (poorly), he would insist that the pro go out on the course with him to tee up every ball. Sometimes people from the company would join him. (Harry Meresman, his accountant, was treasurer of the club). But often he would play alone with the pro. He wasn't out there for the game, anyway; he only played four or five holes to stay in shape for the business. And if he didn't like a shot, he would have the pro tee up another ball and try it again.

As for the *Ultima II*, a sensational yacht which should have served to win *anyone* friends, of a sort, anyway, the guest list was less impressive than the vessel. For many people the idea of being set adrift in large but nonetheless confined quarters with Charles Revson was . . . unappealing. The regulars on the yacht were a group from which he could expect absolutely no competition or argument.

How would Charles Revson spend much of his time in the middle of the Mediterranean? On the radiophone back to the office or the laboratory in New York. And was his yacht named after his wife? Naturally not: it was named after his prestige product line.

Even more than with most entrepreneurs, the story of the man is the story of his business.

(IV)

Yes, He Painted His Nails

Many people achieve a certain success at a given point and take it to a certain level. Being able to sustain it, and then carry it further, all in one man, is very rare. That man must say to himself, "I'm going to rebuild myself. I'm going to broaden my vision, I'm going to think differently, I'm going to change my stature, my appearance, my manner of operating my company, my relationships with my people. And I'm going to go to the next plateau." It takes a very unusual man.
                                             —Sol Levine,
                         Revlon executive vice president

In Revson's last full year at the helm, 1974, Revlon reported sales (rounded off to the nearest $1,000) of $605,937,000. By contrast, in its first nine months of existence, in 1932, sales were $4,055.09—and there was no thought of rounding off the $55.09, because it was enough to pay his salary for two weeks, or two months' rent.

47

The following year, sales rose smartly to $11,246.98. Of this, expenses were as follows:

Merchandise purchased (nail enamel, bottles, caps, brushes, etc.)	$4,792.26
Wages	813.80
Rent	330.00
Miscellaneous taxes	161.29
Trucking and parcel post	345.67
Shipping supplies	71.71
Advertising (in trade journals)	978.32
Telephone	136.88
Traveling and miscellaneous	772.13
	$8,402.06

That left $2,844.92 for the three partners: Charles and Joseph Revson, with 25 percent each, and Charles Lachman, with 50 percent. (The profit in 1974 was $50 million.)

In 1974, Charles Revson had a home in the country, a triplex at 625 Park Avenue, a chauffeur-driven Rolls, and a personal staff (including the crew of his yacht) of forty-four people He drew a $330,000 salary and collected $1,300,000 in dividends He made more than $1 million in charitable donations and paid $131,000 in federal income tax. In 1934, he lived with his father and brother at 625 West 164 Street in Washington Height and rode the subway to work He earned a total of $2,521.60 for the year, $50.79 of which was paid in federal income tax.

The multimillion-dollar account Revlon maintained at the Manufacturers Hanover Trust Company in 1974 was opened on December 20, 1933. For all of 1934, it averaged a $400 balance We know this because even then Harry Meresman was toting up the figures for the firm—on a $15-a-month retainer—and Harry Meresman is not one to throw anything away. Now he sits on the Revlon board and, with former judge Simon Rifkind, executes the Revson estate.

Iris Heller, who subsequently became a major figure in

the beauty business herself, met Charles for the first time in 1933 when she was seventeen She now believes that Charles "killed" her second husband Bill Heller. But for nearly thirty years Charles and Iris got along nicely, and her recollection of their first meeting is vivid.

"I was working for Seligman and Latz," she remembers. "We had thirty or forty beauty salons then, around eight hundred now and we were at 119 West 57 Street. I was going to Barnard at night and had just gotten married the previous December, to the horror of my father . . . I can't explain the pressures of the Depression but I know that my kids used to say to me, 'Tell us a bedtime story, Mommy but don't tell us about when you were poor.' Anyway my boss, Edwin Latz, was taking me to lunch in what used to be the Metropolis Club, and I was hoping to God I'd know which fork to use. We started to go to lunch and there was this attractive young man sitting on a bench in our waiting area Even then I remember that I'd never seen a man with eyes that color. They were kind of no color. Well, I suppose you'd call them gray. It's the kind of gray that makes you think of guns and battleships and storms. [Or at least it made one writer think of those things when she published a roman à clef about Revson twenty-five years later, which may be where Iris got the image.] I'd never seen eyes as cold as that. The other thing about him is that he was wearing a jacket and trousers that did not match. And this was not the era of sports jackets and slacks, *The Great Gatsby* notwithstanding In other words, it was obvious that he just didn't own a whole suit. Which may be one of the reasons that Charles has put such an emphasis since then on clothes.

"Anyway, we went to lunch and we were there a long time and when we came back this guy was still there. I have a fetish about not keeping people waiting, and so I said to Mr. Latz, 'That man was there before we went to lunch and he's still there and we've been gone for a couple of hours.' And he said, 'Find out what he wants.' So I went over to him and asked him what he wanted. He said that Mr. Latz owed him some money. Latz said he didn't owe anyone any money, and Charlie said, 'Oh, yes you do. You owe me forty-eight dollars.'

" 'What for?' asked Latz.

" 'For some nail polish that Mr. Kaplan, your purchasing agent, bought.'

" 'Well, young man, what do you want me to do? Check us with Dun and Bradstreet—our credit's very good.'

"Charlie smiled and said, 'I know *your* credit's very good, but *my* credit's not so good. My brother's walking around downstairs, and we need the money.' Now, Latz swears he said he needed the money so that his mother could buy more ingredients to cook up some more polish on the stove, but I think that's just Latz being dramatic. Anyway, I went to get the money out of petty cash, because it was too late to get a check cashed, and by this time Charles was in Latz's office and they were having a discussion about nail polish and the mechanics of the manicurist, which were certainly different then from today. I think they got twenty-five dollars a week then, plus a small percentage over a certain level. And the idea then was to have the moon and the tips of the nail white, and the center red. At any rate, when he stepped outside I asked my boss what he had wanted, and Latz said Revson had asked whether he wanted to invest five thousand dollars for a half interest in his business. Latz maintains to this day that he said a fifty percent interest. My guess is that he said only 'an interest.'

"One thing I will say that I shared with Charles is instinct. So I said, 'For goodness' sake, do it. This has to be great.' Now, you have to remember that five thousand dollars in 1933 is not five thousand dollars today. But the other nail polishes that were on the market were nothing, and this guy was an intense promoter. People had just begun to talk about his polishes being good. He had color. A whole range. And they stayed on, the others didn't. And manicuring had just begun to come into its own—the longer fingernails and the whole bit.

"Anyway, I told Latz he should do it and he thought it was kind of wacky and he gave me a cliché for which he is famous, about 'a shoemaker sticking to his last.'

50

But I knew this was going to be a great thing so I tore out in the hall after him, and I said, 'Mr. Revson,' and he corrected me and said, 'Charles'—interestingly, not 'Charlie,' I've never heard him pleased at being called Charlie—and I said, 'I haven't got five thousand dollars, but I could probably scrape together five hundred.' (God only knows how I was going to do that.) 'How much of the business could I buy for that?' He said, 'None, but we could have a hell of a week someplace.' Or some funny little remark like that. But even with a twinkle in his eye, you know, he didn't twinkle. There's something about him. It's an iceberg about to mow you down. At any rate, I said, 'Well, I'm married.' And he said, '*You*, married?' You know, I was just a kid. 'Where do you live?' he asked, and I told him. 'Can you cook?' I said, 'Yeah, why?' He said, 'Well, why don't you invite me up for dinner?' And he did subsequently come up for dinner. In fact, he brought his brother, Joe, and his partner Charlie Lachman, without telling me he would, and I just barely had enough hamburger to make it. I cut up more bread and green peppers that night than I've ever in my life done."

Like most companies, Revlon had a humble beginning. What gets lost in the comparison of 1934 and 1974 is the speed with which the company, and with it Charles, became secure. By 1937 he had—by most standards, and certainly by those of the Depression—"made it." In that year he drew a princely $16,500. Sales had multiplied forty-fold in just four years. The average bank balance was up fifty-fold. Even after plowing $62,000 back into advertising, there was an $18,000 profit.

The next year, 1938, the company merely tripled in size. Charles's salary-plus-bonus jumped to $39,000—a lot for a single fellow in those days of the nickel subway ride and the $1,695 Cadillac. Thus, from 1930, when he left his cousin's dress company at the age of twenty-four, to 1937 or so, aged thirty, Charles Revson was struggling to make it; and for the rest of his life he was just struggling to make it bigger.

The year lipstick was added to Revlon's line of

nail-care products, 1940, sales more than doubled over the previous year, to $2.8 million. They sextupled in the forties, septupled in the fifties, and nearly tripled in the sixties, reaching $371 million in 1970. By 1980, one might guess, even though Charles bowed out around the $600-million level, the figure could easily surpass $1 billion or more, particularly with the acquisitions Revson's successor, the man from ITT, is likely to make.

One naturally wonders how this great enterprise was launched.

A company press release from the fifties, leaving out Charles's first wife, his trip to Chicago, and his brief career in the sales-motivation field, romanticizes the founding of Revlon as follows:

It was a bleak November morning back in the depression year of 1931, and Charles Revson, then in his very early twenties [25], badly needed a job. Over a cup of coffee in the Automat, young Revson scanned the sparse Help Wanted ads in the paper—a perusal that similarly occupied thousands of other jobless men at the time.

Two of the ads were for selling jobs; one for a man to sell household appliances—the other, a man to sell cosmetics. Each required applicants to appear in person, and at the same time the following morning. Charles knew there would be a long line at both places. He had never sold either household appliances or cosmetics. So, tossing a nickel in the air, he let chance decide where he would go; heads—cosmetics, tails, household appliances.

The coin landed on the table, heads up, and at dawn the next morning, Charles Revson was waiting for the office to open. He got the job. A little more than a year later, Revlon was born.

That was the last time anything concerning Revlon was left to chance.

There may be in this press release a little of what Charles years later referred to as "honest fiction." "Publicity," he told a gathering of his executives from around the world in 1969, in his own only partially coherent ad-lib style, "is honest fiction. Honest fiction. Now, what does that mean? There is honesty about publicity? But there has to be a basis of fiction about it, otherwise it's not readable. Who the hell wants to read it? Nobody. You want [people] to read about some product being introduced—so [you say], 'The fellow went down forty-six flights of stairs, almost broke his foot, took nine years of suffering'—you see what I mean?—'and he went through all this here and he came out minus three fingers and four toes, but he had the will to get it, and out of that came this great wonderful creativity of this product after years of testing and breaking your neck and everything, tested on ninety-four hundred women and four hundred and sixty-four elephants and out in the desert in 146-degree temperature Fahrenheit and boy!—it almost came to the point of giving up because they never thought they could make it . . .' And that's honest fiction. That's why publicity releases, for my sake, for my purpose, you know what I mean, you all know what you can do with it. You can throw it in the wastepaper basket. I didn't mean that."

Clear?

So maybe he didn't flip a nickel at the Automat to determine his fate. Maybe it was a dime. But the fact remains that he did go to work selling nail polish for a Newark, New Jersey, firm called Elka sometime in 1931. His territory was "Greater New York" and soon he had his older brother Joseph quit work at the General Motors assembly plant in Tarrytown to join him.

At first some of their friends and relations looked askance at the nail polish business. They considered it "sissyish." And cosmetics in those days were reserved largely for actresses and whores. What's more, this Elka firm in Newark did not have a great deal of class. There were just two of them at Elka, an older man who owned the place, and his demonstrator, a hunchback. She would go around to beauty shows pushing Elka's polish. "It was pitiful," Martin recalls.

Elka's product, however, was revolutionary. It was opaque. All the other nail polishes on the market were transparent. Charles saw the potential in this difference.

The others were made with dyes and were limited to three shades of red—light, medium, and dark. Revson felt that polish—"cream enamel," it came to be called—made with pigment so that it would really cover the nails, and made in a wide variety of shades, could capture the market.

He and Joseph were given a few feet of space in a cousin's lamp factory at 38 West 21 Street (the Revsons were never at a loss for cousins), and the tiny firm of Revson Brothers limped along for a year or so selling and distributing Elka nail enamel to beauty salons around New York. Charles began learning everything he could about nail enamel and about the beauty salons that were his customers. He wouldn't just deliver the product and collect his cash. He would find out what was right about it, what was wrong, and what they liked about competitive products. He would put the stuff on his own nails to get the feel of it and he learned to apply it to others' nails by way of demonstration. He became, in effect, one of the few guys in the locker room who could give a really good manicure.

"Yes," he told a reporter in 1949, "I learned how to put it on for demonstration—still can. To this day, I try colors on myself. When you gotta learn, you gotta learn."

His ability to immerse himself in a subject was about to pay off. He began to see that the cosmetics industry, such as it was, was run by weak people; and he began to sense its potential. He asked Elka to expand his distributorship to include the entire country. When Elka turned him down, he went out on his own.

Which brings us to Charles Lachman, who had had the good fortune to marry into a small chemical company—Dresden—in New Rochelle, New York. Dresden made nail polish for other firms to sell. Lachman was interested in selling the stuff direct to beauty salons under his own label. He had heard about the Revson brothers, and he got in touch with them. Or else, as *he* remembers it, they were looking for a supplier, had heard of Dresden, and got in touch with *him*. Either way, it proved to be a very good thing for C. R. Lachman, then thirty-five years old. He and the Revsons agreed to form a separate

54

company—Revlon—which would buy its nail enamel from Dresden. The Revsons were able to scrape together $300, for which, it was agreed, they were entitled to half the new company. Lachman would provide his technical expertise, such as it was, and see that Dresden supplied nail enamel to Revlon on credit. But because Revlon collected cash on delivery, Lachman's "financing" never amounted to more than a few thousand dollars.

It was Charles's first, and undoubtedly his worst, big deal. People used to ask Lachman what he did for the company. "I've got a rake," he would say, "and I rake it in." Still, a deal is a deal, and Charles was not one to renege. Many people have called Charles a son of a bitch, but few ever called him a "lying, cheating son of a bitch." Which is more than can be said for some of the other men who helped-build-America. He lived with his deal with Lachman for a while; and then—and you can hardly blame him—he renegotiated it.

Lachman was described in some stories about Revlon as "a brilliant young chemist." Looking back on Revlon's early days, Martin Revson qualifies that description. "He didn't know his ass from a hole in the ground about chemistry," Martin says. Dresden did not have a better nail polish than Elka; what the Dresden deal offered the Revsons was a stake in their own business. Charlie Lachman did not develop any magic formula; in fact, it was his senior partner at Dresden, a chemist named Dr. Taylor Sherwood, who cooked up the enamel to the Revsons' specifications. Dr. Sherwood's mistake was in not wanting to participate in Revlon himself.

Now, if Charlie Lachman was not a brilliant young chemist, he was not a brilliant young marketing man, either. He did not share Charles's instinct for color, for fashion, or for the consumer. Nor was he by any means as driven. As a result, the brash young Revson and his slower-moving senior partner clashed. "To the point," says Martin, "where Lachman was asked to do nothing. After the first year, he did nothing and was put on the shelf. Absolutely nothing."

According to others who were around in the early days, that may be overstating it—but not by much. Charlie

Lachman was a fundamentally agreeable man, and if Charles Revson wanted him to butt out, why fight? For the next thirty-odd years he drew a substantial salary—plus "bonuses"—and he let Charles make the decisions and do all the work.

Fairly soon, of course, Lachman was smiling broadly. "He was very grateful for his good fortune, I must admit," says Martin. But two of Charles's decisions around 1937 did not sit so well.

The first was his decision to find a new nail enamel supplier. He was not satisfied with the quality of the product coming from Dresden. Charlie Lachman and his wife, Ruth (not to be confused with his second wife, Ruth, or his third wife, Rita), still owned Dresden, and his share in Revlon had not yet made him even his first million (let alone the $100 million or so it came to be worth at its peak)—so he was miffed. A company called Maas & Waldstein, located like Elka in Newark, was given the business and has kept it ever since.

To make matters worse, it was around this time that Charles said to Lachman, in effect: "We're doing all the work and you've got half the company. We ought to be equal partners." Lachman was persuaded to cut his own share back to a third, so that Charles and Joseph would each have a third. At the same time, however, two classes of stock were created in such a way that Lachman retained 50 percent of the voting rights. He could not be ganged up on.

(Later, Lachman recalls, both he and Joseph wanted to cut young Martin into the company, but Charles, he says, was reluctant to go along. They persuaded him, and in the summer of 1938 each of the one-third partners was cut back to 30 percent, freeing up 10 percent of the company for Martin. But this was done in such a way that Lachman *still* controlled half the votes.)

It was probably during the discussion about cutting Lachman's share back from a half to a third, though it might have been in connection with some other dispute, that Lachman grabbed the corporate checkbook and went running out the door.

"Dumb schmuck," Charles is reputed to have said, "*that's* not the business."

Needless to say, Lachman came back. He was not afflicted with the stubborn pride of Martin or Joseph Revson—which wound up costing them tens of millions. He could bend.

"I was in the company a very short time when Lachman appears in my office," recalls a Revlon administrator from the late forties. "He was vice president of the company, a third owner, and half the voting interest. He comes in and introduces himself. He said, 'I'd like to have a pen for my desk set.' I said, 'I'm not in charge of office supplies, but if I can help you . . .' He said, 'No, but your girl is.' The girl I had inherited as my secretary was apparently in charge of such things. I called her in and said, 'Give Mr. Lachman a pen for his desk set.' She said, 'I will not.' I said, 'You *won't*?' She said, 'We're not allowed to give pens to executives for desk sets unless they turn in their old pen, and he loses them all the time. So I'm not giving it to him. That's Mr. Joseph's* orders.' Lachman was standing there listening to all this. I said to her, 'I'll be responsible.' She says to Lachman, 'All right, I'll give you a pen. But don't you lose it again.' People in the office knew he had no authority."

He went on a lot of ski trips, however, and seemed to be having a very nice time. He was seventy-eight in 1975 and going strong on his third pacemaker.

Unlike a silent partner, which is what Charlie Lachman in essence became, an entrepreneur has to work his ass off. He fills eleven jobs himself, he worries about everything, he is driven by a vision, and he is constantly selling different versions of that vision to customers, employees, investors, suppliers—to himself—and to anyone else who will listen. Yet the vision he is selling is not quite the same as the vision that drives him. He can endlessly extol the virtues of his product or service,

---

* "Mr. Joseph," "Mr. Charles," and "Mr. Martin," the brothers were called, plantation style, to avoid confusion. Even after the other two left, it remained "Mr. Charles."

evoking images of a world of whiter washes, fewer cavities, or more brilliant fingernails. And he can be intimately involved, as Charles was, in the creation and the quality of his products. But it is the business, not the product, that obsesses him. He just sells the product; he *owns* the business. He has a vision, quite simply, of hitting the jackpot and winning, along with money: independence, power, and respect—the game.

By one account, Charles Revson was "nurtured on Horatio Alger books." Whether or not this is so—in later life he stuck mainly to paperback Westerns—it is true that he always wanted to make a lot of money and that he never pretended otherwise. He harbored no fond memories of the simple life in Manchester; he got out of there as fast as he could. He harbored no left-wing sympathies, either. His thoughts ran more to the practical than to the intellectual. Looking out the window early one Depression morning as limousine after limousine passed by on the way from Westchester to Manhattan, he was not repelled by such opulence in the midst of widespread national suffering, as some of his peers might have been. Instead, he said, determinedly: "Some day *I'll* have a Cadillac limousine and be driven by my chauffeur to *my* office."

In the meantime, he and Joseph would take the subway from West 164 Street down to the drab, $25-a-month room they had rented at 15 West 44 Street, a few doors down from the Harvard Club and diagonally across from *The New Yorker*.

Charles would carry a soft black sample case full of nail enamel from beauty salon to beauty salon while Joseph remained in the office, keeping meticulous records, watching every penny and paperclip and seeing that Revlon bills were paid on time. If Joseph told a vendor he would have a check by Monday morning, he could bet his life it would be there. "His words are bonds," the yearbook had said of Joseph.

Martin was still working for the brokerage firm of E. A. Pierce, a forerunner of Merrill, Lynch, and did not quit his $35-a-week job to become Revlon's sales manager until 1935. So the only other Revlon employee for much of 1933, not including the boys' mother, who would come down to help out, was a shipping clerk by the name of George Hastell. Hastell came to Revlon fresh from high school and was still with the firm in 1975, a manager in Revlon's large Edison, New Jersey, factory.

George Hàstell

When I came looking for a job, in June of 1933, I remember walking into the lobby with a bewildered look on my face, and a nice young fellow says to me, "You looking for Revlon? Take the elevator up." That was Mr. Charles, though I didn't know it at the time. He was going out to make calls.

I went upstairs and I met Mr. Joseph. There were some other young men there waiting for an interview, also. Mr. Joseph was giving everybody a typing test. He dictated slowly [Joseph did everything slowly], so I was able to type it. Then he asked some other questions and got on the phone to the employment agency and said, "I've decided to take so-and-so." I got up and started to leave and he said, "Come back, come back." I said, "Why?" He said, "I'm hiring you." I said, "But that's not my name." And that's how I got hired. He had gotten the names confused.

I got home and told my wife and parents that I had a job. They said, "Great! Where?" I said, "With the Revlon Company. They make nail polish." My wife said, "*Nail* polish?" It was a dirty word. She never used nail polish or lipstick or anything else in those days.

But I started working, and I had to get there at seven o'clock every morning. Mr. Joseph would open the door and then we would work and leave around five or six. They started me out at $7 a week and said if I worked out they would raise it to $9 after a month, which they did. Then the N.R.A. came in and everybody had to be paid $15 a week.

The office was very small. You walked through the door and there was like an eight-by-eight reception area, with a desk and a typewriter. Behind a partition was a

59

room with two tables, a telephone and a window at the end that looked out on the street. When the four of us were in there—Charles, Joseph, Mrs. Revson, and me—it was crowded.

Our "warehouse" was a metal file cabinet. We had very little stock. We didn't make it ourselves; it came in to us from Dresden in eight-ounce bottles, and we would pour it into quarter-ounce bottles. You held the bottles in your hand and poured from one to the other without spilling. The one thing about nail enamel then was that it had a base, unlike the other nail polishes you could see through, and you had to keep this base in circulation. You couldn't always get it off the bottom, but Mr. Charles taught me how to shake a bottle to get it off. [Mr. Hastell raised both hands, as if held at gunpoint, and then shook them without moving his elbows, as if dancing the hokey-pokey.]

After we filled the bottles and made up the packages, I would go down to the post office. They used to advertise in a beauty shop magazine, in which you sent in sixty cents and we would mail out a bottle of nail enamel. Or we would send it out C.O.D. My first day I came down to the post office loaded with packages and got in line, and when I got up to the window the man says to me, "Oh, you're from Revlon." I said, "Yes." "Another new kid, huh?" I said, "Yes, why?" I thought I was the *only* new kid. He said, "You're not going to last there. Nobody does. They always have a turnover. They work you too hard." Apparently, I was the third or fourth shipping clerk they had had that year.

Another job of mine was to deliver. I had a little black suitcase in which I'd pack the bottles, and I used to travel around on the subway or the trolley car and deliver. Everything was C.O.D.: if I made twelve deliveries, I'd come back with something like $12 or $15. I would usually stop and have a sandwich for a nickel. They had bars where you could go in and get a beer and a sandwich made at the bar right in front of you.

Mr. Joseph worked with me in the office. Mr. Charles was always out selling. Their mother worked in the office, too. She would drop in and help out, filling bottles, putting labels on them—all that sort of thing. Their father would drop in, also, but he didn't take an active interest. You could see he was proud of his sons because they had a going business, though.

Then we started to get busy, and I could see day after day the business kept growing. They got so busy they asked me if I knew anybody who wanted a job, and I said, "Sure." They said, "If you know some nice young guy, bring him in." I brought one in and this is the way it went, bringing in more and more people as we got bigger and bigger.

In that tiny building, 15 West 44 Street, there was a furrier called Sally Studios, and they were growing, too. And pretty soon there became a competition between the two companies of who was going to take up most of the building. Finally, we got so big that we said, "You keep the building and we'll move." And we moved to 125 West 45 Street, above Caruso's Restaurant.

["I used to manage that building," says New York real estate consultant Henry Rice, "and when they moved in, in 1936, they were taking a big leap forward: they were taking a half-floor in a fifty-foot building, for which they were incurring a rent obligation of two hundred dollars a month. It was a very serious question as to whether they were going in over their heads. And in a year or a year-and-a-half's time they expanded to five floors.

"Charles was very affable and charming then, and somewhat . . . servile would not be the word, but he went out of his way to be pleasant. I was important. I was the landlord. When my wife would come into the building, everybody fawned on her. She could never leave without being laden with gift nail polish, gift lipstick, gift anything. Everybody was very nice in those days— they were poor.

"I had staggered the lease expirations on the different floors over about three and a half years, to lock them into the building. They couldn't very well move out half a floor at a time. And when I left the building, and a new landlord came in, he asked me how I could have been so sloppy. He said the first thing he had done was write a new lease to get all the expirations together. I thought to myself, 'You schmuck!' "]

We must have had twenty or thirty people in the factory by the time we moved to Forty-fifth Street, and five or six people in the office. It just grew continuously. It never stopped. On Forty-fourth Street we had no machinery whatsoever. On Forty-fifth we had two machines that I recall- -old machines bought secondhand. One was a makeshift filling machine, so we wouldn't have to fill the bottles one at a time by hand. We put the bottles on wooden trays under a hopper full of four or five gallons of nail enamel. You pushed a pedal and the filling spouts would open up; when the bottles were filled, you'd lift up on the pedal and go to the next row.

And we got a labeling machine. At first we had to put labels on by hand. We had one of those ceramic rollers with water in it that you passed the labels over to wet the glue, and then you positioned the labels on the bottles and the boxes. The dexterity of the people doing this was amazing, that they could put them on straight all the time If we had one that was slightly crooked, we'd scrape it off with a razor blade. But at Forty-fifth Street we got this big old-fashioned machine that would whirl and whirl around and a big arm would come down and put glue on and then come back up again.

When we moved the factory up to [525 West] Fifty-second Street [in 1938], we started getting things like conveyor belts. That's where we did all our assembling. That's when we started with our Christmas sets. We'd make a manicure set with bottles of nail enamel, a tweezer, an orange stick, an emory board . . .

In the early days, I remember particularly Charles always having nail polish on his fingernails, all different colors- -a different shade on each nail. [This saved the expense of printing up a color chart.] Every time a nail polish came in, I'd see him sitting there, putting it on. Then all the girls in the office would have to wear the nail enamel. Same thing with the factory girls: he put the nail enamel on them and said, "You wear that."

When we started with the assembly line operations, this got to be a problem. When a girl was called upstairs, it would disrupt the line.

He was particularly fussy about trimming the applicator brushes. He wanted them even, no straggly bristles on the sides, perfect. He made a fetish of perfection. He wanted perfection and quality. And even then we were throwing batches out if they weren't right.

Joe was very fussy about things, too. He would come into the plant and walk up and down and if he saw something on the floor, he'd give you a lecture. It was like a colonel coming along with a white glove looking for dust —I remember in the Bronx factory he actually did that. Everybody thought he was too finicky. He was finicky about things like that and Charles was finicky about the product.

In the early days, Charles and Joseph seemed to be very equal. It wasn't until later that Charles began to dominate. They each took a different area of responsibility . . . Charles was always the salesman, Joseph was the controller, the bookkeeper, the plant manager. Charles had the vision; he always knew that we would grow bigger and bigger. Joseph was a restraining influence on Charles. He was more straitlaced than Charles.

I remember one of the company parties where we had a bubble dancer who used to dance with a big balloon. I don't think Joseph knew what kind of entertainment we were going to have. But all of a sudden this bubble dancer comes out with the balloon and is dancing with hardly anything on, and he was horrified. But Charles— he wanted to go up and dance with the bubble dancer. Joseph restrained him. As I recall, Charles was out on the dance floor . . . actually sat on the floor and watched her dance.

[Charles liked interesting parties. He would hire mind readers, magicians, graphologists, organize Bingo games— anything, it seemed, to keep from having to stand around talking to people.]

(V)

Charming Charlie

I don't ship shit.
—Charles Revson

"When I started," Charles Revson is supposed to have told Revlon sales managers on more than one occasion, in his own Jimmy Stewart-like, New England-inflected whine. "I used to sell bullshit. I used to walk around— I didn't have anything, didn't even know where I was gonna eat. I used to walk into a store and sell some bullshit, and walk out of the store and say 'Hey, that's pretty good. So I went back and bought the bullshit back for more than I sold it for so I could use it again to sell it for even more than I paid for it."

Though he had failed with the Chicago sales-motivation outfit he briefly represented, Revson apparently learned something about selling and about motivating salesmen from the experience. He was not the smooth-talking, carnation-lapeled hero of *The Music Man*, but his enthusiasm was equally great, and in his youth he cut quite a figure. "Charles personally went out and did the selling," a long-time associate asserts, "personally got the distribution, personally slept with half the girls around the country to get counter space for Revlon. [When he decided to marry Ancky, he had to dispatch a top sales executive to Chicago to break the news to the manager of the Marshall Field's beauty salon—a key account. He didn't have the courage to face her himself.] He was very human, very charming, very witty, smoked three packs of cigarettes a day, and drank bourbon neat. His charisma is what built Revlon—and the rest of the industry as well. All this other stuff . . . his impeccable behavior, dark suits, not laughing, not drinking, not smoking, being very staid and proper and so on . . . all that came later, after the company was of a very sizable dimension."

Although most of them go unrecorded, Charles Revson had some wild times in the thirties—and the forties and the fifties and the sixties, right up until the time he married Lyn. "Charlie was terrific," says one of his first salesmen. "We used to travel together sometimes and get laid every night and have a fantastic time."

Instead of loosening up as he became more successful, he stiffened. Instead of becoming more comfortable with the big world outside, he became more introverted.

Martin recalls that once, around 1936, Charles became so distracted by an affair he was having that for a period of months he neglected the business. It never happened again. And that once around the same time he and Charles were walking down Fifty-seventh Street on a beautiful day and Charles said, "You know, I wouldn't mind going to a baseball game."

"You're going to a baseball game? How can you do that?" Martin asked incredulously.

"Why? There's nothing wrong with that," Charles said.

That exchange has always stuck in Martin's mind, he says, "because of how the man's attitude was at that time, and how it stiffened as time went on."

Almost everyone has tried selling something at one time or another—Girl Scout cookies or Christmas cards, yearbook ads or encyclopedias—and the experience for most people is unsettling. It is lonely, it is embarrassing, and the inevitable rejections are deadening. Tough enough when, in your sales pitch, you can blame your pushiness on a "good cause," like the yearbook; or when you are backed by a well-known name; or when you are calling on people you know; or when you have a supportive sales manager helping to guide you along. But try going cold, a young Jew from Manchester, New Hampshire, on the shortish, thinnish side, into beauty salon after beauty salon where nobody knows you, nobody's heard of you or your product; and try selling it at a premium price, cash on delivery, in the depths of the Depression. Those first few years took the kind of motivation few people have. If Revson hadn't had three big plusses going for him, he might never have made much of a name for himself. But, first, he really did have a much better product (though where had it gotten Elka?); second, he was an attractive young man calling, for the most part, on women (bringing out sexual instincts in some and motherly instincts in others); and third, if he didn't keep selling, how was he going to eat?

The Revson family was getting by all right up in Washington Heights, but it was hardly Fat City. You will recall Charles waiting for two hours at Seligman & Latz to collect his $48, and not having a complete suit to wear. Well, this image is corroborated by another: Charles would occasionally visit the home of another of his cousins, Al Katz, in Philadelphia. Katz was Revlon's first commissioned salesman, then first sales manager. When Charles visited the Katzes, he would have to stay in bed while they took his one suit out to be pressed. "That's a true story," says Sol Levine, an early Revson confidant.

The lean years paid off. Beauty salons that tried the product reordered. Word spread within the beauty trade and among women. Soon Charles was hiring salesmen, attending beauty shows, and signing up beauty supply jobbers to distribute Revlon products in other parts of the country.

Andre Goutal, a Frenchman who thought in French but spoke in English, was given Westchester and Fairfield counties as his exclusive territory—provided he maintain a minimum order level of $60 a month. This agreement was struck in May of 1932, just months after the Revlon partnership was formed. Goutal worked out so well that he became, for a while, Revlon's national sales manager. But at first everything was done on a modest scale: "I have a letter dated November 23, 1933," says Mr. Goutal, now comfortably retired in Cape Cod. "It is signed by Joseph Revson, and he's squawking about two dollars."

Charles could not afford a booth at the 1933 beauty show. A young man he had met while calling on beauty salons, Robert Hoffman, inventor of the Hoffman professional hair drier system, gave him a corner of his own. Charles set up a card table and painted all the nails he could. He collected cash in a cigar box from the sales that resulted. Later, as Revlon grew and the Hoffman hair drier system ran into stiff competition, Hoffman went to work selling for Charles Revson. But for a while he was one of several more established men in the beauty field who took a liking to Charles and tried to help him along (and then wound up working for him).

Hoffman remembers going down to Atlanta to attend the beauty show there. "We drove down to Washington in my old Ford, and took the train from there," he says. "While we were in Washington, he stayed with one of my cousins, and I stayed with another. (Neither one had enough room for both of us, and we couldn't afford a hotel.) He stayed on the couch. The next day, my uncle, who had a potato-chip plant, gave us a huge tin of potato chips to take along on the train. When we got to Atlanta, Charles checked us into the best suite in the hotel, to make an impression . . . but he had no cash. He believed in the best even when he was broke. He was buying made-to-order shoes long before he could afford to. [One of the first tenets of salesmanship: Look successful.]

"He wired Joe for money, and Joe wired back just one word: 'No.'

"We had to entertain, so we went out and bought the cheapest bottle of whiskey we could find, and all our entertaining was done in this big suite with a giant can of potato chips in the middle of the floor."

Charles was the smartest, most dynamic man at the show, all of twenty-seven or twenty-eight years old. People gravitated to him. The phone in their hotel suite never stopped ringing; the women loved him. The only thing that put people off a bit—even then—was that, as Hoffman recalls, "He was the most miserable eater I have ever seen. He would think nothing of sending eggs back three or four times. You know: 'I ordered two-minute eggs, and these are two-and-a-half-minute eggs.' And he would make a scene sometimes." Joseph was the same way. A certain fussiness, meticulousness, attention to detail seemed to run in the family. It was probably inherited from the Major.

At any rate, there was still the matter of the hotel bill to be cleared up, not to mention the train fare he had gambled away at a series of convivial late-night poker games. Joseph had been careful to give his brother a series of future-dated checks, one for each of the weeks he was to be on the road, and he wouldn't send more money. (Without Joseph's small-mindedness and conservatism, Revlon might not have made it through those first difficult years.) Charles managed to borrow some money from another of his mentors at the beauty show, a man named Mike Sager.

Sager used to travel around the country in his Chevrolet selling cosmetics for Hyman & Hyman. He met "Charlie" —as the real old-timers knew him—at a beauty show and, like Hoffman, helped him get in to see the right jobbers. In Boston, Sager saw Charlie sitting on the stairs outside Edward Tower & Company, on Washington Street. He had been waiting for an hour. "I took him right in," Sager says. "I did that with him all over." Eventually, Sager left Hyman & Hyman for Revlon. For a while he had the entire West Coast as his territory. He also helped the company find new products to copy. "Copy everything and you can't go wrong," he remembers Charles telling him. That way—and it was basically Charles's formula for forty-three years—you let the competitors do the groundwork and make the mistakes. And when they hit with something good, you make it better, package it better, advertise it better, and bury them.

Another salesman who traveled with Charles was Jack Price. To conserve funds, one of them would check in and give the bellboy all their luggage; the other would wait a few minutes and then sneak up to the "single" room. "Charlie never went to bed without putting lipstick on his lips and nail polish on his nails," Price says. "He would leave a call with the desk to wake him at two and at four and at six to see how it was wearing."

A small booth at the Midwest Beauty Show, in Chicago's Sherman Hotel in the spring of 1934, resulted in Revson's first big sale. As he told the story to a trade paper years later, with some stilted editing and perhaps just a touch of honest fiction:*

"I started my sales talk by showing the prospect how to apply our cream nail polish, then a new type. Before the week was out, I was teaching beauty shop operators and clerks how to demonstrate and use the polish. That group grew so big I had to rent the booth next to ours, and that additional space made my exhibit larger than our entire plant.

"One afternoon, when I had seven or eight pupils demonstrating, the manager of the beauty salon at Marshall Field & Company stopped by, watched our practical schooling, and from the size of the operation evidently got the idea that we were a big concern. She gave me an order that nearly exhausted our stock. [Later,] I dropped into Marshall Field's and told the salon manager we always followed up our orders and asked could I be of further service . . . She asked about other colors in our line, and I pulled out my order book.

" 'Your company must be a pretty big concern to hold a man over here just to service accounts,' she remarked as she placed an order for a dozen of one number.

" 'Not as large as we hope to be,' I replied.

"As she added another sizable amount on another color, she said, 'This, I am sure, will not delay shipment of the earlier order, for you must have an ample stock.'

" 'Our shipping department has never had to miss a

---

* "The Sale I Never Forgot." *Printers' Ink*, September 15, 1950.

shipping date yet,' I answered, praying that Joseph could live up to that promise.

" 'Didn't the orders at the show overload your facilities?' she asked while adding another item to the order.

" 'No, not necessarily. We have a plentiful supply of raw materials. We try to keep turning that over fast, and the factory is geared to handle anything and everything that comes in,' I replied, wondering how Joseph was going to package and ship show orders alone, not counting this one.

" 'Next time I'm in New York I'd like to go through your plant and meet your chemist,' was her clincher as she added three dozen of another item to the order, darn near filling that sheet.

" 'Yes, do that, but I hope it's not too soon. We are working out an expansion program and the place will be cluttered up for a while.' Of course, I hoped her trip would be delayed.

"I sent the order to Joseph by wire. It was the biggest we'd ever had. [Around $400, by most accounts.]

"He wired back: 'Is this an error in transmission? I couldn't fill it in weeks.' I wired, 'The order is correct.' Then I caught the train back to New York.

"The last of that order went over to the post office at midnight Sunday. Joseph and I dragged our weary bones for a sleep around the clock. We hadn't seen a bed in nearly a week. But we had made our promised shipping date."

And they all lived happily ever after. In fact, there was another big coup at that 1934 beauty show. It was at that show that Charles met A. C. Bailey, of the Bailey Beauty Supply Company in Chicago, which has been distributing Revlon products in that city ever since. Bailey doesn't remember Charles's renting the adjacent booth and setting up shop; he remembers Charles selling alone in a tiny booth a tray of five shades of enamel at $1.25. But he went with Charles nonetheless.

"I went with him," Bailey says, "because I had checked with some of the finest beauty shops in the east, like Michael of the Waldorf, and found that this polish was incredible. It was chip-proof and had more stay-on power,

70

had more gloss and luster, the colors were beautiful, and the formula was just terrific. We were carrying at that time about five brands of nail polish. Blue Bird, Chen-Yu, Glazo and a couple of others. We threw everything else out and carried only Revlon."

Forty-three years later, Mr. Bailey appreciated the chance to characterize Charles Revson: "The most charming man that ever lived, the most dynamic man that ever lived, the greatest salesman that ever drew breath; very charitable, very knowledgeable, a dynamic personality, and a great human being." Which suggests that Charles acted differently with people who bought from him than with people who worked for him. And that he was easier to love from a thousand miles away than from down the hall. But Bailey's warm feelings are understandable. Revlon *built* jobbers like A. C. Bailey. The demand among beauty salons for Revlon nail enamel became so great, to the virtual exclusion of any other brand, that the jobber in each city fortunate enough to have the Revlon line was almost assured of success. And only one jobber would be franchised in any area. Many beauty salons would simply refer to this jobber as "the Revlon jobber." As Revlon grew and added more products, so did the jobber. Even so, many of them hated Revson. He pushed them for all he could.

In 1935, Martin joined Revlon full-time as sales manager. If Joseph was the old-fashioned elementary-school teacher, explaining everything very slowly, twice, and putting a great premium on neatness . . . Martin was the demanding but popular high-school football coach, who "actually believed all the things he said," as one incredulous associate put it. Martin had many of Charles's dynamic qualities ("The Jewish Cary Grant," they used to call him), but not the brilliance—or the mean streak. Martin was more ebullient, would shout, throw things out the window, pound the table; Charles never raised his voice. Yet people feared Charles; they liked Martin.

When Revlon signed on Batten, Barton, Durstine & Osborn as its ad agency, Martin coined a slogan: "Go, go, go! With B.B.D. and O.!" He would ask his salesmen,

71

"Are you marking time or making time?" And he would tell them, "You're the greatest, Revlon's the greatest, so get in there and *fight!*"

"Tough traveling these days," he wrote one of his salesmen from a hotel in Memphis during the war, "but we Revlon guys can take it. Expected to be in New Orleans today but my spirits are high, ah those spirits." A handwritten note to Jack Price, circa 1938: "We've come a long way together, kid, (how well you and I remember the old days when people wondered how we ate and traveled just selling Revlon) and we'll go a long way farther. When you first came with us we were puffing along proudly on less than $100,000 [sales]; and then before we knew it, we were over the hump, yes, sir, $1,000,000; and it won't be long now before we'll be hitting $5,000,000. That's us, kid, always feeling proud, whether it's $50,000 or $5,000,000. Nothing can stop us."

He went so far as to name his first son "Peter Jeffrey Revlon Revson"—a name Peter hated until the day he died.

"I traveled all over the country with Martin and he was fantastic," says ad man Norman Norman. "It was our job to give sales presentations to department stores. We'd go to a city, then only a struggling cosmetic company doing twenty-three or twenty-five million . . . we were pretty exciting already but by no means the largest thing that ever happened. We'd take the biggest suite in a hotel and meet with nobody but the president of the store. It didn't matter what chain, we met the president. 'I'm Martin Revson, V.P. of the company. I'm entitled to see you. We're going to be the biggest cosmetic company in the country and I'm here to work out with you the details of how that's going to happen.' That was the way he would talk. He'd say: 'I've been downstairs and you've only given us eleven feet of space and you've got twenty-nine feet for Charles of the Ritz. That's wrong. They're not going to be in first place. Now, you tell me the timetable you want; we'll do whatever is necessary to get there.' First the president would laugh, then he'd take him seriously, and before you knew it, an hour and a half later they were working out the details . . . Martin was one of the most brilliant sales managers I've ever seen in my life and it was all homegrown and natural. I don't think he ever took a course."

Martin developed "Psycho-Revlons," where salesmen would act out selling situations in front of a group and have their performances criticized. At the time, this sort of role-playing exercise was novel. Psycho-Revlons even became the subject of an S. J. Perelman *New Yorker* parody. (Charles would not subject himself to group criticism, but in the early days he did keep a recording device in his apartment to practice pitches and pep talks.)

Martin's sales force quickly grew to cover the whole country. By 1937, they were selling to department stores, and then drugstores, as well as beauty salons. It was an aggressive sales force; slackers were not tolerated. The pressure from the top came right down through the ranks to the salesmen. One district sales manager required a lagging salesman to call in *every two hours* to report on his progress until his performance improved. And since drugstores were often open until ten at night, salesmen were expected to work very long days, if necessary, to meet their quotas.

Periodically, other cosmetics firms would attempt to encroach on Revlon's territory, and competitive battles would ensue. The Revlon salesmen were expected to win. If a Chen-Yu nail enamel color chart somehow walked out of a store in a salesman's briefcase . . . well, it could always be replaced by a Revlon color chart. If the bottle caps on some Chen-Yu nail enamel were loosened a bit and the enamel hardened . . . well, the store, or the consumer, would know not to buy an inferior brand again. If, in an attempt to secure counter space, a salesman should spread his arms out, accidentally sweeping the competitive product off either end of the counter onto the floor . . . well, the salesmen were authorized to buy up the damaged merchandise at the retailer's cost and replace it with Revlon product. And if there were a particularly intractable marketing problem, Mickey Soroko might be sent in to take care of it.

Mark D. Soroko—the strong-arm man, the problem-solver, the enforcer, the house dick. A character lifted straight from the pages of Damon Runyan. Soroko was in some ways the most valuable player in the company, after Charles, for twenty-five years. The son of orthodox Russian Jews, he grew up milking cows in Chelsea, Massachusetts, and almost finished the eighth grade. He was a process server, tracking down people to serve with subpoenas. He ran a collection agency, frightening or threatening people into paying off their debts. He was the kind of guy, he acknowledges, who would go out of his way for a fight.

Mickey met Charles through a cousin—the mind boggles at all Charles's cousins—and then, when he was going through a messy divorce and was down on his luck, in the midthirties, he moved in with the Revson boys, who were sharing a suite at the Cameron Hotel on Eighty-sixth Street. Martin and Charles slept in one bedroom, Joe slept in the other, and Mickey slept on the couch. Joe snored. At first Mickey was reluctant when they asked him to join Revlon. "I thought it was a feminine business," he says. "I was surprised later on when I found out it was one of the roughest businesses you can have. Especially due to the fact that outside of Helena Rubinstein, who was a questionable Jew [less than gung-ho, that is],we were the only Jews in the business. And we were not welcome."

If the beauty business was a "pretty rough one," it was partly because Mickey Soroko was in it. Mickey was the kind to shout and threaten and slam his fist on the table . . . even, some said, to carry a gun (though not to use it)—or, at least, to show up on occasion with someone who did carry a gun. Yet most people could not help liking him.

Fiercely loyal to Charles and to the company, he would always wait around at night until Charles left the office. And Charles, though undoubtedly a little afraid of Mickey, recognized his indispensability and rewarded him appropriately. He made a gentleman of Mickey: Hand-tailored suits, Havana cigars (smoked all the way down to the stubs), and yellow Cadillacs that were his trademark in

Larchmont. As a final gesture, in 1971 Charles made him a member of Revlon's board of directors.

Charles liked street fighters, liked to think of himself as one, and had his man in Mickey Soroko. No one knew exactly how Mickey did what he did—there were plenty of rumors—but he got things done. Presumably, those people he couldn't scare into doing what he wanted he could cajole, and those people he couldn't cajole he could pay off. He had signing privileges on a special Revlon bank account. And no Revlon controller was about to question any of his expense vouchers. In one town ages ago there was a problem with fire regulations, which would not permit the sale of nail enamel, a flammable substance. A couple of weeks later, one of the *fire trucks* went around delivering the nail enamel that had been held up. How did this happen? Mickey won't say.

During the war, he managed to land some sizable government contracts. And somehow Revlon had an easier time than its competitors in obtaining the raw materials and packaging materials it needed for its cosmetics.

Mickey's charm and his lavish entertaining endeared him to a most remarkable assortment of people. People in government, detectives, dermatologists, prominent Jews. It was Godfatherlike. Trivial example: A Revlon executive was in a rush to get a driver's license, but failed the test. Someone told him to see Mickey. Mickey sent him down to see a friend of his, who turned out to be the Commissioner of Sanitation. The Commissioner of Sanitation walked him over to the Commissioner of Motor Vehicles, who put him in line, got him a test, waived the thirty-day waiting period, and got him the license on the spot.

As for Mickey's own driving habits, he used to park those yellow Cadillacs anywhere. If he got a parking ticket, he would look around for another Cadillac to pin it to, and very frequently it would get paid. If it didn't, well, Mickey had his own way of living and he always managed to come out ahead somehow.

He was responsible for all Revlon's product liability cases, which is why he became so thick with the derma-

75

tologists. They could alert him to problems; they would be loathe to testify against Revlon in court. (A Revlon base-coat called "Ever-On" in the early days was so effective that it may have been responsible for the devastation of a great many fingernails and perhaps even one amputation. The product was withdrawn, of course, and Mickey went dashing around the country settling what might otherwise have been scores of costly lawsuits. Without Mickey, Revlon might then and there have gone the way of Bon Vivant vichyssoise.) He was responsible for dealing with the Food and Drug Administration. He was responsible at first for labor negotiations. And for internal security. And for enforcement of Revlon's selective distribution policies—cracking down on black market operations in Revlon merchandise. Anything that needed doing where you might have to get your hands a little dirty, Mickey stood ready to do.

Clearly then, despite Revlon's reputation as a one-man success story, Charles had some invaluable help. In the early years, brother Martin and Mickey Soroko were among the major contributors. Others came on board as the company grew. And there were also a great, great many minor contributors.

One such was David Kreloff, who in 1975 was completing his thirty-sixth year of service to the company, about as loyal a soldier as one could find. Kreloff was around early enough to see Revlon in its adolescent stage.

Dave Kreloff

I love my work and the company, and I don't let anyone cheat Revlon. I don't let anyone throw things away in the wastebasket, for example, if they can be used. It hurts. It's a waste of money and ridiculous. That's my outlook.

When I first joined the company in March of 1939, Revlon was already substantial. They had enamels and the manicure products, but they did not have lipstick. They came out with lipstick in 1940, and it was unbelievably exciting. I was in the mail department and it

76

was a six-day week, until noon on Saturday. I had a desk on the same floor where they had a small lab room, although the real lab was up at the factory on West Fifty-second Street. Charles would spend his time in this little room with Lillian Dunn, and his whole life was nail enamel.

[Lillian Dunn recalls sitting across the manicurist's table from Revson, applying nail enamel to his nails, and he to hers. "In the early days," she says, "we worked pretty much seven days a week. He taught me how to put it on, how to look at it, feel it, evaluate it—how it flowed, how it dried, how it set, how it wore. He taught me to use it as a professional and to misuse it as a consumer—I had to know both. And for months, hours at a time; he just taught me nail enamel."]

I wasn't in the mail room long. I'm always thinking of ways to improve things, and I went to the controller and said I wanted to make some suggestions but I didn't know who to talk to . . . and a week later I was made head of the mail department. And six months after that I was brought up into the sales department.

Whenever they had any function, a show or anything, I went to it. I remember at the Statler Hilton there was the International Beauty Show every year. Charles would be in a booth with his products. I would come on Saturdays and Sundays to help set up the booth. That wasn't my job, but I wanted to get into the display department. Charles had brought out Aquamarine hand cream, and he had the lab bring down a stainless steel bowl full of it. They also brought down stainless steel spatulas, and everyone who came near us was supposed to get a sample on their hand. And I was helping him do this, so this is how he got to know me.

In those days, Charles would hold a sales meeting every Saturday on the fifth floor of our offices, at 125 West 45 Street. The conference room was right next to the mail room on that floor. He would come in in the morning, take off his jacket, roll up his sleeves, and stay in there for the whole day. The meetings lasted all day. When I finished my work I would go in there and do whatever they wanted me to do. I used to run over to the

Gaiety Deli on Forty-sixth Street, off Seventh Avenue, and get them all sandwiches.

He was the greatest salesman ever. Martin was the sales manager, but Charles was the salesman. I'd listen to him talk about why you can be successful and why you should be successful and how you can be. He always said you had to have the will to win. And you couldn't help yourself—you had to believe him. I watched him sell his bottle of nail enamel to two department store buyers one day. They just couldn't resist him. He didn't scream or badger; he told them what the future would be. That the whole fashion world was going to come along, and that this is what it would be like. They believed him and he was right.

He said one day that he would be known as the king in the fragrance world—and at that time he didn't even *have* a fragrance. Aquamarine is the first fragrance he came out with, many, many years later. [And now Revlon's got Norell and Intimate and Ciara and Cerissa and Charlie.]

They say he's a murderer, he fires people, he insults them and so forth . . . okay, he's a businessman, and 90 percent of the people he murdered deserved it. But he's really a very warm guy. He was never aloof; it was easy to be with him. The last fifteen years it hasn't been easy to be with him because he's on a different level in the world.

When those Saturday sales meetings were over, then he liked a good time and a lot of fun. I think this was at the Commodore Hotel, one time they took the mattresses off the twin beds, put one on top of the other, and they were shooting dice. Throwing dice against the headboard. That day Charles came in with a brand-new, ivory-color suit, tropical suit, and everybody was teasing him about the suit, and he was so proud of it. (This was before he got into the dark suit bit.)

I guess everyone had a cocktail too much and in those days they had an inkwell on the desk with a pointed pen. They didn't have ballpoint pens in those days. I don't know if Mickey [Soroko] was winning or losing, but he picked up the inkwell and went over to Charles and threw

78

it all over his new ivory suit. [He was probably losing.] Charles just stood there, looking at the mess all over his suit. He didn't say a word and he went into the bathroom and he took the wastebasket in the bathroom, filled it with the toilet bowl water, and just poured it all over Mickey.

That started it, and they started to throw things at each other. Food . . . whatever was in the room. I'm not sure of the figure, but I do think the hotel bill was $1,700 to restore the room. This was around 1941. I remember hiding under a bed for the next half hour because the lamps were flying, they were unscrewing the light bulbs and throwing them at each other . . .*

And Joseph's reaction when he got the hotel bill?

Not good.

Can you remember anything about Joseph?

Well, if something was on the floor, even a piece of paper, he'd have a meeting and make a big fuss about it. He would make an issue over it. I remember rubber bands. But he was a nice guy . . .

The Revlon Company would have a Christmas party every year for the entire company, five or six hundred people, at the Biltmore or the Roosevelt. When we moved to the Squibb Building [in 1943], they had beautiful showrooms, very plush, and the parties would be held there. Reuben's, which was down in the building, would come up and set up the food and the tables and so on . . . very nice parties. And then the parties were stopped. And in my opinion they were stopped because at the last party, Joseph Revson, who was a rather straight guy,

---

* Another night early in Revlon's corporate history, Charles and one of his henchmen returned to their hotel suite with a couple of "potential Revlon customers," shall we say, they had picked up on Sixth Avenue, not far from Times Square. Al Katz, Charles's cousin and first salesman, was asleep. Charles went into the bathroom, mixed some toothpaste in a glass of water, and emptied the glass over the most sensitive part of his cousin's body. Whereupon his cousin, fully aroused and in considerable pain, went for a shaving cream bomb and took after Charles. The two potential Revlon customers looked on patiently as Charles and his cousin destroyed the hotel suite. It was only later that Charles became such a party pooper.

was walking to one of the showrooms with a drink in his hand, and an employee, a girl who weighed about 170 or 180 pounds, maybe had had too many drinks and suddenly leaped off a chair and threw her arms around him, spilling her drink all over him, and his drink all over him. And that was the last party we ever had.

What about Martin?

Well, I remember one day I was sitting in on a sales meeting he had called . . . I was pinch-hitting for my boss, Lester Herzog . . . and Martin was wearing a checkered shirt. This was about ten years after the ivory-suit incident I described to you, and Charles was now wearing only dark suits. So Martin's door opened and Charles walked in. And you could see it and you couldn't: a little flicker of change came over Martin because big brother was looking over his shoulder, Charles being as critical as he is. As Charles walked in Martin kept talking, but his tone had changed. Less self-confident. And Charles just wandered around making everyone feel totally uncomfortable.

He says to Martin, "Hey, that's some shirt you're wearing, kid." Lester and the others he called "kiddie," but Martin he called "kid," which I don't think he liked. He just broke up the meeting because of Martin's shirt. Martin said something like, "I'm glad you like it; I'll get you one"—it was just joking; but the meeting went nowhere until Charles left the room.

(VI)

Life Without Father

Probably the biggest failure in his life is his family.
— John Revson

Johanna Catharina Christina de Knecht was in America. The beautiful daughter of an important Dutch publisher and the former wife of a French count, she had sailed from Europe in 1939 with a group of friends aboard a yacht belonging to Baron Johnnie Empain. The baron was a European banker/industrialist, said to have an income even then in excess of a million dollars a year, and it had been his intention to sail to the Philippines via the Suez Canal, with a brief layover at his home in Egypt. Bad weather precluded passage in that direction, however, and so the party sailed the other way, via Monte Carlo, to Cuba instead. From there young Johanna had gone with some friends to New York, staying at the Sherry-Netherland Hotel and planning to return in two weeks to Paris. (Where, on the Quai de Bethune, she had a beautiful apartment in a building that was owned, coincidentally, by Madame Helena Rubinstein.)

But war broke out, and travel plans were again upended. Worse, the flow of funds from abroad was interrupted, and the twenty-five-year-old ex-countess found herself modeling for Saks Fifth Avenue.

She and some other models were returning from a photo session at the 1939 World's Fair one March day when they stopped at a beauty show being held in the Sixty-fifth Street armory. While waiting for one of the models to have her picture taken, Johanna Catharina Christina de Knecht, who spoke four languages (if you included English, which there was no overwhelming reason to do), was approached by a kinky-haired gentleman who introduced himself as Lester Herzog. He invited her to have her nails done at the Revlon booth. Ancky Christina, as she was known for modeling purposes, accepted.

"The first time I saw her," Charles recalled ten years later, "she had the wrong shade of lipstick. She needed an education and I had a lot of trouble with her." Perhaps—but he was taken with her nonetheless. He asked her out for the evening. In fact, he took eight or ten people out on the town that night, as he often would in those days (many of them buyers), darting into one nightclub for a drink or two and then out to another and another and another—and another. "I said to myself, 'This man must be rolling in money. He's crazy!'" Ancky recalls.

Charles took Ancky home. "He gave me his card and said, 'Call me.' And that was the beginning, I vood say."

At first, though Charles seemed like "a very nice man, very dynamic," it was really the opportunity of modeling for Revlon that interested Ancky. "It was a working arrangement, you might say." (Ancky was neither the first model nor the last to have such an arrangement with Charles.) But over a period of about a year—and a great many American Beauty roses, which were his trademark, three dozen at a clip—Ancky began seeing less and less of Phillips Holmes, a movie actor she thought drank too much, and more and more of Charles Revson.

82

Sitting on the veranda of her magnificent Palm Beach home, a few doors down from Estée Lauder's place, fifteen years divorced from Charles but in love with him still, Ancky recalled the unorthodox way he went about wooing her:

"Charles kept on saying, 'I'm never going to get married, I'm never going to get married.' So one day after about six months I said to him, 'Charles, I'm not getting any younger, you're never going to get married, it's been nice knowing you, we had a marvelous time—think we've got to say bye-bye.'

"So he kept on saying, 'I'm never going to get married.' So I said, finally, good-bye. And we got married four days later.

"We nearly didn't, though, because I remember Charles coming up to the apartment I was sharing with some other girls, an enormous apartment on Fifth Avenue . . . one of my friends, Gloria Swanson, is living there now . . . and he didn't want me to keep anything I had. My clothes, made in Paris; my jewelry. He said, 'No, give this away.' He was more or less the kind of person, I vood say, who wanted you to come naked to the party. He just wanted me to break completely with my old life, I suppose. He didn't even want me to keep my jewelry—it was amazing."

The wedding was held on October 26, 1940, in a judge's chambers in New York. Charles was thirty-four. During the course of the ceremony, he started to laugh. Heh, heh. "He wasn't laughing purposely," Martin recalls, "or making fun of the ceremony—he was laughing nervously." But Judge Eder didn't know that. He departed from the traditional text long enough to remind the groom of "the seriousness of marriage."

Marriage was not Charles Revson's forte; he was not entirely enthusiastic about the concept. No doubt this was partially the result of his first one. Indeed, when Charles and Ancky went for their marriage license and Charles was asked by the clerk for the name of his first wife, Charles—though he readily admitted there had been a first wife—simply could not remember her name. Ancky had to supply it for him.

After the wedding itself there was a big reception that

Charles had wanted to hold at Bill's Gay Nineties, his favorite night spot. "Nothing doing," Ancky said. The party was held at a posh midtown hotel. So it shouldn't be a total loss, Charles commandeered the Gay Nineties' piano player.

Their week-long honeymoon was in Hot Springs, Arkansas, where, perhaps not coincidentally, Charles was also able to take care of some business with an important department store. "I think that was our trouble," Ancky reflects. "It was always business. Always business. I think he lived his whole life for business."

The Revsons were married in October, and in January, Ancky, who had always gone to Switzerland in the wintertime, said, "C'mon, Charles, it's time to go skiing." Charles said he was sorry, but he couldn't take a vacation just then. "Well, I *always* go skiing," Ancky said, "that's just a normal thing!" So Charles asked, "Which would you rather: skiing or a mink coat?"

"And that," says Ancky, "is how I got my first mink coat." Charles wouldn't consider letting Ancky go without him, with her friends. "The wife should be barefoot and pregnant, as they say—that was his philosophy of life," Ancky says. "The wife stays home and he does his business."

Ancky won her second mink coat in a bet. When she would complain about his working too hard, he would say he was going to retire when the business reached $3 million in sales. Ancky bet him a carton of cigarettes against a mink coat that he voodn't. (Then he said he would retire at $10 million; and he once told Martin, when sales were running over $20 million, that a company like theirs shouldn't grow any bigger—it would lose its prestige image.)

"The first year," Ancky remembers, "we used to go to lots of good places. We saw every show. Charles was a big theatergoer, and we used to sometimes get into a little argument. If the play was no good, he'd say, 'C'mon, let's go.' I'd say, 'Oh, let's stay, it might get better.' Maybe that's why he made three or four nightclubs in one night—he was impatient. He didn't like something, he'd walk out and go to the next place. He was usually right when he said, 'It won't get any better.' "

The Revsons always ate out—at Pavillon, the Colony, or at Ronnie's Steak House, a Revson favorite. "He'd say, 'Let's have dinner around seven-thirty.' I'd say, 'Fine,' and show up at the office at seven-thirty. And I vood sit and sit in the waiting room, sometimes until nine o'clock, and it was getting to be a little . . . So I said, 'Charles, I won't come, I won't pick you up, I won't wait, I'll meet you in a restaurant. And if you say we are going to have dinner at eight, we meet at the restaurant at eight.' Then he came on time, I suppose because he didn't want me to sit there by myself. Otherwise you had to wait for him, because business came first."

(Dave Kreloff used to sit with Ancky when she was in the office with nothing to do, even before she married Charles. They would read children's books together to improve her English. "She would read the books and ask me how her pronunciation was," Kreloff says. Mike Sager remembers Ancky coming to the office on Saturdays with Charles and darning his socks.)

Every so often the dashing young couple would go to Ben Marden's casino, a big nightclub over in Jersey well known for its activities upstairs. "Everybody went there," says Ancky, "all of New York." They used to let Ancky win at blackjack just to keep her away from Charles, who was playing on the "real" table for big stakes. By dealing Ancky winning hands, they had her begging Charles to stay just a little longer, and sometimes he would. Later he learned to set in advance exactly how long he would play—rarely more than half an hour—and when time was up, he quit. He would win a lot and he would lose a lot, but he would never get carried away. (When he was losing big, Ancky used to give her 13-carat diamond ring a half turn so only the band was showing and say: "You see this big ring?" People would say: "What big ring?" And Ancky would say: "Charles just lost it."

Several times a year they would go out to the track, also, and for a short period in his life Charles became absorbed in the horses. He would sit in the office betting twenty races a day. He enjoyed gambling on tips in the stock market, too. He was not one to buy and hold, he was after *action*. Yet in business, he was not a gambler. The business was not to be fooled with or jeopardized in any way. Without the business, the rest of this would not have been possible and Charles knew it.

In 1942 Ancky became pregnant with John. "I was excited about it," she says, "because from the day I got married I wanted to get pregnant—and it wasn't easy." One reason must have been that for a time Charles didn't want to have children. "I wanted to have five," Ancky says, "but he said it wasn't a good idea to bring children into 'this miserable world.' The war was going on and there was a lot of tension." High as Charles was riding by 1942, it still seemed to him a miserable world. He saw life through hypercritical glasses.

Ancky had John, then a miscarriage, then Charles, Jr., then another miscarriage. But later she adopted a daughter (as a final attempt, some said, to regain Charles's attention before their divorce in 1960); and still later, with her new husband, she adopted two more children— so she wound up with five after all.

During the war, Martin was in the navy and Joe was in the army. Ancky worked for the Red Cross every day from ten to four; she worked for Bundles for Britain and Bundles for America; and she would sometimes get up at five in the morning to go down to the boats that were arriving with wounded soldiers and accompany them in the ambulances to lift their spirits. For recreation, she attended aviation college two nights a week. She learned to fly, but not yet being a citizen could not get her license. (Charles would never fly without two pilots in the cockpit—and Ancky was not one of them. "He said he would never go up in a plane with me," she says. He preferred boats to planes, anyway.)

While Ancky was working day and night on her charities, her husband was working day and night on the government contracts Mickey Soroko had somehow managed to land him, and on Revlon. Besides assembling first-aid kits, he was charged with producing dye-markers

86

for the navy and hand-grenades for the army. To do this he set up the Vorset Corporation in Oxford, New Jersey. The plant was carefully divided into eighteen separate buildings so that a mistake in one would not necessarily obliterate all the others.

Vorset was not unprofitable and it kept Charles out of the army. It also performed for the war effort with such distinction as to receive, in July 1944, the army/navy "E"—an "award of excellence" for "achievement in production." This was no routine accolade. As the local New Jersey paper reported at the time: "The little town of Oxford was agog Friday, when more distinguished visitors visited in one day than had ever visited it before in its entire history." Food was by Louis Sherry, music by Charles Knecht and his orchestra, and "The Star-Spangled Banner" by radio star Florence Edison. An "E" pennant was presented and "E" pins were given to every employee of the plant. Charles was justifiably proud. He had set out to make the best damn dye-markers the navy had ever seen, and he had succeeded. Dye-markers are not as easy to make as they sound, given, for one thing, the varying colors and temperatures of water in different parts of the ocean, and given—as Charles later demonstrated to the navy that he had been—faulty specifications. He had had to come up with his own recipe for dye-markers.

There is a story that, in the course of the trial and error this effort entailed, the Vorset plant one day turned the Raritan River green. And there is a story that when Charles was in Washington discussing one of his contracts, a procurement officer asked him whether he knew anything about "powder." Meaning gunpowder. Charles, thinking in his own terms, said he knew "everything" about powder, and so was given the go-ahead. There is even a story that one day Charles—who was not a man to panic—saw a grenade somehow get its pin plucked. Supposedly, thinking fast, he lunged for it and tossed it out the window.

Revlon, meanwhile, was in a holding pattern. Distribution was extended and sales grew, but supplies were scarce. Glass bottles were rationed. Lipsticks were deemed important for morale, but their metal cases had to be replaced, first with plastic, then with paper. And castor oil, a key component in lipstick, was so hard to come by that when Revson's young chemist, Ray Stetzer, heard of a warehouse-full in Tennessee, he immediately headed south to arrange purchase. He had to devise a quick quality check, and wound up sticking his finger in each of dozens of forty-gallon drums, sniffing and licking. He bought out the whole stock and spent the rest of his trip on the toilet.

Even harder to come by than castor oil were nylons, which led Charles to throw his beret into the leg makeup market that had sprung up. He invested $68,000 in such a product and was about to ship his first few hundred cases when a letter arrived informing him that United Drug (Rexall) had already registered the name he had chosen. He became so disgusted with the whole thing that, rather than change the name or go to court, he sold his entire stock to a cosmetics bootlegger for $8,000 and washed his hands of it. (If he did not become the leg makeup king during World War II, neither, many years later, did his introduction of a male genitalia deodorant spray—Private—win him a place in the marketing hall of fame.)

The Revsons didn't see each other much during the war years; both were working hard. But they didn't see all that much more of each other after the war, either. Ancky slowed her pace; Charles did not. Ancky would come up to the Squibb Building and say: "Charles, Charles—when are you coming *home*?"

It was his routine throughout life to sleep late and work late. When he was first married he would rise around ten-thirty. But once up, he was too preoccupied to take time for the breakfast Ancky soon stopped bothering to make. He would work until ten-thirty or eleven at night.

They lived in Manhattan, first in the Warwick Hotel, then across the street in a gigantic three-bedroom, three-bath duplex apartment at the Dorset, on Fifty-fourth Street just off Fifth Avenue. The bedrooms were upstairs, overlooking a huge two-story living room.

"Even then he had a fantastic life-style," says Irving

Botwin, who first met Charles in 1943, when Ancky was pregnant with John. "He invited us to dinner at Ronnie's Steak House. It was during the war, when steaks were at a premium. There were five of us—Charles, Ancky, Lester, myself, and one other man. And before you knew it, the table had grown to ten. He had the first round table, the captain's table. He was only thirty-six then, but there was something about him . . . he never came on too strong, he was low-key . . . he just had winner written all over him. I looked at the prices on the menu, $3.50 for a steak, $1 for a shrimp cocktail—that was a lot of money in those days and I didn't want to impose on the guy, but he insisted I have something first. He was always a good host; and if he wasn't the host, he was a lousy guest, as is usually the case."

After their dinner, his overcoat draped over his shoulders, cape-like, Charles decided to stroll into the Warwick drugstore to see what was cooking. He told Ancky he would meet her back at the apartment shortly. He spent two hours in that drugstore, Irving says, grilling the man behind the counter, studying the terrain, observing the behavior of the customers.

Martin, meanwhile, was living in Westchester with his wife, Julie, whom he had married in 1938, and with their young son, Peter. Julie Phelps Hall had been a nightclub singer before she married Martin. One of the men she had dated before Martin was (just to keep things interesting) . . . Charles. For years the two families were very close; it was Julie, by one account at least, who helped persuade the Charles Revsons to move up to Westchester. Shortly after Johnnie was born in 1943, Charles plunked down $90,000 for a ten-acre home in Rye, formerly the home of Cluett Peabody. Charles described "Holly House," as it was called, as "early Tudor." It came with a tennis court and they soon added a pool. Not for Charles, who was too embarrassed by his skinny legs ever to wear a swimsuit or short pants, but for Ancky, who loved to swim. (Her home in Palm Beach has a pool and a private tunnel to the ocean.) To help her keep Holly House in order, she had a cook, a butler, and an upstairs maid. To help with the children there was Katie Lowery, a governess who came to help out for six weeks in the summer of 1945 and wound up staying thirty years. (After the divorce she remained with Ancky to look after her adopted children.)

The Revsons were now Westchesterites, but they did not give up the apartment at the Dorset until the late fifties, when they moved into the Pierre. In addition, for a dozen years or more Charles shared an apartment at 240 Central Park South with his bachelor friend Lester Herzog ("the king's pimp," as some knew him). Charles would stay in town Monday, Tuesday, and Thursday nights; by the fifties, he would often stay in town Wednesday nights, too. Ancky would come in Monday nights for the opera. Both boys attended Rye Country Day School from the age of four through the ninth grade, when they were sent to Deerfield.

On weekends, Holly House was like a country club: There were always twenty cars in the driveway (several of them their own) . . . people would be playing tennis or taking lessons from a local pro, Joe Sobek . . . swimming . . . "always big parties, sandwiches for everybody," Ancky recalls. "It was lots of fun in those days. You know, I miss it." In the wintertime there were sleigh rides followed by hot chocolate.

Saturday night they played gin. Charles didn't like bridge. "We'd have maybe four tables, sixteen people would come over," says Ancky, "and then at eleven o'clock or midnight we'd have a big buffet with all kinds of food and everybody would stop playing. And after that everybody would go back to playing cards. Charles was always a gambler. He was very good at gin." Except that there was one guy who took him for $200 almost every week. "Charles was like his private patsy," Harry Meresman says. "His mind wanders, like mine. Finally he owned up to it and quit, cold turkey."

Charles was a gambler; Ancky was a collector. She collected porcelain shoes and report cards and Red Cross citations and the notes that came with gifts and . . . She even collected dogs, or so it must have seemed to Charles. There was an Irish setter named King, a gift

90

of the Meresmans; a cocker spaniel named Dynamite; and quite a procession of others. Charles did not get along with dogs. Big ones, Ancky suggests, may have frightened him a little. When Ancky went to buy a poodle, but was told by the owner that she could only have it if she also bought "the boxer that came with it," and so bought the boxer, too—Charles put his foot down. "Either it goes or I go," he said of the boxer, and it went. Charles's younger son (and the poodle) were disconsolate, but his older son, John, was not. John blew hot and cold with dogs. On one occasion he tired of King and Dynamite and buried them in an underground garbage can. (They survived.)

Sunday for Charles would begin with a late-morning perusal of the papers, noting the news and poring over his own and competitors' ads. Then there might be more tennis, or possibly a trip to the factory or the lab. Ancky had to try on all the lipsticks, and then wear them into the hotbox to see how they stood up in heat and humidity. It was hell, she says.

For a time Charles had a box at Yankee Stadium, and would take his boys out to the ball park. "He liked to go shopping at the A & P, also" says Ancky—"Can you imagine that? Charles Revson shopping at the A & P? Going to the ball game? So he wasn't always the way he became later on." He would play Monopoly with the children. He once built a rowboat with them, from a kit, with the help of the tennis pro. On rare occasions, he would drive the family up to Moosehead Lake, in Maine, to go fishing. "I must say," Ancky says, "when he was home he spent a lot of time with the children. The trouble was, he wasn't home that often."

Christmas was a warm family occasion. The Revsons always had two trees. Max, the gardener, would string the lights, but Charles insisted on decorating the main tree with Ancky on Christmas Eve after the boys had gone to sleep. Even on Christmas day he would not rise until around eleven, while the boys, naturally, if they could sleep at all in the face of such impending munificence, were up at seven. Thus, the second, smaller tree upstairs. It was stocked with just enough minor attractions

91

to keep the boys occupied until Charles was ready for Christmas to begin.

Santa was good to the Revsons. They were never a deprived family. The boys had to wash cars for their allowance, it's true—but look what they were washing. The family fleet consisted, around 1957, of a chauffeured limousine; a tangerine-colored Eldorado Charles had had specially made for Ancky to match one of his new lipstick shades (years earlier there had been an ultraviolet Chrysler); a Corvette and a Thunderbird both purchased in one day; a station wagon; an old three-wheeled Cushman scooter they called "the putt-putt," which Charles enjoyed driving into town for a laugh; and a lawn-mower-motor "car" for the kids to drive around the property.

(With that many cars there had to be accidents. Looking out his office window one afternoon, Charles noticed a bashed-up tangerine-colored Cadillac being towed down Fifth Avenue. He knew Ancky had had an accident even before she called him from the hospital, unhurt, to break the news. He himself was once helping the Meresmans dig one of their cars out of the snow. It was their car and their driveway, but he had taken charge of the operation. Finally the tires caught hold as he gunned the engine into a frenzy—and the car into the garage wall. "Well, you win some and you lose some," the Meresmans recall his saying. In much the same spirit, John once managed to back the Eldorado into the Thunderbird.)

Charles was thirty-nine when his second son arrived, in March 1946. He wanted to name him Joseph, as he did not expect his brother to marry and have a son of his own. (Joe did marry, the following year—Charles was best man at the wedding—and had two sons and a daughter.) But Ancky hated the name Joseph . . . had never liked her own name, Johanna . . . and so, for the first week of his life, the second son was known as "Mr. X." Finally, they agreed to name him Charles Haskell Revson, Jr. His mother has always called him Boochie; others knew him as Boochie, Junior, or Charles. For the longest time he felt uncomfortable being introduced to people as "Charles Revson," with all that that implied.

"I never really knew my father," Charles, Jr., says.

"I would see him one out of every five or six nights maybe. He'd come home Friday night, we'd be watching television or something and would come down to say hello to him, kiss him on the cheek, and then go back upstairs. I'd see him maybe Saturday. He did always insist on our kissing him, but he wasn't the type you'd just put your arms around and hug. If anything was wrong, I could always count on his help; but when I was growing up, I didn't see him that much."

Nor was Ancky what Charles, Jr., would call a "mother's mother." "When she was younger," he says, "she was a glamorous, beautiful-looking woman. She didn't want to sit around. She always wanted to go out and be seen . . . I'm very close to my nurse, Katie—she brought me up." Charles left it to Katie to provide the discipline. He never spanked the children or commanded them to do anything. "What he would do," Charles, Jr., says, "is nag and nag and keep at you. And when he stopped nagging, then you knew you were in trouble. Because then he'd cut you off completely.

"He paraded himself around with the feeling that he was something very, very special. He was like a head-master, like a teacher who's always right. You never got to know him. He never let you get close.

"He used to drive me nuts. He didn't want me to wear a pompadour in the third grade like everyone else. 'That's for sissies . . . you can't wear that . . . you've got to be a man.' One time we went to Saks when I was seven or eight. My father drove the tailor absolutely nuts. I was so embarrassed! He could embarrass you quite often."

If in other respects Charles Revson was not the perfect family man, there was one circumstance under which he would call an immediate truce with his brothers; one visitor to the office who would never be kept waiting and before whom his speech would be reduced to the purest civility. That man was, of course, the Major.

"He was really a very fine man," says Ancky, "but I must say he was quite difficult, very spoiled. Very spoiled. He used to get so mad if he couldn't have the car and chauffeur! If Daddy had tickets to the theater and the secretary had forgotten to pick them up . . . boy, he was pretty upset. Believe you me, he liked to live very well.

"I always had a box at the opera, at the Met, and he used to go with me and I'd say, 'Please, Daddy, be quiet,' because he used to sing along with the opera. He knew every opera. Any music you vood hear, he could tell you, 'That's from such-and-such opera.' He knew the composer and everything."

(Charles would drop in on the opera only occasionally. It was a box for eight, so there was always room. He might arrive at ten, sit through the end of *Rigoletto*, and then take Ancky and her friends out to eat.)

"A funny story . . . I'm going to tell it—I know Charles gets annoyed, but it's an idiosyncrasy people have. The Major wouldn't use the phone in his room. You know, the hotel used to charge you . . . it was a nickel in those days . . . so the hotel would charge ten cents or fifteen for each call. He'd rather go downstairs and call you from a pay phone. It was really silly. An idiosyncrasy, you know."

In 1949, the Major died. One might have expected the cause to be cancer: The Major not only rolled and packed cigars, he inhaled them. But it was a heart attack. Lillian Dunn remembers going to the funeral. "That's the last of the Major," Charles told her sadly.

There were two impediments to a perfect marriage between Charles and Johanna Revson. First, Charles was never home. Second, they were both strong, stubborn people. Charles could—and did—spend two hours arguing with Ancky on a transatlantic phone call. Usually their disagreements related to the children.

For one thing, Ancky wasn't Jewish. Charles himself was not particularly religious (even though "Revson" means "rabbi's son"); but he was not about to have his sons singing "Jesus Loves Me," either. Imagine his surprise, as they say, therefore, when he came downstairs unusually early one Sunday morning, around eleven, to see his two boys all dressed up. Where were they going? More to the point, it turned out, where had they been?

94

Indeed, *where had they been going every Sunday morning for two years* while their father was asleep upstairs? Sunday School. (This despite the fact that Ancky was not particularly religious, either.) They never went again.

Charles didn't want his sons going to a Protestant Sunday School, but he did want them to go to camp. Ancky did not, and they wound up not going. He also wanted them to go to prep school, which they did. Charles wanted Boochie to take Saturday morning boxing lessons. Ancky was unalterably opposed to the idea. (Charles, Jr., didn't like it either.)

But the biggest problem was competition from the business. "Charles, why do you *work* so hard," Ancky would ask as he got richer and richer. "It's easy to get to the top," Charles would reply. "The hard thing is to stay there." Ancky was itching to go to the parties and balls that, years later, Charles would begin to go to with his third wife, Lyn. "If he might have been more social," she says, "I might still be married to him. It's just that I got tired of sitting at home and not doing anything. I feel if you sit home too much your life is passing you by completely."

He was, besides being tired when he got home from work, shy. He felt most uncomfortable making small talk with polished New York socialites. He was more at home with Lester and a couple of broads. And that brings up the painful issue of Charles's fidelity. Charles never had any serious affairs while he was married to Ancky—and *that*, one of his long-time associates and screwing buddies told me, is the important thing. But there is little doubt that on a night-to-night basis he was a firm believer in the double standard. He called Ancky frequently to find out just what she was doing at all times, but did not hold himself equally accountable.

Once, about halfway through their marriage, Ancky arrived elegantly attired in his outer office. Charles had altogether forgotten that he was to take her to the opera. He turned to one of his men and started to attack him in front of Ancky. "*Now* you've got to call a meeting? You couldn't take care of this this morning? This afternoon? I promised my wife I would take her to the opera!"

The executive, who hadn't called a meeting at all, but who thought it best to play along, apologized, explaining that it was a terrible emergency. Charles dispatched Lester to put Ancky in a cab and told her he would be along as soon as he could break loose. When Lester came back upstairs, he asked, "Did she go?" And when Lester said she had, he said, "Okay, what have you got for me tonight?"

Sales manager Jack Price, now retired in Scottsdale, Arizona, with his wife of forty-seven years, claims to have been one of Charles's chief procurers until he left Revlon in 1944. "Charlie Revson never lived a healthy day of his life without screwing at least three times," he says. "He did it anytime he wanted, and he always paid for it. He never romanced any of the girls—he didn't have the time or the interest." He did it in the office, he did it on the road, and most of all he did it up in the apartment at 240 Central Park South that was registered in Lester Herzog's name.

The apartment, to which only Price, Herzog, and Revson had keys, consisted of a large living room, a large kitchen, and a long bedroom with three beds. It was used to entertain visiting buyers as well as Revson and his inner circle. There was the evening, for example, that Charlie, Lester, Al Katz, a Revlon salesman, and a jobber from out of town were all sitting on the floor playing strip poker. Four women whom Price had arranged for were already stripped and looking on. Price himself, of course, was only an observer: "He never saw me naked unless I had just come out of the shower." Charlie, on the other hand, was exceptionally well endowed, Price says (holding his hands apart as though boasting about a fish he had caught) and he was not averse to letting people in on the secret.

The poker game progressed and the Revlon salesman, a New England family man, was losing badly. Finally, Price says, he loses everything, "and he has to lay one of the broads in front of everybody." He doesn't want to. He says, "Charlie, look, I've been married fourteen years . . . Please . . ." Revson says: "You got into it, you started with it, you gotta go through with it." Then he

96

turns to Price and says: "If he doesn't, I want him canned tomorrow morning." He turns back to the salesman and says, "What the hell do you care? These girls aren't going to say anything. They don't care. Take off your clothes and fuck. If I were you, Maurie," he advises icily, "I'd do it. You got yourself into this."

So he did.

"The greatest orgy I ever saw in my life happened in the Drake Hotel in Chicago," Price says. "It was an enormous suite on the third floor, around 1943. We were all sitting around and the madam comes to me and says, 'Jack, there's a girl here I haven't sent out too much. She hasn't had much contact with men. She's not a virgin, but she told me she's never had an orgasm.' She was a slender young girl, around twenty-one, and kind of pretty—but scared. I told Charlie and he went over and talked to her. He told me later that he offered her a hundred dollars if she did have an orgasm. The girl goes into another bedroom with the madam and finally she comes out with a kimono on. She lays down on the floor right in front of everyone. This is part of Charlie's deal, it's got to be in front of everybody else. He always did it in front of people. And sometimes right in the middle he'd look around to see everyone else's reaction.

"So Charlie starts on her. They're both naked. One of the Revlon jobbers, a short, cocky guy, is running around with nothing but his socks on, with a hernia as big as a baseball. [Price has an eye for the tasteful detail.] Charlie keeps pumping and pumping and nothing is happening. He could go longer without an orgasm than anyone else I knew. A doctor once told me that the larger you are, the longer it takes. He kept after that girl for an hour at least, in front of everybody. Suddenly she got it—this is no fake and he and everyone else knew it. She threw her arms around him . . . and then it was over. They were both soaking wet. She immediately ran to the bathroom, and by the time she came back Charlie had his shorts on and was no longer interested."

This was in 1943, and Charles did not grow more faithful to Ancky with time. Yet he didn't want Ancky to leave him, as she began threatening she would. In fact, when in 1960 she actually decided to get a divorce, he offered her her full $2.5 million settlement plus a magnificent ruby necklace if she would stay.

Revson attributed his marital problems to his marrying women less intelligent than he, and with whom he thus had difficulty communicating. But given his character, it would be a rare woman indeed who could have satisfied him and maintained her dignity at the same time.

"He liked to tell you everything you should do," Ancky says. "He didn't want to have any aggravation; he wanted you to agree with him on everything."

He would tell Ancky how to make up. "I have big eyes and I wanted to make them look larger and he always said, 'You shouldn't do that.'" He would tell her not to go water-skiing. "But Charles, I *love* to go water-skiing! Why shouldn't I go water-skiing?" He would tell her where she could and could not go. "I was on a trip once with friends. I went to Holland and Paris, but I could not go any farther south than Paris. He made great stipulations. It was silly—if you want to do something bad in Europe it's very easy; you don't have to go to the Riviera. But he had very little belief in people. It was his character. He didn't trust people, I think."

Charles became more demanding and difficult as he got older. It got to be his way or no way. "He was a man," Ancky says, "who always wanted to be right. That was his character. And nine out of ten times he *was* right!" (The tenth time he could usually wrangle out of admitting he was wrong. "He was very good at shifting the blame for things," Charles, Jr., says.)

Though she divorced him, Ancky loved Charles to the end. "How can I explain?" she reflects. "Charles expected you to be completely in the background. I think now that you know me a little, you know I am not a background girl. You must be a person. That's the way I feel, anyhow. You cannot be somebody's slave . . . that's very difficult. For me it's difficult. And yet I don't know how to describe him, because he could be the most thoughtful man. I remember once he was in Europe and he brought me back beautiful Dutch Delft. Or he'd bring me caviar from Paris. I never felt left behind with Charles

98

—I really mean that." Yet Charles would never allow Ancky to accompany him on business trips. It was a strict company policy that wives be left at home, regardless of who might be willing to pay their travel expenses.

Near the end, Ancky frequently threatened Charles with divorce. Finally she went into his office one day and saw a photograph of him and the Princess Borghese, namesake of one of his cosmetics lines. Charles was wearing tails. "I was so mad," Ancky says, "because so many times I had asked him to wear tails for some function I had arranged, for one of my charities or something—and he would never do it for me. But for the business, he was wearing tails. I looked at him and I said, 'I want a divorce.' And that was it."

(VII)

But You Wouldn't Want
to Work There

All I demand is perfection.
—Charles Revson

By the late forties, Revlon was already ensconced in the Squibb Building, at 745 Fifth Avenue, and had more than a thousand employees on the payroll, there and at the plant. The Revsons had had fifteen years or so to learn how to deal with employees. Yet turnover of clerical personnel was running at 166 percent a year—the average girl lasted seven months—and executive turnover was nearly as bad.

People were like checkers in the Revson style of management. One personnel man from the early fifties, now head of personnel for a *Fortune*-500 company, would have to fire thirty people in the office when business slacked off, then go out and hire thirty more on Monday when business picked back up.

An earlier Revlon personnel manager, Walter Ronner, joined the company in 1947 and was immediately thrown into such a situation. "I arrived on a Friday," he remembers, "and I wasn't there more than three minutes when I got a call from Joseph Danilek, the comptroller of the company. He said, 'We are going to lay off about forty people today. You have them laid off; we are going on an austerity program.' So I asked him, 'How do we do this? By seniority or by job classification?' And he says to me, 'Look, I've got orders from management to lay off forty people. I don't care how you do it, but get rid of them. By the way, we quit here at five-fifteen, so don't notify anybody until five o'clock. We want a day's work out of them.'

"We had two full floors in the Squibb building, all open offices, typewriters, calculators, NCR operators and so on. And I didn't know who any of these people were. I visualized . . . here I am, coming in as a new man, and the first thing I do is discharge forty people. So I said to Danilek, 'I refuse to do it.' He says, 'Do you mean what you say?' I said, 'Yes.' He was not my superior; we were on the same level of authority. 'If that's the case,' he says, 'I'll have to do it myself.'

"Forty people were picked at random, and at five o'clock Danilek lined them up on the stairs between the fifth and sixth floors—so the others wouldn't see—and he gave them a little lecture about lack of work and handed them their severance checks and let them go.

"On Monday morning there was a call from Charles's secretary: 'Mr. Charles wants to see you.' So I went to see him. There was a tray on his desk with mashed peas, a glass of milk, and crackers. He was on one of his diets. The first thing he said to me was, 'Are you a Socialist?' He said, 'You know, when you get orders from top management, your job is to carry them out. It looks like you and I are not going to get along at all.' So I said, 'You can't fire me for refusing that kind of instructions. You and I have a contract.' He said, 'Who the hell gave you a contract? You haven't got a contract.' I said, 'Yes, I do. I have a contract with this company that is superior and takes precedence over any written agreement. I'm supposed to make money for the company. If you ordered me to take ten thousand dollars

101

and dump it in the Hudson River, I have the right to refuse it. This is what you did Friday.'

"He said, 'How did we throw the money away?' I said, 'We shouldn't have given those people severance pay. On the basis of two weeks' average, it came out to almost ten thousand dollars.' He said, 'That's our policy, to give severance pay.' I said, 'Not if people quit. We have thirty-five to forty people quitting here every week.* All you have to do is wait a week and we'll lose them and we'd save the ten thousand. In addition to that, we have damages that we can't calculate. You've got people looking through desks to see how things were done, where things stood . . . you have no continuity, no orderly transition. And the rest of them are busily looking in the paper seeing what jobs they can get elsewhere. So what you've done is a great big loss and I refuse to participate in it.'

"Charles asks me with a sort of a twinkle, 'Does that mean that thirty-five people will leave next week too?' I said, 'Yes.' He said, 'How do you know?' I said, 'Because we keep turnover figures in this company, but nobody pays attention to them.' "

That week there was such demoralization in the office over the previous week's bloodletting that more than thirty-five people left, Ronner says. He went to the art department and had a giant invoice made up in the amount of $1,500,000 for "labor turnover for the year," addressed to Revlon and stamped PAID. He sent it through the regular inter-office mail to Charles.

"I got called again to come see Charles," Ronner says. "It made an impact on him because he understood advertising. That was the only way you could communicate with him, through some kind of dramatic thing. And you had to stand up to him. I learned very early about him: He was like a tiger. If he was in a cage with you and he smelled your fright, he'd jump you. That was the

* This was an exaggeration. With 275 office workers then at 745 Fifth Avenue, it normally took about four weeks for that many to turn over.

end of you. But if you stood up to him, you gained his respect. I had pretty free rein after that."

Ronner instituted a security system under which one couldn't be dismissed unless he was given a warning first, and unless the dismissal was agreed to by a three-man security board. Turnover, he says, abated dramatically. But before the security board system had been devised, in 1949, and after it faded from the scene with Ronner's departure in 1952, people were being fired like popguns. A beauty consultant had to go because, in Charles's words, she had a smelly ----. Receptionists were chosen to match the decor—and since the decor of the reception area was changed at least twice a year to match each new shade promotion, the average receptionist was fortunate to last six months. To Charles, she was the central character in what was really one enormous walk-in window display. But rather than have Personnel line up a dozen prospects for him to audition, Charles would just requisition "a blonde" or "a brunette." Then, in passing through the reception area, he would decide that the woman was no good—she wasn't a *natural* blonde, or her complexion was too dark, or she wasn't tall enough —get rid of her. By the time the right girl had been installed, a new promotion would be on its way, and the call would go out for a redhead. Personnel tried to transfer used receptionists into other jobs, but most of them were aspiring actresses or models who would have no part of, nor skills for, secretarial work. (So stories about turnover of Revlon receptionists, chosen to match the decor, are true. But some of the women, at least, knew in advance they were signing on for limited engagements.)

Longevity with the firm was inversely proportional to proximity to Charles. You get close to the fire, you get burned. With a few notable exceptions, like Ruth Harvey, Charles went through secretaries like a leper through a crowd. One of his secretaries had a mustache of sorts. Get rid of her. Another was the "Secretary of the Year" before he hired her. It was a disaster. Here she was, all efficient and organized and professional; and here was Charles, always running late, keeping his records in his head, and expecting her to take his shirts and his dirty

103

handkerchiefs to the laundry. He virtually never dictated a letter and virtually never wrote—or read—memos. If his secretary gave him mail that had to be answered, he'd say, "Give it to So-and-so . . . find somebody to take care of it." The letters that did go out over his signature were all written by her. Besides sorting his dirty laundry, she would go down to the kitchen three times a day and prepare his special tray of food—which he would sometimes just push away in disgust.

One of his secretaries had a law degree, great secretarial skills, and a knowledge of several languages. He hated her with a passion. But as he never fired anyone himself, he called Mickey in to do it. Mickey supposedly walked up to her desk and said, simply, "Get out of here." See how easy it is to communicate with people?

You would think that a secretary would require very little urging to leave such a boss, despite the money and status that went with the job. But it was difficult to get a secretary for Charles Revson who would not fall in love with him. However inconsiderate or abusive he could be, he had that tremendous magnetism.

At Revlon, fear was the dominant emotion, particularly among those whose intercoms might crackle at any time with a call from Charles. The tension started at the top. Each of the brothers was strong-willed and outspoken, even if Charles was clearly dominant. Their battles were frequent and bloody. To quote Carl Erbe, their public-relations counsel for many years, and a close friend of Martin's: "There was a tremendous emotional clash among the brothers. They would fight and not talk for three or four days. But the end result was good, because what they were fighting for was a better business." (It was a situation Charles would not tolerate forever, however.)

Physically, the fraternal summit meetings were extraordinary. Joseph was a sniffler. He had allergies, Martin had a nervous cough and kept a spittoon nearby. And Charles, who had digestive problems, belched a great deal. Together, they sounded like a sputtering Model T Ford.

To deal with the fear and tension in the Revlon organization, Erbe initiated a series of comic films, slide shows, and theatricals. The idea was to improve morale by demonstrating that the Revsons could laugh at themselves. A thirty-minute film called *Inside Revlon* included a shot of Lester Herzog whipping a Revlon sales manager, stripped to the waist and bloody. (Casting Charles in this role might have hit a little *too* close to home.) A spoof called *Breath of a Salesman*, staged partly to counter the negativism of *Death of a Salesman*, which opened on Broadway in 1949, and which Martin, particularly, deplored, had a scene where the man playing Joseph Revson was to enter the strong room, dust off the money, laugh maniacally, and then wheel the money back into the safe. Erbe chose a man named Eli Davidson for the part, but fear of the Revsons was such that Davidson refused it. He was certain he would be fired. No manner of verbal assurances could persuade him. Joseph had to write out an affidavit guaranteeing his job before he would take the part. His performance turned out to be the hit of the show—which, Erbe says, "created a marked difference in the atmosphere in the company for a period of time." The problem was, it wasn't a terribly long period of time.

Charles wanted the fabric of his organization to be tight. If a girl went to the ladies' room, she was goofing off. "You treat your secretary like a sister," he often chided executives. He told Jerry Juliber, for a long time his personnel manager and number-one snitcher, "The thing that has ruined companies is when looseness sets in. You got to keep tight at the ass. The day we get soft, we'll go down fast." He spent his own money lavishly and was generous with salaries, but he was also capable of saying to a woman who tossed a paperclip into the ashtray of his conference table, "I *paid* for that paperclip!" And mean it.

He had a great fear of being taken. He would go to any expense to get an ad perfect, yet he hated to let his creative people shoot ads on location. Locations tended to be in rather sensational vacation spots, and Charles was afraid he was being taken. At one meeting up in his skyscraper office with a bunch of advertising and agency people, he stopped in midsentence when a passing jet plane caught his eye. "There goes another art director," he said ruefully. A New York photographer's studio once had to be transformed into a Caribbean paradise, palm trees and all, at enormous cost, because Charles refused to have three or four of his people fly down to shoot the ad.

Not only were people "fucking on the company," as Charles put it; they weren't coming in to work on time. This may have had something to do with the fact that Charles himself never arrived at the office much before eleven or twelve, but it was no less deplorable. (Charles knew about the lateness of others throughout his network of informants.) At various times in the company's history, therefore—and as late as 1971, when Revlon was supposedly a modern corporation—everyone was required to sign in in the morning. *Everyone.* Even Charles signed in. One day, when Revlon was in the process of moving from 666 Fifth Avenue up to the General Motors Building, in 1969, Charles sauntered in and began to look over the sign-in sheet. The receptionist, who was new, says, "I'm sorry, sir, you can't do that." Charles says, "Yes I can." "No sir," she says, "I have strict orders that no one is to remove the list; you'll have to put it back." This goes back and forth for a while with the receptionist being very courteous, as all Revlon receptionists are, and finally Charles says, "Do you know who I am?" And she says, "No, sir, I don't." "Well, when you pick up your final paycheck this afternoon, ask 'em to tell ya."

If Revlon was a difficult place to work, particularly in the forties and fifties, it was not without its rewards. George Hastell, Revlon's most senior employee, got his first Christmas bonus after only three or four years with the firm. He was making $28 a week by then, when Joseph called him in and handed him an envelope; George thanked him and started to walk out. "Aren't you going to open it?" Joseph asked. "All right, I'll open it," George said, "but whatever it is, I'm happy." He opened the envelope and found $150 in cash inside. It was more money than he had ever seen in his life. "I'm flabber-gasted," he said.

He had been with the company twenty-three or twenty-four years when Charles, Joseph, and Charlie Lachman took him to lunch at the Savoy Plaza and presented him with a gold watch for twenty years' service. "I felt very ill at ease," he remembers. "I had never been in their company socially; they were the bosses. I'm sure they felt awkward, too."

And on his fortieth anniversary with the company, in 1973, by which time a full-scale personnel department had professionalized much of the haphazard employee relations of the early days, they surprised him with a free trip anywhere in the world. He and his wife chose the Orient, and Revlon paid for everything. (Not all long-time Revlon employees were by any means as fortunate.)

Upper-echelon executives were treated to stock options along with their salaries; but particularly before Revlon went public, and afterward as well, the Christmas bonus was used as the chief expression of appreciation. Charles never praised anyone's work. But the fact that an executive was still on the payroll meant he was doing okay, and the size of his Christmas check signified just how well. Joseph would distribute the checks promptly to the operations people who worked under him. Charles would keep *his* batch of checks in his vest pocket for months. People were standing around with their tongues hanging out. Christmas went by, New Year's went by, Washington's Birthday . . . Then Charles would pull out one of the crumpled checks, with the ink practically worn off, and he'd say, "Here, kiddie, here's a check for you." By the time the guy actually got the bonus, he'd lost his taste for it. But Charles looked on these bonuses as gifts. Nobody should tell him when they were to be given. If they were required of him, they weren't gifts. This way, he had everyone on a string.

The clerical and factory workers, at first, got no Christmas bonuses. They got Thanksgiving turkeys. A choice: kosher or non-kosher. Anytime anything came up, no matter what, Charles and Joseph would say to Ronner, the personnel man, "Look at these goddamn people. We give them turkeys and look what they do to us."

"I was getting kind of tired of hearing about turkeys all the time," Ronner says, "and Dave Livingston, the head of District Sixty-five, knew it. He said to me one time in the middle of our negotiations, 'You know, Ronner, we only have to eat those turkeys once a year. You've got to eat them all year round. Why don't we discontinue the turkeys? We don't want them.'"

The next time Charles said something about the turkeys, Ronner told him that the union had requested that they be discontinued. "You mean they don't want them?" Charles asked. "Why not?" "Because they don't think they should sell their soul for a turkey," Ronner replied. "Would you?"

Unions made Charles very uneasy. When Eli Tarplin was first interviewed for a marketing job in 1949, Charles noted that he had taken a course in labor relations. "Are you a Commie?" he asked Tarplin. "Are you an agitator? I don't want any agitators: we have a lot of labor problems and I don't need that." Charles never dealt with unions himself, leaving that first to Mickey Soroko, and later to his personnel managers—Ronner, succeeded by Jerry Juliber, succeeded by Jay Bennett.

The first attempts to organize Revlon workers came in the late thirties, while the company was still on Forty-fifth Street. The union organizers had gotten some Revlon employees along with some noncompany people to form a picket line. Mickey Soroko arranged to have all the nonstrikers meet at the Bloomingdale's subway exit and drive across town to Revlon's offices in cars he had hired, walk through the jeering picketers and into the building. "Mickey made a real thriller out of it," says one who was around at the time, "and the funny part is, he really didn't have to." The people who missed the cars just walked calmly up the street and into the building. After about a week, the picketers threw in the towel. In the midforties, however, Revlon was organized by District 65 of the Distributive Workers of America, then a very left-wing outfit.

Mickey's dealings with the unions ranged from the

heavy hand to the glad hand. During a strike in 1947, he came down with the flu and had the entire union negotiating committee bussed up to his home in Larchmont. Someone suggested to Charles that this might not be so smart, bringing the workers to posh surroundings to tell them the few cents an hour raise they were demanding was excessive. But Charles supposedly said, "What are you talking about, posh? His home is a nothing. It's a piece of junk." As, by Charles's standards, it was. But the workers were impressed. They liked the swings in the yard—just the kind of playground they wanted for their kids—and they were delighted to find a bartender in a white jacket waiting for them inside with an open bar, hors d'oeuvres, and the like. Indeed, rather than feel any great sympathy for Mickey, who came down in his pajamas and bathrobe for the negotiations, some of them began to feel nine feet tall from the drinks.

Still, even if it cost a little more than it might have to settle the strike, Revlon could afford it. And it was worth the money to get those workers to stop slipping little "fuck you" notes into the compacts, the way in later years disgruntled automotive workers would toss a loose bolt into the deep recesses of the odd Cadillac or Continental.

Subsequently, Jerry Juliber somehow befriended the head of District 65—became, in fact, his best friend and neighbor, Juliber says—and there was relative harmony between Revlon and its union for the next twenty-five years.

(The ex-president of one of Revlon's former subsidiaries, whose workers were organized by a different union, makes no attempt to conceal his hatred of Charles Revson. He claims that Revson and Revlon were forever paying people off, including labor leaders. He says that one day he agreed to a 3 percent wage increase for the workers in his company, and that that evening he got a call direct from Charles ordering him to rescind the raise. The next day, he says, one of Charles's men arrived at his place with a bag full of money for the union leaders, but that he refused to go along with the attempted bribe.)

Charles himself never attended labor negotiations and

rarely visited the factory. He was much more interested in the laboratory and in the marketing end of his business—the creative side. Joseph was at least nominally in charge of overseeing Operations.

Joseph would arrive at the 134th Street plant every Tuesday for inspection. Knowing Joseph's routine, the workers, who arrived at the plant at eight, would spend the morning cleaning and sweeping and dusting until Joseph came. They would not run any of their production lines, because there was no way to do so without messing things up. Management cooperated in this farce because management's neck was on the line, too. As Joseph's car pulled up to the plant, the word would go around to get ready. And as soon as he approached a work area, the conveyer belts would be started up. Joseph would go through and see everyone working and everything spotless, just the way a plant should be. No boxes on the floor, nothing out of place.

Joseph would not tolerate smoking anywhere in the plant. A hazard. So on Tuesdays no one smoked until after he had left. There was an elevator operator, an Italian, who used to afford himself the luxury of a single cigarette every day after lunch, down in the basement by the oil furnace. One day Joseph decided to inspect the boiler room, which he had never done before. He catches this elevator operator smoking, next to the raging furnace, and fires him on the spot. The union (not District 65, a different one) threatened to shut down the plant if this man was not reinstated, which would have crippled the company right in the middle of a successful promotion—for a lipstick shade, if you can believe the neatness of the story, called *Where's the Fire?* Charles was apprised of the situation and reason prevailed.

Joseph was forever being countermanded by his brighter, brasher, younger brother. "You idiot!" Charles would say in front of others as he launched into criticism of something Joseph had done. Or else he might just come in and make a broadside attack: "Joseph," he would say, "do you know what's going on in that factory of yours? Do you *know?*" And then he'd turn on his heel and leave. This tended to have an unsettling effect.

110

Poor Joseph. His speech was extremely hesitant and riddled with even more "in turns" than Charles's was. His two next most frequent phrases were, in turn, "by executive directive" and "in that sense there."

"He was dull," says Irving Botwin. "You couldn't get two words out of him. I could never figure him out. When I first met Charles, Joe was in the Quartermaster Corps, stationed in Virginia. Lester Herzog told me once that Joseph wanted to donate a swimming pool for the camp, because it was very hot there, and that the army wasn't permitted to accept it. Joseph was the weirdest guy."

But great on the small stuff. "Joseph would come down and argue with me about the way I lettered the file cabinets," Eli Tarplin recalls. "One time I was sitting in a room arguing with him about spray cans. It was one of our first hair sprays—I think Satin Silk. I was inexperienced and I hadn't ordered enough cans, and I came back to him and said I wanted to increase the order. He said, 'You can't.' I said, 'What do you mean I can't? We're sold out!" He said, 'If you go to school and you fail your examination, you can't, in turn, take the examination over again, can you?' I said, 'No.' He said, 'Well, in that sense there, that was your projection, and, in turn, you can't do it again.' I said, 'But, Joseph, this is business!'

"So I had to go to Charles to get the extra spray cans. But in that conversation with Joseph I had said, 'Joseph, you can't do that, you'll reap a hardship.' Meaning that we'd lose sales if we didn't get the cans. And Joseph said to me, 'Eli, what are you trying to say? Were you being insulting?' He apparently thought I meant 'reek,' not 'reap.' We went and got a dictionary and looked up the word 'reap,' and he said, as he sniffed—he always put one finger on the side of his nose—he said, 'That's a new word. In the future, don't use words that I don't understand.' " In that sense there.

So Joseph's method, if you made a mistake, was to make you live with it (or fire you). Martin's philosophy was frequently articulated this way: "Kiddie, I'm running a bank. You make deposits, you make withdrawals— you're human. You got enough deposits to cover your

111

withdrawals? You got an account." Once he called in a man who had really blown it and was expecting big trouble. Martin walked over and put his hand on the man's shoulder and said, "Kiddie, you've got the deposits; don't make no more withdrawals." And that was the end of it.

Charles could take an equally broadminded view of mistakes if they were made honestly and were admitted openly. But Bill Mandel, who worked head to head with Charles for fifteen years, makes an additional point, regarding Charles's sense of proportion: "I've often said," he says, "that I could come up with a product that would sell twenty-two million dollars' worth. And the next night I could go to dinner with Charles, and if I order the wrong champagne—that's one for me, the twenty-two-million-dollar product; and one against me, the champagne. They're equal. That's my description of Charles."

It was Joseph's conservatism combined with a clash of stubborn brotherly pride that led to his departure from the company in 1955, shortly before the public offering. Joseph thought it might be risky to take Revlon public and was against the move. His partners were for it. Furthermore, Charles had decided he had had enough of arguing. There could only be one man in charge. If his partners wanted to stay in the company, they would have to enter into a voting trust agreement, assigning the voting power of their stock to him. Joseph refused. He offered to buy Charles out. But he couldn't afford to buy out Lachman as well—and Lachman, wisely, was not about to entrust the company to Joseph. So it was agreed that Revlon would buy back Joseph's stock.

Harry Meresman was sent up to Joseph's place in the country to try to mediate and persuade Joseph to sign the voting trust agreement so that he could remain in the company, but he still refused. Meresman recalls asking Joseph how he would feel if, after the company went public, the stock proved to be worth much more than he would be getting for it from the company. Joseph said that sometimes a man had to put principle ahead of money. And so he sold his 30 percent share in Revlon back to the company for $2,528,000, leaving his brothers and Lachman with all the stock.

Revlon went public on December 7, 1955, at $12 a share, six months after *The $64,000 Question* debuted. Within weeks it hit $30. By mid-1956 it had split two-for-one (as it did again in 1961, and three-for-two in 1969) and by the end of 1956 it was listed on the New York Stock Exchange.

That Charles, Martin, and Charlie Lachman had not expected this kind of instant success was evidenced by their selling 101,833 shares as part of the public offering. Thirty-four Revlon employees, meanwhile, were permitted to buy an average of 3,000 shares each at $11 a share, $1 below the opening price. Those who held on for just four years realized a 1,000 percent gain, or something more than $300,000 apiece—which was separate and apart from the stock options they were soon granted.

Had Joseph waited four years, his Revlon stock would have brought $35 million. Joseph later said that if he had known Charles wanted him to stay in the company, and that it was Charles who had sent Harry, he would have stayed. Meresman asks, dryly, "Who did he *think* was sending me?"

But unlike Charles, Joseph could live easily off the income from $2.5 million. He led a very quiet, lonely life after leaving Revlon. It was not long afterward that his wife, Elise, separated from him, leaving him even more isolated. He spent much of his time in his apartment at the Carlton House, on Sixty-first and Madison. He liked to paint.

A friend saw him sitting stiffly in the dining room of the Savoy Plaza Hotel, lunching one Saturday afternoon with his young son. On Monday, he called Joseph, and asked if he might make a suggestion: "Wouldn't it be better to take your boy to a ball game or something?" Joseph thought that was an excellent idea and thanked him for suggesting it.

Joseph would walk, alone, along Central Park South or down Fifth Avenue, wearing an overcoat sometimes even in July. One evening in December 1971, Carl Erbe saw him walking down Fifty-seventh Street. "Joe, for

113

Christ's sake, you don't look good," said Erbe. "Have you been to the doctor?" Joe said: "I'm going now." He died of a heart attack the next day. Charles attended the funeral but did not speak.

Joseph's estate was valued at $2,531,873, almost exactly what he had received for his share in the business sixteen years earlier. This was divided among his wife, Elise, and his three children, Joanne, Thomas J., and James A. Revson.

(VIII)

Fire and Ice and
Everything Nice

In the factory, we make cosmetics;
in the store, we sell hope.
　　　　　—Charles Revson

Marketing is strategy. Instinctively or consciously,
Charles plotted a shrewd one. From the beginning, Revlon's approach was that nail enamel was a fashion acces-
sory, not a mere beauty aid, and that women should use
different shades to suit different outfits, moods, and
occasions. This automatically broadened the market.
Where before a woman might not have bought a new
bottle of nail enamel until the old one was empty, now
she might keep half a dozen or more on her dresser . . .
particularly because fashions, and with them Revlon's
colors, kept changing so fast. Like General Motors, a
company Revson greatly admired, Revlon instituted the
model change and, with it, planned obsolescence. Revlon
would bring out a new color every fall and spring. By
the midforties, its semiannual shade promotions were as

115

much an event to women as Detroit's new-car introductions were to men. The most popular colors would remain in Revlon's line for years; but when the new color was announced, smart women just had to add it to their collection.

Later, with General Motors as his model, Charles developed separate cosmetic lines, similar to GM's divisions, to go after each segment of the market. Revlon itself was the popular-priced line (which Charles preferred to liken to Pontiac rather than Chevrolet); Natural Wonder, the youth line; Moon Drops, the dry-skin line; Etherea, the hypoallergenic line; Marcella Borghese, the high-class line with an international flavor; and Ultima II, the top of the line. Likewise the fragrance lines. And the strategy worked as well for Revlon as it had for GM.

Although Revlon was born of the Depression, Charles chose to compete not on price (there were nail polishes around for a dime), but on quality. Furthermore, he understood what he was really selling. He wasn't telling the fact that his polish was made with pigment, and thus fully covered the nails; he was selling the chance that it might turn the right head, or lend "a touch of class." He wasn't selling a very deep red polish; he was selling *Cherries in the Snow* and *Fire and Ice* and *Fifth Avenue Red*—and with the colors, excitement, fun, and a fantasy. Since it didn't cost any more to make dark red polish called *Berry Bon Bon* than to make plain dark red polish, and the one could be sold for six times the price of the other, this was not a bad strategy.

In order to sell the excitement, fun, and fantasy—indeed, in order to create it—Revlon always advertised very heavily in relation to its sales. One result was that beauty salons and competitors got the impression Revlon was a much larger concern than it really was—which was part of the idea. (The company borrowed privately for years before going for its first bank loan, in order not to reveal its modest balance sheet. Only the Revsons, Charlie Lachman, and Harry Meresman knew the figures; and it was Harry who arranged for the early financing, at 2 percent a month, through an arm of his accounting firm. Later, when Revlon did go to Manufacturers Hanover

116

Trust, the bank had to agree to accept only a balance sheet —no income statement—and to keep just one copy of it, sealed in an envelope in the loan officer's desk drawer.)

Revlon's first ad outside the trade journals appeared in the summer of 1935 in *The New Yorker*. This may have had something to do with Charles's passing their offices each day on the way to and from his own, but more likely it was that *The New Yorker* woman was exactly the kind of "classy dame" with which he wanted Revlon associated. The ninth-of-a-page ad read:

The New Yorker . . . The House of Revlon . . . a New York socialite . . . Saks Fifth Avenue. It's the image that counts, never mind the fact that "the House of Revlon" was a few bare rooms where people poured from big bottles into little ones and trimmed applicator brushes; or that Charles didn't even *know* a New York socialite; or that that ad, which cost $335.56, was Revlon's total consumer advertising budget for the year. (In

1975, Revlon was spending $75,000 in *The New Yorker*, and perhaps $65 million elsewhere.) As for Revlon's being available at Saks, an early departure from Revlon's beauty salon exclusivity, the only thing more important to Charles than being in Saks was life itself—and it was a toss-up, at that. Saks was everything this boy from the west side of Manchester wanted to be.

Whatever profit Revlon made was plowed back into advertising. At first the company even borrowed to advertise. The result was enormous demand at the beauty salons for the latest Revlon color. And the mechanics of a manicurist's tray being what they were (particularly the trays Revlon designed), it was much easier to carry just one line of nail enamel than several. It was also less of an investment. Revlon became not just the General Motors of nail enamels in the beauty salon field; it became the AT&T.

In its first five years, Revlon dealt exclusively with the beauty trade. That in itself was a selling point to the beauticians; and since the company couldn't sell everyone at once anyway, it was good strategy to start here. What better advertisement than to have Revlon used by the professionals? What more ideal arrangement than to have women *pay* to have ten samples of the product painted onto their nails, to be shown around town for the rest of the week? At ten to the customer, Revlon calculated in 1948, within a week or two of introducing a new shade upwards of 50,000,000 freshly manicured samples would be strumming the national tablecloth.

It was only natural that women whose nails were done with Revlon enamel upstairs in a department store beauty salon would then demand the product downstairs at the cosmetics counter. Revlon soon obliged. And after selected department stores were opened, selected drugstores were offered the opportunity of carrying the Revlon line, as well. "Selected," because a Revlon product was not just any commodity, like soap powder, to be found on every corner. The trick was to make it nearly as available and yet maintain the aura of exclusivity. By limiting the Revlon "franchise" to the best outlets, Revlon also gained more leverage with each one, and the ability to demand the kind of attention and promotion it could not otherwise expect.

Revson understood the difference between a differentiable product and a commodity. It is the difference tween Morton's salt, at ten cents a pound, and Lawry's seasoned salt, at $1.79. Both have brand names, true, but there is not much you can do to distinguish one pure salt from another. You compete on price and on the efficiencies of your operation. Revson didn't want to compete on price, and his operation was not all that efficient. He wanted to compete on the creativity of his products and on his company's marketing skill. Example: buoyed by the incredible advertising power of *The $64,000 Question*, Revlon hair spray sales reached a volume of $15 million or more, and was a substantial part of the business. But hair spray, like soap or deodorant, was more of a commodity than a fashion accessory, and Charles saw that the margins were going out of the business. So, rather than lower his price to meet the growing competition, or advertise aggressively to maintain the market share built up by *The $64,000 Question*, Charles made the strategic decision to "milk" the product. He kept his price high and cut back his advertising. His profit on each can sold, with fewer ads to pay for, was juicy, even though, predictably, the sales volume began a steady decline. It was a profitable way to bow out of a market Revson felt wasn't worth fighting for.

"Cost-of-goods"—the cost of the product itself and its packaging—was the fundamental number in Revson's business equation. Charles liked products that cost little to make, relative to what he could sell them for. If his cost-of-goods was low enough, he could advertise heavily; he could afford severe quality standards; he could make mistakes; he could operate his impressive research facility; and he could still make a good profit.

Many manufacturers will sell a product for twice what it costs them to make, applying the rest of the money to indirect costs like advertising, sales commissions, management, overhead, interest and, they hope, profits. Revson tried to sell his products for quadruple, not just double, their cost. The distributors and stores to whom the products were sold would then approximately double the price once more.

Cost figures are carefully guarded. However, those that follow, from 1962, are fairly representative of Revlon's costs throughout its history. Cosmetics have gone up in price since 1962, of course, as have Revlon's costs—but the *ratios* have not changed that much. Costs at Revlon rose relative to selling prices during the sixties but then began falling significantly as, in the last few years, a professional management group began to manage the operations of the company as shrewdly as Charles was managing its marketing.

The cost-of-materials table on page 122 affords a glimpse of the heart of Revlon's business.* Notice, for example, that the materials in a seventy-five-cent bottle of cream nail enamel cost Revlon only one tenth of that. (The enamel itself, minus bottle and box, cost practically nothing.) A two-ounce bottle of Eterna 27, the magic wrinkle remover, sold for $8.00 and cost just fifty cents (plus labor and overhead) to produce. Other products allowed less generous markups (like the hair sprays), while some allowed more. Nail polish remover didn't allow as good a markup, presumably because it's not what you'd call a high-fashion item. *This* commodity, however, had the very considerable advantage of being carried along by the rest of the Revlon line. Futurama lipstick cases, including one in sterling silver for $47.50, had modest markups relative to those of the lipstick refills— the old "give away the razors to sell the blades" ploy, only not quite so generous.

Note also the dynamics of "economy sizes." In 1962 you could buy three times as much Revlon Velvety Nail Enamel Remover for sixty cents as you could for thirty-

---

* Cost-of-materials includes the bottle, can, or case; the goo inside; the label; the box—everything but factory labor and overhead. And there's a good deal less labor involved in putting together a lipstick than, say, a watch. Revson's rule of thumb was to keep his cost-of-materials under 20 percent of his whole-sale price, and to keep his cost-of-goods—materials *plus* labor and overhead—under 33 percent.

five cents. But you weren't hurting Revlon; the extra two ounces, including the larger package, cost a mere 3.3 cents. The markup on the extra two ounces was even greater than on the first ounce.

And note, finally, the impact volume can have on costs. The little one and a quarter-ounce purse-size Living Curl Hair sprays actually cost Revlon more than each regular seven-ounce can—presumably because there were twenty times as many regular-size cans being made.

One reason for Revlon's hefty markups is that the consumer is paying for a lot of advertising. Professor Theodore Levitt of Harvard Business School, among others, argues that advertising and packaging are as much a part of cosmetic products as alcohol or lanolin, and so a justifiable, albeit very large, part of the cost. Would an unadvertised private-label lipstick in a plain package afford a woman as much satisfaction as a Revlon lipstick at twice the price? Would she be participating in the fun and fantasy? If the answer is yes, then Safeway is missing a bet. But women, by and large, don't want elegance on sale. It is a marketing cliché that with certain ailing products the way to boost sales is not to cut prices but to *hike* them.

Revlon's fashion strategy came into its own in 1940, with the "Matching Lips and Fingertips" campaign and the introduction of Revlon lipstick. For the first time, Revlon ads, like its products, were in full color, and spread over two pages in such magazines as *Vogue* and *Harper's Bazaar*. "Pick up a tea-cup, light a cigarette, draw on a glove. Your slightest gesture delights the eye . . . with lips and fingertips accented vitally, fashionably by Revlon Nail Enamel." Crudely put, Revlon was selling "class to the masses"; a chance to be fashionable for the price of a lipstick.

Matching lips and fingertips was a canny way to enter the lipstick business. The only way to match your lips with Revlon fingertips was, of course, with Revlon lipstick. Neat. Interestingly, "matching lips and fingertips" was not an original Revlon idea. Another firm had used the theme in its ads a few years earlier. The difference

REVLON COST-OF-MATERIALS, JUNE 1962
(Selected Products)

Product		Retail Price	Cost	Cost as % of Retail	Cost As % of Wholesale	Units Sold First Six Months 1962
Nail Enamel						
Cream	½ oz.	75¢	7.5¢	10%	17%	3,509,737
Frosted	½ oz.	95¢	12.1¢	12%	21%	2,087,846
Transparent	½ oz.	75¢	7.3¢	9%	16%	165,032
Removers						
Velvety	1 oz.	35¢	6.2¢	17%	30%	36,336
"	3 oz.	60¢	9.6¢	16%	27%	27,856
Nonsmudge	5½ oz.	65¢	9.6¢	14%	25%	254,682
Lipsticks						
Lanolite		$1.10	9.5¢	9%	15%	1,890,584
Lustrous		$1.10	9.6¢	9%	15%	4,034,352
Super-Lustrous		$1.25	11.5¢	9%	15%	3,310,727
Futurama Cases						
Petite Diamond		$1.75	32.0¢	18%	36%	Not yet on
Brushed Gold		$4.00	79.0¢	20%	33%	the market
Sterling Silver		$47.50	$9.41	20%	33%	

Makeup

Touch & Glow Liquid	1 oz.	$1.50	8.6¢	6%	10%	1,590,166
Cake Rouge		$1.50	29.6¢	20%	33%	97,667
Ultima Liquid Makeup	1½ oz.	$3.75	21.4¢	6%	10%	127,447
Ultima Face Powder	2½ oz.	$3.75	43.3¢	12%	19%	36,648

Eyeliner

Roll-On Mascara		$2.00	26.9¢	13%	22%	225,896
Brush-On Mascara		$2.00	17.4¢	9%	15%	488,881
Cake Mascara		$1.35	14.6¢	11%	18%	64,802
Liquid Eyeliner		$1.50	10.7¢	7%	12%	290,516
Eyeliner Pencil	¼ oz.	$1.00	9.0¢	9%	15%	232,113

Creams and Lotions

Moon Drops						
Moisture Balm	1 oz.	$2.00	17.4¢	9%	15%	70,143
Ultima Cream	2 oz.	$5.00	44.0¢	9%	15%	10,930
Clean & Clear	5½ oz.	$1.25	16.4¢	14%	22%	359,013
Eterna 27	2 oz.	$8.00	49.1¢	6%	10%	188,622
"	4 oz.	$13.50	87.0¢	6%	11%	57,285

Living Curl Hair Spray

Purse Size Regular	1¼ oz.	$1.00	25.6¢	26%	43%	47,222
Regular	7 oz.	$1.50	20.9¢	14%	23%	1,044,004

was, as with so many other things he copied—Revson made it work.

It wasn't until 1944 (*Pink Lightning*) that the full-scale color promotions were begun. Prior to that there had been advertising campaigns like "Expect Great Things From Revlon," and "Morale Is A Woman's Business." Kickier, and more Revlon-like, was the first ad to run in *Vogue*, in June 1936, reproduced on this page. It had what came to be known as "the Revlon touch," that little extra creative twist that people found hard to define, but to which they all referred.

Scandal in the
REVLON nail polish family!

Revlon's "G"* Woman, famous for gathering advance style information and creating new exclusive nail polish shades to harmonize, has been running after the men.

But she was doing it for you, my lady. So if you have seen her talking to strangers, please be tolerant. She was merely finding out what nail polish shades "He" prefers for you this summer.

"He" likes "Bimi" and "Sudan." You will, too. New. Timely. And they wear and wear. Sun-fast. Lustrous.

*Gadabout

REVLON NAIL ENAMEL CORPORATION
125 West 45th Street, New York City

The shade promotions allowed for total "theming" of the marketing effort. To introduce *Fatal Apple* in 1945— "the most tempting color since Eve winked at Adam"— color spreads were place in the fashion magazines; department stores were furnished with window displays; the Revlon showroom was decorated to match; and Revlon's publicity director, Bea Castle, arranged an elaborate press party that featured not only Maurice the Mind-reader, but also a snake and snake charmer from the William Morris Agency, a hollow gold apple door prize from Cartier, a grove of miniature apple trees from the Washington State apple-growers' association, and fashions from Forever Eve. All New York's top editors and publishers were invited to this party and some of them came. Charles himself remained in the background, but loved it. He had taken particular interest in the menu: lobster and rice, meatballs and spaghetti—this was a cocktail party, but he felt that people coming from work wanted more than just cheese on a cracker. They wanted entertainment and something good to eat along with their drinks.

When *Plumb Beautiful* was introduced in 1949, Bergdorf Goodman devoted eight windows to the promotion, where Russian sables, chinchilla, ermine, and mink were the background for Revlon's sixty-cent nail enamel. Such was (and is) the power of a Revlon promotion in the fashion world.

In 1950, Revlon kicked off its new color with a full-page teaser in *The New York Times*. Smoke was curling from the burning edges of a hole in the center of the page. At first glance, the hole and the smoke looked real. The headline was, WHERE'S THE FIRE? And that's all. No Revlon signature, no copy, nothing. Shortly thereafter, *Where's the Fire?* was introduced as Revlon's new shade.

(Revlon had no monopoly on cleverness. To launch Heaven Sent in the late forties, Madame Helena Rubinstein floated hundreds of pale blue balloons down on Fifth Avenue, each bearing a sample of the fragrance.)

The shade promotion to end all others was Revlon's *Fire and Ice*, in the fall of 1952. "You could hardly pick up a general-circulation or fashion magazine this week," *Business Week* led off a major story, "without seeing the [*Fire and Ice*] advertisement . . . To much of the industry, this was one of the most effective ads in cosmetics history. In a sense, it marked a new height in an industry where advertising is all-important (cosmetics are second only to food in advertising volume). Perhaps more than

125

any previous ad, this one successfully combines dignity, class, and glamour (a trade euphemism for sex.)"

The two-page spread consisted of a dazzling model, Dorian Leigh, in an icy silver-sequin dress with a fiery scarlet cape; and on the facing page, the headline, ARE YOU MADE FOR 'FIRE AND ICE?' You were, the ad stated, if you could answer eight of the following fifteen questions in the affirmative:

Have you ever danced with your shoes off?

Did you ever wish on a new moon?

Do you blush when you find yourself flirting?

When a recipe calls for one dash of bitters, do you think it's better with two?

Do you secretly hope the next man you meet will be a psychiatrist?

Do you sometimes feel that other women resent you?

Have you ever wanted to wear an ankle bracelet?

Do sables excite you, even on other women?

Do you love to look up at a man?

Do you face crowded parties with panic—then wind up having a wonderful time?

Does gypsy music make you sad?

Do you think any man really understands you?

Would you streak your hair with platinum without consulting your husband?

If tourist flights were running, would you take a trip to Mars?

Do you close your eyes when you're kissed?

The idea behind this campaign, besides playing on the "duality of women," was to create a sense of indignation at all the attention European women had lately been getting at the expense of the supposedly more tame American women. Press releases stressed this theme, and Carl Erbe invented the American Institute for the Recognition of "Fire and Ice" to fan the flames.

The response to the promotion was sensational. (It didn't hurt the other forty-eight shades of lipstick and nail enamel in the Revlon line, either.) Nine thousand window displays were devoted to *Fire and Ice*. Every newspaper and magazine wrote about it and every radio announcer made reference to it. *Fire and Ice* beauty contests were conducted around the country. Disc jockeys and newspaper editors were sent questionnaires ("In your field, you are a pulse-taker and an opinion-maker. Your ideas are very important . . ."); and the uncynical responses that were returned, by the hundreds, were consistent with the times. Pat Chamburs of radio station WFLA in Tampa answered this way:

Which qualities do you think make for Fire and Ice in women?

1. Ever so slightly pouted lips.
2. Smoldering, sad eyes with a "I wanta, but only with you" look.
3. Lovely, large, and prominently displayed bust.

Would you marry a Fire and Ice girl?

Yes, Yes, Yes, Yes, Yes, Yes, Yes, Yes, Yes, Yes, YES!!! (Could we take my wife along?)

Name a few of the women who epitomize Fire and Ice to you?

Marilyn Monroe, Antonel la Lualdi, Rossana Podesta, Silvano Mangano, Linda Darnell, Marilyn Monroe. [You can see that the European "threat" had some basis.]

The managing editor of the Waukegan, Illinois, *News-Sun* answered: "I don't know any, and I don't know what a *Fire and Ice* girl is . . . but I'm for 'em."

The editor of the Wesleyan College paper wrote at the bottom of his questionnaire, "Please send me more information."

Twenty-two hotels, from the Plaza in New York to the Cornhusker in Lincoln, Nebraska, were induced to stage *Fire and Ice* preview parties. Rudy Vallee, starring at the Sheraton Biltmore in Providence, talked about the *Fire and Ice* party all week.

Judges in the Hollywood *Fire and Ice* beauty contest included David Niven, Robert Stack, and Ray Milland.

Arthur Godfrey, Jimmy Durante, and Steve Allen managed to play on the promotion. Dave Garroway gave the *Fire and Ice* quiz to one of his secretaries on the *Today* show; *Beat the Clock* and *Search for Tomorrow* also found ways to work it in. Bob Ferris, of radio station KNX in Los Angeles, went through a "Firewater and

Dice" routine. ("Do sables excite you?" "No, I never cared for the smell of horses.")

Revlon's advertising muscle never hurt in getting plugs like these. "Those things are done sort of inadvertently," Martin once explained to *Business Week*. "What you do is go to see Hope or Skelton or somebody of that nature and tell them about your new product coming out with, oh, a couple of million dollars in advertising, and then the script writer writes it in . . . So that's the way we get it in—sort of inadvertently." Commented S. J. Perelman: "The easy negligence of the whole thing is truly captivating. For sheer insouciance, nothing could surpass the spectacle of an incipient Mark Twain grinding out cosmetic yaks with a two-million-dollar pitchfork lightly pinking his bottom."

The *Fire and Ice* campaign definitely had "the Revlon touch." "There's a little bit of bad in every good woman," Revlon marketers felt, and it was to this that Revlon always tried to appeal. It was a matter of giving women what Kay Daly called "a little immoral support." Revson wanted his models to be "Park Avenue whores"—elegant, but with the sexual thing underneath. The *Fire and Ice* copy asked: "What is the American girl made of? Sugar and spice and everything nice? Not since the days of the Gibson Girl! There's a *new* American beauty . . . she's tease and temptress, siren and gamin, dynamic and demure. Men find her slightly, delightfully baffling. Sometimes a little maddening. Yet they admit she's *easily* the most exciting woman in the world! She's the 1952 American beauty, with a foolproof formula for melting a male! She's the '*Fire and Ice*' girl. (Are you?)"

"Our ads were more strongly read than the editorial copy in the magazines where we advertised, and that was given to us as a goal," says Norman B. Norman, who headed Revlon's advertising from the agency side in the late forties and into the midfifties. "All Revlon advertising had to do with emotions . . . how women thought, how they lived, how they loved . . . and we wove in our products. That's quite different from what most companies do, where they describe their products, the benefits of them. Revlon never did that, which was a brilliance

128

of its own." (In later years Revlon did do that, particularly when it had unique treatment products to sell which could be differentiated from the competition on their merits.)

Fire and Ice was just the kind of manufactured national event that *The Great Gatsby*, from Paramount Pictures, would be twenty-odd years later. Paramount had a somewhat more jaded press and populace to try to excite; but they also had a classic novel, a nostalgia craze, and Robert Redford to work with. Revlon had a red lipstick.

Who didn't?

Now, the question naturally arises, who was the genius behind this campaign and the others? And the first part of the answer is that it was not Charles. Yes, Charles had the judgment most of the time to know what was good and what was not, in itself no small talent. But he was no David Ogilvy. As a copywriter, Charles could not have commanded $100 a week. It was not he who came up with names like *Paint the Town Pink* or *Rosy Future* or *Pink Vanilla*. His creativity lay in the product end. As a marketer, he was shrewd rather than creative. He liked to think of himself as a great editor. "The trick isn't to know when you have it," he used to say, "the trick is to know when you don't." His forte was criticism, not enthusiasm.

No one could match his scrutiny of the color in an ad, or his sense of how the model's eyebrows should look, or his patience in endlessly improving a package design. But he needed a good deal of coaching when it came to words. "Look," he told his marketing people once, "all of us can't write. All of us are not endowed with the ability to write. All of us don't know how to put the words together. But at the least—the very, very least—all of us who are connected with marketing, regardless of what, should try to learn what they are and become editors, at least, of words."

Those who worked with him closely say that his editing had two consistent and allied characteristics. The first was to make things "safer." Where he made change after change, the trend was often away from the daring or the risky or the bold to the more conventional. Secondly, his

129

renowned "perfectionism" to some degree was, rather, the grip of indecision. He would redo and redo and change and change past one deadline after another, not so much to make each version better than the last—which they often were not—but because of the fear of letting loose something that might be no good. He was a terrible procrastinator because, egotist though he was, like anyone else he was unsure of his judgments and afraid of making a mistake.

Revlon's creativity was the product of a few key people within the company and an endless succession of agency people. Bea Castle was one of the company's creative mainstays, responsible for many of the early shade names.

"*Fire and Ice* was my name," she remembers. "The color we had for that particular fall was not a very exciting color . . . it was red. How much can you say about red? But it was the color that women were going to use, and it was the season when the Italian starlets first came into being. We were struggling with names, trying to do a red that had meaning. So Kay Daly and I, who worked together as a team for a long time, were knocking around themes and names, names and themes, over breakfast one morning at Reuben's. As we were talking, I said: 'Let's talk about what a woman is. That's what we're really talking about. A woman is hot and cold, good or bad, a lady and a tramp . . . a woman is *fire and ice*.' At which point Kay said, 'Just a minute, I've got an idea.' We both agreed it was a corny name, but that we could do something with it by doing a questionnaire. Kay did half of the questions and I did half. Then we decided to use Suzy Parker as the model. [Actually, it was Suzy's sister, Dorian Leigh.] I took her over to the Waldorf and said, 'Put a streak of silver in her hair. That's the ice.' Kay went to a designer and had him do up an all-glitter dress with a red coat.' "

And so the creative process unfolds. In more ways than one. Kay Daly's version of the genesis of *Fire and Ice* differs only on the essentials: 'I once used 'fire and ice' in a piece of copy that went, 'all sugar and spice in the sunlight, all fire and ice at night,' " Kay explains, "so I pulled that phrase *Fire and Ice* as a shade name, and

130

it was approved. Bea had nothing to do with this. Charles then said, 'I would like to see an ad that would be an answer to all the publicity going on that Italian women are the most exciting women in the world.' I had to give it to him by Monday, so I spent the whole weekend working on it. I wrote a kind of *Time/Life* essay on American women . . . and it seemed dull. Finally I decided at the last minute Sunday night to do it as a questionnaire.

"Since advertising was supposed to be Martin's function, Charles didn't get into it as much then as he did later. He would just come in at the end and kill it all, usually, or change it all. But when he read this copy . . . I remember there were a lot of people sitting around the boardroom table in the old Squibb Building, and Charles sauntered in as he does [at a bit of a tilt, elbows close to his sides], and he sat down at the end of the table reading this thing. He was very intent on it, and then he looked up with a grin on his face—which was very unusual—and he looked right around the table to me and said, 'Who wrote this crap?' And that's the only compliment I ever considered he paid me. He said it with a smile, meaning, 'I adore it, but I'd never tell you that.' "

And Bea Castle? "She hated it, as a matter of fact," Kay remembers. "Bea and I had a kind of iffy relationship, although we did get along very well for two women in the same business. Martin called Bea in and showed her the *Fire and Ice* photo of Dorian Leigh by Avedon and asked what she thought of it. Bea looked at it and sort of didn't say anything, and so Martin said, 'Do you think it's too rich looking?' And Bea said, 'I think she looks like a little tootsie whom the Aga Kahn would have spotted on the Riviera and he would have said, "Here's some money, go to Dior and blow it." ' And that was Bea's comment on the photo. I had to take it to the editor of *Vogue*, Jessica Davies, to have her opinion on it before Martin would go with it, and she thought it was the classiest thing she had ever seen, and they did a whole issue on *Fire and Ice*."

Kay's original ad copy was barely changed at all, which was almost unheard of at Revlon. "Bea did add one question, which was, 'Does gypsy music make you sad?' I didn't like it, but I went along with it."

As for the famous *Fire and Ice* photograph: "I had had an idea of what the costume should look like," Kay says. "A long turtleneck sweater made of rhinestones. Dick [Avedon] and I always talked out all the details before we took any pictures, and he said the costume should have more contrast. I had seen a Balenciaga cape when I was in Paris and we had it copied. The dress was more of a problem, because I couldn't ask a Norell to sew on all those rhinestones, so I called a strange little man I knew who designed G-strings and clothes for strippers and gave him a hundred-and-fifty-dollar down payment. He didn't have enough help to sew on all the rhinestones, so my assistant and I sat sewing with him until we had enough for the photograph. There really was no back to the dress, just a front. If you turned the model around, there would be just a bra and a girdle and big safety pins holding it all together. We got Dorian into it, and Dick is absolutely marvelous with models. He said to her, 'How *dare* you look like that? How *dare* you look so beautiful?' And her face just lit up."

How did the average American woman score on the *Fire and Ice* test? "It wasn't that serious," Kay explains. "I think women had a lot more humor about themselves at that time than advertisers gave them credit for. The things that I did for Revlon I always did sort of tongue-in-cheek, feeling that women would be amused."

Fire and Ice was picked as the best ad of the year by *Advertising Age*.

Charles was an instinctive rather than a professional marketing man. He had little regard for a company like Procter & Gamble, even though to most marketers P&G is about as good as you can get. The modus operandi at Procter & Gamble is market research and testing. Testing new products, testing new ads, testing alternative promotions . . . the science of marketing. The modus operandi at Revlon was instinct . . . the art of marketing. Fashions changed too fast to allow test marketing. Where P&G might take four years to launch a new product, Revlon

132

could be in national distribution in six months. Charles had to anticipate the market and run on instinct. He would get the opinions of those around him—Revlon secretaries were particularly important in this regard—and that was it. (He did test market, in a sense, by allowing his competitors to make many of the innovations—and the mistakes—for him.) Nor did he bother to commission market research to determine by questionnaire what women wanted, what they liked about competitive products, and how they thought of Revlon. He relied largely on his own intimate understanding of his products and of his market. He was his own walking market survey, asking questions of retailers and consumers wherever he went. He did credit himself with "sensitivity," but lost patience with people who ascribed his success to some sort of magic touch. As he himself put it: "Jesus Christ, I graduated from school—I wasn't considered a genius. I never was an outstanding success from the day I went to work. I never had any whatever it is. The only thing you can say about me is that if I have something to do, I'll learn everything about it—that I will. I'm nosy as a son of a gun. I am nosy. There's nothing about it I won't learn."

Remembering their childhood, Martin says: "He was always a curious boy, he always had to ask questions—sometimes to the disgust of Joe and me. In those days I guess we were insecure, and a guy always asking questions—you'd say: 'Why don't you stop it by now? Why be a pest?'"

Charles had to know how things *worked*. If man is motivated by his need to control his environment, Charles seemed to be doubly so. And to control things, one must first understand how they work.

"If I pick up this cigarette lighter," says Robert Armstrong, picking up his gold Tiffany lighter, "to me it's something to light a cigarette with. Charles would pick it up and he'd ask what it cost. Solid gold? He'd look at the mechanism. How is it put together? He'd look at it from all angles. Why is it designed this way? What kind of hinge is there? Is there money in this? He'd make a thorough analysis, and he would learn something from this lighter that he would store away in his mind and use someday in connection with something else."

"When we went on trips together," says Mrs. Jack Friedman, "he and Jack and I would disappear. The three of us would walk around the smallest town in Greece or Italy and check out factories. If there wasn't a factory there, we'd check out a grocery store and dissect it and analyze it and talk to the owner and find out where he gets his stuff from and so on." A *grocery* store? Charles explained: "You must understand grocery stores, food stores, whatever it is—it's related." At one point he became intrigued by McDonald's, and would drive around on weekends with the Friedmans' then thirteen-year-old son, watching how the McDonald's operations worked.

What's more, he was an enormous reader. Cowboy books for escape, yes, but piles of magazines of all sorts, too. "He was more up to date than anybody," says Bill Mandel.

Better than anything else, Charles knew women. Not how to live with them, maybe, or how to respect them, but how they should look and what they would buy.

"I always felt that when Charles looked at a woman, and I'm including myself, it was like being behind an X-ray machine," Kay Daly says. "Charles knew if I had a slip on, if my underwear was clean . . . About fifteen years ago he told me he had thought about it and had decided how I should dress. 'You don't have a look,' he said. 'You dress well, but you don't have a look. Any woman has to have a look. The Duchess of Windsor has a look, and like it or not, it's a look.' I was very skinny at the time, and he said, 'You've got good legs and you should always wear a plain pump and never ankle straps,' which Bea Castle wore always and he couldn't stand it— sort of Joan Crawford shoes. He said: 'You should always wear full skirts and very wide belts and a shirtwaist top.'

"It was a very good formula for the way I was built at the time. Charles just had an innate feel for these things. He had terrible taste in furniture and decor [gold on gold], but the way a woman should look was native to him."

He had an almost irresistible urge to make people

over—men or women. He would lecture men on the virtues of jacket cuffs with buttons that really buttoned (he used to roll up his jacket sleeves along with his shirt sleeves); he would go up to women he didn't even know—in an elevator, for example—and say, "Excuse me, but if I may make a little criticism . . ."

"Why do you wear your hair that way?" he once asked Iris Heller, almost stamping his foot in frustration. It bothered him, as a sour note would bother a sensitive musician.

The Friedmans had Charles over for dinner one evening along with one of their sons and his date, who hadn't been to the house before. The young couple excused themselves to go out, and the older people around the table began remarking on how really beautiful the girl was. "She's going to have a double chin in ten years," Charles said. He knew.

One day Charles and Suzanne Grayson were talking and Charles looked up at her and said, "You're going to have a baby." Which was true, but "I don't think even my mother knew at the time. I knew, but I wasn't even fat, and I was sitting down when he said it—he just knew. He was a very perceptive man." This remarkable sensitivity, combined with his Pygmaliomania, led him to eventually to "redo" tens of millions of women throughout the world.

(IX)

The Revlon Girl(s)

I did not like him.
—Suzy Parker

As one of the largest advertisers in the fashion business, Revlon's appetite for beautiful women was insatiable. Just as a great many of New York's ad men and designers passed through Revlon's mill at one time or another, so did a great many models. Candice Bergen was at school in Philadelphia when Revlon's Sandy Buchsbaum "discovered" her and spread her across the pages of *Vogue*. Barbara Feldon came rolling out of a rug in a commercial for Chemstrand when Revson happened to be watching television. She was signed to an exclusive contract. (After three years with Revlon, she became *Get Smart* Agent 99.) Mary Bacon was a jockey—and, it turned out later much to Revlon's embarrassment, a Ku Klux Klanswoman—before she became a "Charlie girl." Most models were sent to Revlon by agencies for specific assignments. Model mogul Wilhelmina herself posed for Revlon. Just four women—Dorian Leigh and her sister Suzy Parker, Barbara Britton and Lauren Hutton—became so closely identified with the company over a period of years that they were, in effect, "the Revlon girl."

Dorian Leigh, the stunning redhead in the *Fire and Ice* ad, was already a top model when she did *Fatal Apple*, her first Revlon spread, in 1945. From then on Revson considered her "lucky" and used her in shade promotion after shade promotion. But he barely knew her while she was "the Revlon girl." "He only became very very friendly with me," she says, "when I came to Europe and he came here." In Europe still, running a restaurant she calls Chez Dorian about an hour outside Paris, she says that in the fifties Revson became "very romantic" with her—but that he didn't get very far. "He was used to buying everything he wanted," she says, as though writing jacket copy for a pulp novel, "and in me he met someone he couldn't buy."

Still, there was the weekend in 1959 when she kept inviting him down to her place in Portofino, letting it be known, according to one of those at lunch, that she was wearing no bra. (In 1959 that made Ms. Leigh a swinger.) So they were at least, as she says, "very very friendly."

"When I knew him," she says, "he couldn't make up his mind whether to really divorce [Ancky]. He didn't want to divorce her until he found something better, you see?" One candidate who apparently crossed his mind was Dorian herself—an excellent cook, very well spoken, cultivated, glamorous, and beautiful.

"The last time I saw him in Paris, in 1959," she says, "I was just about to get married again. And he was advising me against it, naturally. [Because he was interested himself? "Yes, that's right, more or less."] And he sent me a tremendous thing of orchids—I think probably there must have been forty different varieties of orchids. I don't know where he bought it, but a tremendous thing. And I called him up and said, 'Charles, that's just about the most vulgar thing I ever saw in my life!' And he said, 'Well, I didn't want to send you the *money* . . .'"

137

He did have a tendency to overdo. Having become so rich so fast, it would take him a while to develop a light touch. When Barbara Britton, Revlon spokeswoman, opened on Broadway in *Thee and Me*, co-starring Derwood Kirby, Charles sent two *enormous*, waist-high vases of roses. "One would really have been more than enough." Ms. Britton can't help smiling. Particularly as the play closed that same night.

Later, when she and Revlon parted on friendly terms after twelve years, she got not so much as a thank-you note from Charles. She was no longer important to the business, so what was the point? "I must admit I was a little bit piqued," she says.

She had, in the early years, been anchoring nine commercials a week: three each on *The $64,000 Question*, *The $64,000 Challenge*, and *The Walter Winchell File*. Models would play out the scenes in the ads, but she did all the talking. In her busiest year she earned $130,000—more than twice what the president of TWA was making. Her work load diminished after the quiz-show era passed, and when taped commercials replaced live. But her famous line—"If it's the finest of its kind it's by Revlon—Revlon London, Paris and New York"—opened *The Ed Sullivan Show* week after week. "And now here's the *star* of our show," she would continue, a gracious version of jolly Ed McMahon, "Ed *Sullivan!*"

While Barbara was integrity-grace-and-beauty on television, Suzy Parker was the same, only with a dollop of elegant come-hither thrown in, in print. Born "Cecilia" Parker (in 1932), she now lives in California with her husband, actor Bradford Dillman. She became an even better-known model than her older sister, Dorian. *Life* magazine devoted a cover to her in 1957, and no less an authority than *The New York Times*, in their obituary of Kay Daly, incorrectly credited her with the *Fire and Ice* ad.

Charles was wild for Suzy Parker, at least professionally. "They don't make combos like that anymore," he said of the two sisters. But when B.B.D.&O., the ad agency, suggested that she be put under exclusive contract—a novel concept at the time—he said no. The agency was talking about a lot of money; Charles wouldn't even throw out a counteroffer. "He thought I should be working for the sheer joy of working for Revlon," she says. Her $120-an-hour fee might have been more than fair for most kinds of work, but these Revlon shade promotions involved a single session, three or four hours, and that was *the* ad for the season. "So I finally said screw him," she says. "The next time they wanted me for an ad I said no thank you. Then the war was on. He hated me. He absolutely hated me. He said, 'I can't stand the girl's face, I don't want to see it anymore.' Which was okay by me—I had other accounts and I was interested in movies.

"As time went on it became really very funny. They did this particular Cleopatra ad and shot it with ten or twelve different black-haired girls, at great expense. It wasn't the photographer's fault; it was just that they couldn't choose the model. So they had to keep paying Avedon for the pictures. It was a disaster. Finally, at the last minute, they brought me in and put a black wig on me and they never let Revson know it was me in the ad. He never realized." (He doubtless realized full well. Out of pride he may have pretended he didn't.)

Earlier she had done a similar last-minute bailout retake on *Stormy Pink*. "We worked at night [double the fee] off Montauk Point, in the ocean, and I had to hold a stallion. We really did that. It was very dangerous because it was windy and the pebbles kept rolling out from under the horse's feet, and I'm trying to hold him down. We worked on that for almost six hours in the middle of the night, in the middle of the ocean [well, not quite], and I was in a chiffon dress. I think the reason I was such a good model wasn't that I was such a particular beauty or anything, but that I was as strong as a horse. And that occasion proved it!"

The Revson/Parker relationship was such that when *Time* sent a photographer around in 1956, Charles had to pay her to appear—as if it were a modeling session and not a simple publicity shot. (See photo.) While the photographer was setting up in Revson's office, Parker was dressing in the ladies' room and putting on her false

139

fingernails. "I wore false ones in all the ads because I've never had long fingernails," she says. "I had gotten them all glued on, rather unsatisfactorily, and I was trussing my white mink, and I make my entrance and everyone says, 'Wow, wow,' and all that—and I lose one of the damn fingernails."

"I'm crawling under the desk and the *Time* man says, 'What are you doing?' 'I'm looking for my blinking, bloody fingernail,' I said—and Charles turned absolutely beet-red. 'You mean you wear *false fingernails?*' the photographer asked. He thought it was a riot. I thought Charles was going to explode with rage, because I said, 'Of course I do, I always have—in all those ads.' At which point Charles turns to me and says, 'All right, let's change the subject.' He thought I had done it deliberately . . . and I don't know that I didn't."

And yet, even after he turned her down for the contract she wanted, she kept doing the ads. "It was my own vanity, I suppose . . . my own challenge that I could come in after they'd spent all that time and money trying with other girls and in two or three hours do the ad."

In terms of exclusive contracts, she says, she paved the way for Lauren Hutton. "But," she adds, laughing, "Lauren should really get her own expression. She's still using mine."

Mary Laurence "Lauren" Hutton, as practically any red-blooded American knows, *is* Ultima II and gets a bit more than $200,000 a year to play the role. Less well known is that before he signed Lauren, Revson was considering Racquel Welch for a similar job, presumably at a higher price. He got as far as summoning her then husband, Patrick Curtis, to a meeting in his office at which he proceeded to tell him, in front of several others, that Racquel had no taste—or at least came off *appearing* as if she had no taste—and that she didn't know how to dress. He would have to make her over. Curtis played along, saying he would be willing to allow Charles to buy her a new wardrobe, and from there they went over to the Waldorf Towers to meet the sex symbol herself. Whether Charles was unimpressed, the money was too much, or Curtis/Welch nixed the idea—most probably the last—it went no farther. Had it, Revlon would have taken on a rather different image from the ones projected around Barbara Britton and Lauren Hutton.

Contrary to publicity photos, and certainly contrary to rumor, there was nothing between Lauren Hutton and Charles Revson beyond a friendly mutual respect. She was not Revson's discovery; she was, she says, just the logical choice: "I was the only big brand-name model in the country." Nor did she meet him during the five months of negotiations that led to her exclusive Revlon engagement. It was only at the signing, in 1973, that they met for the first time—and established a rapport.

It was photographer Richard Avedon who had sold Revson on the twenty-eight-year-old one-time Playboy bunny. And now, for the signing, he was asking her to be on her best behavior—to appear, not in jeans, which was more her off-camera style, but in "high drag," as she puts it. She complied. She even agreed to wear her "tooth," the dental falsie that bridges the gap in her smile. She didn't want to, "because it always creates an artificial situation," but she wore it anyway.

They were all sitting around stiffly—she and Avedon, Charles and Paul Woolard, agents and lawyers—having tea. When the crumpets came around, she grabbed one, completely forgetting about her tooth. Naturally it got caught in a wad of crumpet—and she cracked up. She looked over at Avedon, who was a nervous wreck, and gave him a grin—with a big black gap in the middle of her teeth. He sort of choked on his tea. Not knowing what else to do, she just made an announcement. "You'll have to forgive me," she said in her backwoods-Florida, liberated-hip mellow-dy, "but my tooth is stuck in a wad of crumpet here and we'll have to do something about it because it cost fifty dollars and I'm not going to lose it." Charles laughed. (Yes, Charles laughed.) Lauren retrieved her tooth. She went back to behaving, she says, and sitting there silently. Avedon, trying anything he could think of to make conversation, and knowing that Revson liked to vacation in Mexico, mentioned that Lauren was trying to buy some land there. Charles asked where. Suddenly she got this vision of the monster tycoon

141

going in and stealing her land. "Outside Acapulco," she said reluctantly. "Where outside Acapulco? I know the whole area." "Down the coast." "East or west?" "East." Eventually he got her into a corner. "I got real paranoid and I said: 'All right, I'll tell you where—but you better not get my land.' And that really cracked him up. Here I am telling this giant tycoon to lay off my land. I think it was basically that thing that made us become friends."

Revson liked her candor and her spunk. He used to refer to the "chicory in her soul."

As for her having an affair with him—or with Julie Christie, as was also rumored—she says that their total contact was confined to five or six "high teas," like the first, and to one dinner at the Beverly Hills Hotel—at which several others were present. She was in Mexico (not on *that* land, she never did get *that* land), virtually incommunicado for two or three months, when the story broke that she and Julie Christie were buying a house in New Jersey and living together. She had never even met Julie Christie, she says, and only found out about the story when she called the Ford modeling agency to find out whether she had any business to attend to. ("What are you doing in Mexico?" her agent joked. "You're supposed to be living in New Jersey with Julie Christie.") She ignored the story, which took on a life of its own, and eventually returned to New York, where she was ushered in to another tea with Charles to discuss her next picture session. At the end of the meeting he said: "I just want you to know that I don't care what you do with your private life . . . I just think you should be a little discreet." "I had no idea what he was talking about because I had forgotten all about it. And I kept looking at him and he kept avoiding my eyes. He kept talking around it—and finally I caught on. I started laughing." She assured him there was nothing to the rumor.

A couple of weeks later, the news of his own divorce broke, along with the word that he was leaving Lyn for Lauren. (Or else Lee Radziwell, which was equally absurd.) At their next meeting she told him that a friend had called to say he didn't care what she did with her private life, but that he thought she ought to be a little more discreet. She suggested that they run an ad with the three of them—he, Julie, and she—in a big four-poster bed, peeking out from under the ruffled coverlet. "He didn't go for it, but he thought it was funny."

Lauren Hutton is one of the few who credit Revson with having had "a wonderful sense of humor. We always joked back and forth," she says. She also appreciated what she saw as his courtliness.

If only he had been as charming with everyone else.

(X)

But You Still Wouldn't
Want to Work There

If there is any feature of his personality that remains in my mind as the dominant, motivating force in that company, above everything else, it is his primary concern about people. I don't mean concern in the sense that he cared about them, because he didn't. I mean his concern that they weren't good enough in their jobs, so get rid of them. He was constantly tearing guys apart. Forever.

—Sidney G. Stricker
 former Revlon vice president

As good as Charles Revson was with products, that's how bad he was with people. He was a savvy marketing man and a lousy boss. He had qualities of great leadership, and could milk the most out of many of his people, but he was about the last man in the world any but a very special breed would want to work for. He was sort of a cross between a Vince Lombardi—tough, demanding, but you would give your life for him—and a Captain

Queeg—petty, demeaning, paranoid. He also paid very well.

A lot depended on you:

If you were a bright guy with a flashy résumé, a wife and kids in Mamaroneck, and a nine-to-six professional executive's mentality, you could be in for trouble. You would represent a challenge to Revson, for one thing—a chance for the crude, self-educated, self-made Revson to take on your Princeton B.A. and your Chicago M.B.A. and your upper-middle-class upbringing, and win. Could you possibly be as good as you had cracked yourself up to be? Could you offer the kind of dedication this fanatic wanted of all his people? Could you even understand what it was he was trying to say to you?

But if you were street-smart, and tough, and not easily cowed, but ready to give your heart and soul for the company; if you never tried to bullshit him, but knew how to "handle" him nonetheless; if the chemistry were right and you really had the talent . . . then you might last for some time.

If the "divorce" did come, be you wife, brother, or executive, you might never talk to him again, no matter how long you had known him. (He wouldn't let Ancky or Lyn visit him in the hospital when he was dying.)

Generally, if you were a hotshot, you peaked remarkably early. And then, even if it were not for another year, you were as good as gone. Revson would fire you in his mind a year before anyone else knew it, explains Bill Mandel, for years the heir apparent.

Many men should probably never have been hired in the first place. But Revson was always after some brilliant new executive or creative talent whom he just *had* to have; whom he had to overpay to get; and with whom he would quickly become disenchanted. One out of ten might pay off, he figured, and the other nine were just a necessary cost of finding the tenth.

One creative star who did not pay off was Joel Schumacher, the then twenty-three-year-old designer behind Paraphernalia, a successful New York boutique. He was lured to Revlon in 1965 with a two-year contract at $60,-000 a year plus $15,000 expenses and a stock option.

145

(Youth was big in the sixties.) He is more honest than most about why it didn't work out. "I just hated it from the minute I got there. I had made a terrible blunder, and they had, too. ["It was a mistake," admits Jay Bennett, Revlon's chief headhunter.] I didn't belong there. Paraphernalia was a very rebellious concept, and there I was, going into the middle of the Establishment. I hated the atmosphere. Black suits and so on . . . dress regulations. I considered myself a great dresser—I was hired for my style—and I didn't want to be told what to wear.

"The first real problem was over publicity. Victor Barnett called me into his office and said that Mr. Revson was aware that everybody knew how much I had gotten to come with the company, and he was not pleased. I took it very immaturely . . . 'fuck you' . . . I was interested only in my own stardom, and I liked all the publicity I was getting in *Women's Wear*. Barnett said that Mr. Revson did not like it, which makes sense from their side—the publicity is supposed to be for Revlon, not Joel Schumacher."

"Did Victor Barnett hate you?" Schumacher is asked.

"I think so. But he couldn't have hated me as much as I hated him. We traded mean words."

Two more different people than Joel Schumacher and Victor Barnett are hard to imagine. For his own style of dress and general bearing, Mr. Victor was known to some around Revlon as the Mortician. Charles Revson was one of the few people who appreciated him, and with whom he was on good terms. Harry Meresman, his father-in-law, was another. Sir Isaac Wolfson, his uncle, was a third. (Never has life imitated caricature quite so wonderfully as at Charles Revson's funeral. While everyone else simply walked into the temple and took a seat, the Mortician—attired as usual—walked busily up and down the center aisle, back and forth, escorting people to their seats and solemnly surveying the crowd—looking grieved, to be sure, but for all the world as though this were his day.)

"Naturally my work suffered," Schumacher continues. "I was functioning at my worst and I knew it. Barnett called me in and told me I was doing a terrible job, and

I sort of told him if they didn't like it they could fire me. They didn't want to fire me because they would have to pay off my contract. And I couldn't afford to walk out.

"They took away all my designing responsibilities, all my privileges"—the star had a limousine for a while"—and they started questioning every lunch, every phone call. They were trying to drive me out. They put me in this office on the worst floor, down with the auditors and the secretarial pool, with no phone and no secretary, and they told my lawyer that I was expected to be there from nine to five. My hours were checked, and if I left early, they called my lawyer and said I was in breach of contract. I spent two months like that while my lawyer was trying to get me out of my contract with a settlement. The only project they gave me to do was a window for The House of Revlon, and I deliberately did terrible sketches. I did one which was three blow-ups of calendar pages, exploding, like, with wigs coming out of them. Terrible! We were at war."

Revlon wound up settling the balance of Schumacher's contract, as it settled so many other contracts of high-priced men who found themselves working down in that same Siberia, for something in excess of $50,000. And it's easy to see how, in this case at least, Revlon considered itself the victim and not the villain. Like many who spun through the revolving door, Schumacher got more out of the company than he put in.

But rather than try to apportion the blame for the extreme brevity of this marriage, Schumacher summarizes the syndrome:

"Nobody goes to work for Revlon unless he was a star before," he says. "Then Revlon overpays you, you get bought for so much money that it's an offer you can't refuse. Then you get there and you are the prisoner of your own greed and Revson is sitting there with those piercing eyes representing what you have done to yourself. Once he buys you, how can he respect you? And how could I respect him when I knew he had bought me and I didn't respect myself?"

Most of the stars Revlon hired were not quite so

147

creative or far out as Joel Schumacher. There was Mort Green, brought in in the late fifties as the TV messiah, who wore *green* velvet suits (get it?) and who once danced a marengue on the conference-room table to illustrate his idea for *el Flama Grande*, the new Revlon shade. But by and large, the creative talent Revson wrung out and discarded was more in the Brooks Brothers/Madison Avenue mold.

The turnover among executives was unbelievable. Part of the problem may have been Charles's need to eat executives for breakfast, to feed his own ego and assuage his insecurities. Part of it must have been his impatience with men not as bright as he and not nearly as knowledgeable about the business. He would frequently feign a sort of sarcastic simplemindedness when he wasn't satisfied with the answers he was getting. "La-aa-arry," he would whine in mock befuddlement, "what's she *saying* to me, La-aa-arry?" He would force people to repeat their statements three and four times—which begins to crack anyone's self-confidence. Or sometimes he would just forget their names.

One Wall Street analyst was working on a report titled, "Twelve Coming Executives at Revlon," to prove that the company had developed depth of management. Only two of the twelve were around by the time the man finally gave up in disgust. A purchasing post was filled six times in a single year. Suzanne Grayson, who later left Revlon to open The Face Factory (a Baskin-Robbins approach to lipstick), went to work at Revlon on a Thursday, and her boss was fired the following week. It happened all the time. *Ad Age* referred to it as "the grand march from Revlon."

(One face that remained the same in the annual reports all the way from 1966 to 1975 was Charles's own. From 1966 on, the same photo was used . . . cropped differently each year . . . and Charles did not look a day older to his shareholders in 1975 than he did in 1966.)

By the midsixties the turnover slowed, in part because Charles was directing some of his attention to other things, such as acquisitions. He acquired and then dis-

148

posed of—hired and fired—almost as many companies as executives. And then there were Revlon presidents to court, marry, and divorce (three of them, between 1965 and 1971: George Murphy, Dan Rodgers, and Joe Anderer); hair stylists in the extravagant Revlon salon to get rid of; Lyn and the yacht and the triplex apartment to remodel, all at great expense; and international operations and the pharmaceutical company to oversee. It was only natural that Charles would have less of an impact on the nuts and the bolts of each ad and the hiring and firing of each middle manager. Moreover, the brilliant-if-abrasive marketing whiz, Bill Mandel, had risen in the company to the point where he could stand up to Charles and, largely, keep him away from the rest of the troops.

(Mandel was one of the few who could make Charles laugh. He used to laugh at Mandel's jokes and then feel so embarrassed that he'd make a remark like, "Oh, you're always *doing* that sort of thing!" He'd laugh hysterically and then catch himself and say, "You've got to stop *doing* that." It was almost as if he felt guilty laughing or having a good time—as perhaps he did. Here they were talking about something as serious as the tag line for a new makeup—Charles wanted to call it "an ingenious potpourri of makeup coloring"—and Mandel blurts out, "If you keep that up, Charles, you won't have a pot left to pourri in." Mandel could get away with murder, Kay Daly says. After Mandel left the company—Charles, it seemed, had the last laugh—Stan Kohlenberg was one of those who could stand in as company comic. "I was kind of the village idiot sometimes because of the way I'd try to get some of the pressure off. I could get him to laugh. He wouldn't show me he was laughing, but he would put his hand over his face and sort of shake his head.")

Despite Revson's fearsome reputation for chewing people up, a lot of very talented men and women were attracted to the company over the years (women were restricted to creative posts). Revlon represented the challenge of the big leagues, and never hurt anyone's résumé.

149

What's more, you could actually form quite an affection and respect for this dynamic, single-minded, slightly insane, often infuriating, galloping egomaniac, even if he never did say thank you. His aloofness and never being satisfied enhanced his magnetism. "You got the feeling from him," Kay Daly said, "that no matter what you did, you were never going to please him. And this is something that is very interesting to women. Martin doesn't have that because he's too nice and too much of a good egg. But Charles had this *edge* . . ."

And then there was the money. Revson paid premium wages (coupled with lucrative stock options) because he could never have gotten top people to work with him, and to work those hours, if he had not. And once a man worth $25,000 anywhere else had gotten used to a $35,000 lifestyle, Revson owned him. He could abuse him all day long, and the man would take it because he couldn't afford to leave. "It was the most overpaid company in the business," asserts an alumnus, "and that was Revson's luxury for telling them anything he wanted."

Additionally, he would pay almost any price for what he wanted; never wanted to be thought of as cheap (least of all "a cheap Jew"); and lacked the patience to negotiate. When he wanted something, he wanted it now—and that costs money.

"If the job is right and the money is right," he asked one man who had left Revlon, "will you come back?"

"Well, I, uh—" stuttered the man, caught by the directness of the question.

"Not, 'Well, I, uh,' goddamn it—*yes or no?*"

"If the job is right and the money is right? Well, yes!"

"Okay, Jay," Charles said to Jay Bennett, who was sitting with them, "take care of it."

"What would it take to get you back," Bennett asked one such man. "Sixty? Seventy? Eighty?" To which the man replied, "Well, you just ruled out sixty and seventy."

In the days when Charles handled these things himself, he was an equally soft touch. In 1947, Charles was looking for "a publicity girl" and Bea Castle came recommended to him. "I asked him how much money I'd be making," she remembers, "and he named a figure. I had

150

always worked by the week, and this was the yearly figure, and I was stunned. The figure he named was something like $10,000, which looked like a million to me. He saw my expression and quickly added $1,000 to it."

If $10,000 looked like a million dollars to Bea Castle in 1947, we can only wonder what $125,000 looked like to Kay Daly, in the fifties. Or what a million looked like to Bill Mandel in 1966, when Charles promised it to him out of his own pocket if his stock options did not earn him at least that much. (They did.) Or what *two* million looked like to Sol Levine, the brilliant, funny, effective head of Revlon plant operations, when, through a complicated deal, it was paid to him as a bonus for signing back on with Revlon in 1969. Or, finally, what a $3.1 million five-year contract looked like to Michel Bergerac when he was signed on as Charles's successor in 1974—plus, oh yes, a 70,000-share stock option worth another $2.8 million on paper less than a year later.

In a marketing business like Revlon or a research business like U.S.V., Revlon's pharmaceutical company, it pays to get the top creative talent, because what you are really selling, as opposed to raw materials or labor, is the product of a few good brains. But talent always seemed brighter outside the company. Once it was working for Revlon, it lost much of its mystique. So there was little advancement from within the ranks, and the salary increases were not nearly as lavish as that initial deal. And here was the catch: In order to get a big raise or a promotion, you generally had to threaten to leave for the competition (or actually do so and then be wooed back). But once you did that you were a marked man. Charles took that sort of thing personally. Your disloyalty to him and to Revlon would not be forgotten. Your salary would be raised, and the search would begin for your successor. He would get even with you and regain the dominant position in the relationship by paying enough to keep you—and then forcing you out. It was the old "You can't fire me; I quit" syndrome, in reverse. There were exceptions, but it was a familiar Revson pattern.

Charles was a demanding, often abusive employer, no question about it. He had this relentless intensity . . .

151

like a man too excited by his ideas and his work to fall asleep as, in fact, Revson had difficulty doing. He would call Ray Stetzer at the lab every day without fail. And then he would call him at home on Sunday night. Sunday night conversations with Stetzer could run nonstop from seven-thirty to eleven—three and a half hours on the phone—because Charles had that many questions to ask, that many products to discuss, and that much stamina. And then Monday morning, as every other morning, the phone would ring up at the lab at ten o'clock, and Charles would be asking Ray what progress had been made on the things they had discussed the night before. Agh! He had tremendous patience—who else could spend three and a half hours on the phone in a sitting?—and tremendous, nagging impatience—who else would call the next morning to find out what had been done?

He even offered Stetzer two acres of his own property in Rye if he would only build a house there. It wasn't enough that he would call Stetzer at three or four in the morning from Tokyo (well, it wasn't three or four in *Tokyo*); or that once in the late forties he had the Royal Canadian Mounted Police track the Stetzers down in the midst of their vacation to have him rush back to the office; or that in 1952 a police gondola in Venice came out to get them in the middle of the Grand Canal for the same purpose. He wanted them to live next door.

That Stetzer died of a heart attack at forty-nine (as did Bill Heller) was not entirely unrelated to "the Revlon experience." Said an ex-personnel manager: "I left because I just didn't think I could take the Charles Revson routine. You know, a lot of the people who were close to him are dead now. I'm not sure I'd be alive today if I had stayed."

That's putting it strongly, to be sure—but what *about* all these charges of "owning" executives and "murdering" them and such? Someone once confronted Charles directly on these points:

Charles was dining at The Four Seasons with this man, whom he very much wanted to hire—the woo-ee, we'll call him. Now a top Revlon executive, the woo-ee was then quite comfortable and secure where he was, thank

Family Portrait, 1912. Charles, aged five, is seated at lower left.

CHARLES REVSON

"Chick."

JOSEPH REVSON

"Joe." "Red."

ORACLE STAFF

Back row: William Couser, Wilmot Frear, Alice Coyne, Marion McQuesten, Edwin Flanders, Joseph Revson. *Front row:* Lionel Whitten, Margaret Curran, Leonie Chandonnet, Beulah Omand, Irene Cote, Rosalind Parker, Charles Revson.

Above: Classmates "Chick" and "Red" Revson—one liked to argue, the other to recite. These are two pages from the 1923 Manchester High School yearbook. Charles was sixteen. **Top right:** At first, Ancky says, she and Charles had "a working relationship." **Bottom right:** It's hard to guess from his expression which he loved more, rowing or having his picture taken.

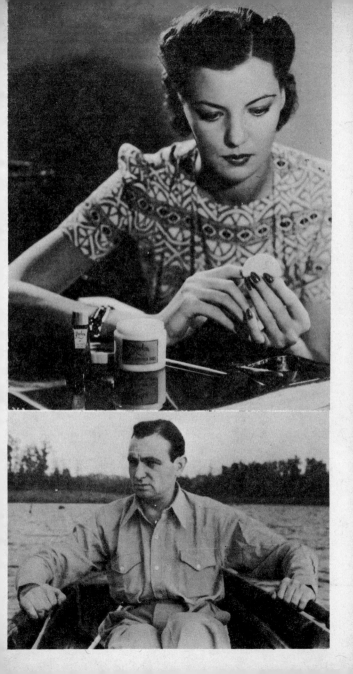

Above: Summer, 1939, with brother Joseph (right), out on the town. Right: He always liked hats. In 1939 he was on a beret kick. Below: Martin's sons, Douglas (right) and Peter Jeffrey Revlon Revson (left), took boxing lessons from Dr. Mac. Charles wanted his boys to, as well, but Ancky wouldn't hear of it. 1948. Opposite: Smile, Charles—you're on your honeymoon! (Hot Springs, Arkansas, October, 1940)

Left: Daddy and Johnny, July, 1943. Below: Accepting the Army/Navy "E" award, July, 1944. "What do you know about powder?" the officer had asked, meaning gunpowder. "Everything," Charles replied, thinking in his own terms. Right: Christmas circa 1947. There was a tree upstairs as well, with gifts to keep the boys occupied until Charles was ready for the holiday to begin.

Top left: The Major with chauffeur, Eric, in the late forties. He had no trouble adapting to the new lifestyle his boys provided him—not one bit. Bottom left: Aboard the Queen Mary, August, 1952. "He could be the most thoughtful, considerate man." Right: Suzy Parker—strong as a horse.

Does any man really understand you?

Who knows you as you really are? Does _he_?

Who knows the secret hopes that warm your heart?

Who knows the dreams you dream, the words you've left unspoken?

Who knows the black-lace thoughts you think while shopping in a gingham frock?

Who knows you sometimes long to sleep in pure-silk sheets?

Who knows you'd love to meet a man who'd hold your hand and listen...

    while you say nothing at all?

Who knows there was a morning when your orange juice sparkled like champagne?

Who knows the secret, siren side of you that's female as a silken cat?

Who else but Revlon understands you as you really are...

    a trifle shy, but oh-so-warm...and just a little reckless,

deep inside...as strange and unexpected as cherries in the snow.

Revlon's 'Cherrie

Above: Dorian Leigh, 1953. "It was only later that we became very, very friendly." Left: The Fatal Apple promotion—1945. Right: The Bachelor's Carnation promotion—1946.

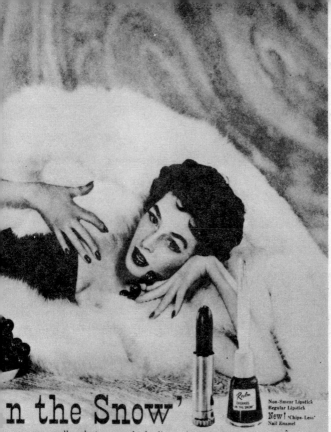

n the Snow'

new <u>madly</u> voluptuous scarlet for lips and matching fingertips

Non-Smear Lipstick
Regular Lipstick
New! 'Chips-Less'
Nail Enamel

to flirt with fire...

...thin ice...

'Fire and Ice

...matching fingertips.

...dancing on the moon

Above: Suzy Parker? No, her sister, Dorian Leigh. Right: "If it's the finest of its kind, it's by Revlon," Barbara Britton would say. "And now, here's the star of our show—Ed Sullivan." With her are her son and daughter and assorted entertainers.

ARE <u>YOU</u>

MADE FOR 'FIRE AND ICE?'

Try this quiz and see!

What is the American girl made of? Sugar and spice and
everything nice? Not since the days of the Gibson Girl! There's
a new American beauty . . . she's tease and temptress, siren and
gamin, dynamic and demure. Men find her slightly, delightfully
baffling. Sometimes a little maddening. Yet they admit she's ready
the most exciting woman in all the world! She's the 1952
American beauty with a foolproof formula for melting a male!
She's the "Fire and Ice" girl. (Are you?)

Have you ever danced with your shoes off?	yes ☐	no ☐
Did you ever wish on a new moon?	yes ☐	no ☐
Do you blush when you find yourself flirting?	yes ☐	no ☐
When a recipe calls for one dash of bitters, do you think it's better with two?	yes ☐	no ☐
Do you secretly hope the next man you meet will be a psychiatrist?	yes ☐	no ☐
Do you sometimes feel that other women resent you?	yes ☐	no ☐
Have you ever wanted to wear an ankle bracelet?	yes ☐	no ☐
Do ashblonde excite you, even in other women?	yes ☐	no ☐
Do you hate to look up at a man?	yes ☐	no ☐
Do you face crowded parties with panic—then wind up having a wonderful time?	yes ☐	no ☐
Does gypsy music make you sad?	yes ☐	no ☐
Do you think any man really understands you?	yes ☐	no ☐
Would you streak your hair with platinum without consulting your husband?	yes ☐	no ☐
If tonight were raining, would you take a trip to Mars?	yes ☐	no ☐
Do you close your eyes when you're kissed?	yes ☐	no ☐

Can you honestly answer "yes" to at least eight of these questions?
Then you're made of "Fire and Ice" And Revlon's high-
and passionate scarlet was made just for you—a daring projection
of your sexy hidden personality! Wear it tonight.
It may be the night of your lifetime!

Charles, lipstick patches on his palm, looks admiringly at Suzy Parker (whom he had to pay to appear for this publicity shot). Bea Castle looks doleful. Mandel looks genuinely interested. George Abrams, with an eye for publicity, looks straight into the camera. Martin looks knowingly over at Charles. Ancky, framed on Charles's desk, forces a smile.

Leonard McCombe, Time-Life Picture Agency. © Time Inc.

1. (SILENT FOOTAGE)

2. WOMAN: I want a word with all you tigers.

3. Oh, you men know which ones you are. Grrr, I like you. But I don't like ...

4. lions.

5. You know, men with wild, dry manes.

6. The kind with lots of - uh - dandruff.

OOK as only *Revlon* does it!

pyramids, shocked the world! see-at-night eyes...
ay...and the deadly ingredients (redistilled) are these:

phinx Eyes

idea in eye makeup! Madly mysterious! Egypt-inspired!
newly shaped...elongated...darkly outlined for depth,
gorous lids, lightened with beige, shadowed with smoky
The effect? Unforgettable! (And almost *unforgettable*!)

w down | beach | pink | nouveau | super-
pink ! | peach ! | cognito ! | peach ! | natural !

Revlon's (not a cliché in a carload)

'colors avant garde'

10 new potent pales for lips and nails!

New low-key look for today's new breed of
beauty...bored with yesterday's fashion
clichés, restless for tomorrow's look today!

nes the evolution! No harsh or hackneyed reds, no pedestrian pinks! These
ow-key colors—so new they're barely born! Sensuously soft. Shatteringly chic.
'll love them on sight. Scoop up Revlon's COLORS AVANT GARDE—all 10 at a clip!

Above: Bella Abzug? No, Suzy Parker again—
1962. Right and Left: Barbara Feldon in
1963...

13. See, it says right here, Top Brass has medicated ingredients to fight dandruff.

14. And Top Brass is non-greasy.

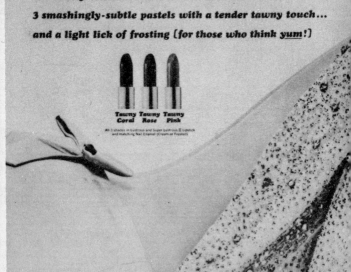

Revlon says: Coming in now...

the tawny-toned mouth...sexiest understatement of the year!

3 smashingly-subtle pastels with a tender tawny touch...

and a light lick of frosting (for those who think *yum*!)

Tawny Coral Tawny Rose Tawny Pink

All 3 shades in Lustrous and Super Lustrous II Lipstick and matching Nail Enamel (Cream or Frosted)

15. So remember that, tiger. Get the medicated hair dressing, Top Brass and sic 'em.

...before she and Don Adams "Got Smart." Charles had mixed feelings about television advertising—it was not his dish of wax. Below: Candy Bergen? Yes! Candy Bergen—1964.

Watch the tawny-toned mouth take over the town... creating quiet havoc wherever it glows!

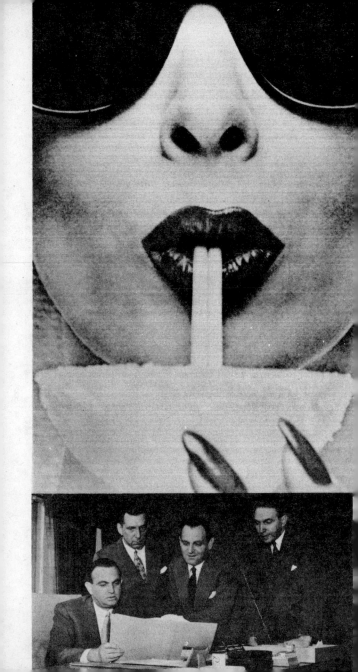

Revlon invents wet lipstick

(it's actually filled with ⅓ moisturizers!)

First lipstick that does for lips what moisture lotion does for skin — actually feeds moisture into lips to keep them soft, supple…makes dry lips obsolete!

Wet lipstick means we've practically reinvented lipstick. This new formula (brimful of *penetrating* moisture) changes the look, feel and function of lipstick. But completely. And it could change the lips of a whole generation of women. Starting with you.

The feel is fantastic. Greaseless. Non-gooky. Intangibly light. It almost *skims* on (other lipsticks seem to *drag* on by comparison). The look is smashing. The colors (there are 20!) have a new subtle shimmer. Soft, soft, soft. *Distractingly* sensuous.

This is the Big Change in lipstick that simply *had* to happen. But nobody (not even Revlon) could bring it off till now. Don't ask how we did it. Our lips are sealed.

New 'Moon Drops' Lipstick

Above: Wet lips—they belong to none other than model mogul Wilhelmina herself—1972. Left: The partners circa 1950: Charles, Charlie Lachman, Martin and Joseph.

Above: Lauren Hutton, 1975, her false tooth firmly in place. Left: Kay Daly, at the time (1963) perhaps the first woman executive in the country. Right: Sales meeting 1941. Charles is flanked by Martin and Jack Price on his left, Howard Pims and Mickey Soroko on his right.

It's hard to believe a makeup
that feels this light and looks this natural
could cover this well.

'Beautiful Creme Makeup' is so natural-looking you never
look 'made up,' even in sunlight. And even if your skin isn't perfect, this
exclusive gel formula makeup covers perfectly. It wears beautifully in
humid or rainy weather too,
because it's waterproof.
'Beautiful Creme Makeup' is
matte enough for normal or even
oily skin. Yet it's moist enough for
dry skin with tiny lines to hide. The
result is believably beautiful skin.
For hours and hours.

'ULTIMA' II
REVSON

REVLON SALES MEETING
JANUARY 3, 1941

STANDARD FLASHLIGHT CO.

Four frames from Inside Revlon, the film Carl Erbe made in 1950 to try to ease corporate tension. It worked, but not for long.

Lester Herzog "whipping" a stockaded Revlon salesperson. "If brains were dynamite," one wag had said of him, "Lester couldn't even have blown his nose."

Office of the President.

"If it wasn't terrible, it wouldn't be my life."

Top: Charles and Lester at an early promotion. Above: When Charles used to visit Al Katz (pointing) in Philadelphia, he would have to stay in bed while they took his one suit out to be pressed. Joseph (in uniform) was "weird."

Mr. Charles Revson—distinguished president of Revlon Products Corp.—started as a retail clerk, became a packer in the garment industry, then sold cosmetics. Mr. Revson was so impressed with the growing demand for nail enamel that, in 1932, with his brother and a chemist friend, he started his own firm—and developed a superior nail enamel, "Revlon". He has since marketed other products—and made Revlon nail enamel the world's largest seller.

It is for men like Mr. Revson who seek a finer whiskey that Lord Calvert is *Custom Distilled* and blended . . . to achieve an outstanding combination of rare taste and distinctive, satin-smooth lightness. So jealously is Lord Calvert's *Custom Distilled* quality guarded that each bottle is numbered and recorded at the distillery. Tonight, discover how *Custom Distilled* Lord Calvert, the "whiskey of distinction," can make your next drink a far, far *better* drink.

For Men of Distinction . . . LORD CALVERT

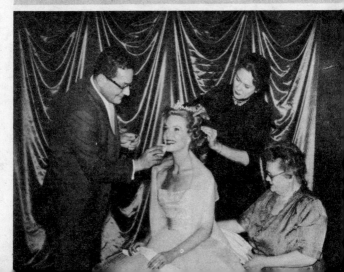

Top left: Not only was he a Calvert "Man of Distinction" (above), he also won the Horatio Alger Award in 1950 and was selected as "One of America's Ten Best Groomed Men" by the Barber's Journal & Men's Hairstylist. Bottom left: Readying the spokeswoman: a lot had to go right when you were doing nine live commercials a week in front of fifty million people. Top right: Hal March quizzes shoemaker Gino Prato on opera. Above the silhouetted isolation booth is Revlon's name in lights. Bottom right: March introduces Mabel Morris.

Above: Charles presents the first $64,000 check to a marine captain named McCutchen who knew all about food. Left: George Beck with fourth bride, Marlene, 1964. Bottom left: Al Katz, La Verne Johnson (director of Revlon's beauty consultants), Lester Herzog and moustachioed Bill Heller at 1951 sales conference.

Above: The magnifying mirror on Revson's toilet seat was placed at just the right angle. Right: "Gargling Cepacol by the gallon"—one of several medicine chests aboard Ultima II. Below: Exercising in 1965 with Dr. Mac. He did this every morning for twenty years. Note the custom-designed pajamas.

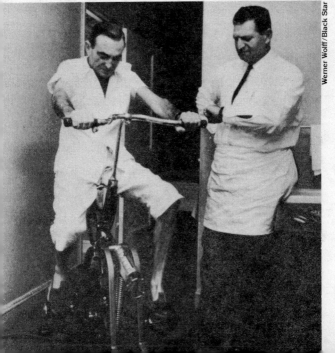

This announcement is neither an offer to sell nor a solicitation of an offer to buy any of these securities.
The offering is made only by the Prospectus.

December 7, 1955

373,900 Shares

Revlon, Inc.

Common Stock
(Par Value $1.00 per share)

Price $12 Per Share

Copies of the Prospectus may be obtained from the undersigned.

Reynolds & Co., Inc.

Hornblower & Weeks	Paine, Webber, Jackson & Curtis
Francis I. duPont & Co.	Laurence M. Marks & Co.
G. H. Walker & Co.	Bache & Co.	Goodbody & Co.

Top left: That Man, circa 1945. Above: Twenty years after the publication of this original "tombstone," Revlon stock, adjusted for splits, hovered near $500. Left: John Lindsay and Jacob Javits managed to get their photos in, too, and Robert Redford got his name mentioned as a regular member—but Lyn Revson, shown here after her divorce, dominated the New York Post's coverage of a new oh-so-chic tennis club.

Sidney Stricker

Top: Building the image: Charles lands on the Breakers golf course with Lyn and (far left) Bill Mandel to referee an oh-so-chic beauty contest. Middle: They actually became quite the loving couple. Above: Charles, flanked by Lyn and Ancky, is impatient. John is forty-five minutes late for his own wedding. Ben Johnson, Ancky's husband, is at far right; Susan Sheresky, Lyn's daughter, at far left.

Graduation day. John Revson had two shadows to grow up in, not just one. His father, at right, and his cousin, Peter, below.

Above: Sixteen bathrooms, twenty-two phones, $20,000 for a tank of gas. The Ultima II (right) was thirty feet long, air-conditioned—and sat unobtrusively on the deck of the Ultima II (above).

Charlie

A most original fragrance   by REVLON

It's Charlie's first Christmas!
So it's only right she never
found under her tree before.
Give it to her now—any one of
six beautiful ways.

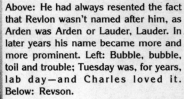

Above: He had always resented the fact that Revlon wasn't named after him, as Arden was Arden or Lauder, Lauder. In later years his name became more and more prominent. Left: Bubble, bubble, toil and trouble; Tuesday was, for years, lab day—and Charles loved it. Below: Revson.

Bergerac. Now it's up to him.

you, and so felt he had nothing to lose by being frank.

"Mr. Revson," he said, "I'm intrigued by what you're offering me, but—excuse me for being blunt—I hear you're a real shit. That you devour people, that you think you own them seven days a week . . . You've got a lousy reputation, and I really would like your response to that."

The thrust of Revson's answer was that he's honest, he's straight, and, yes, he is demanding. And he thinks he got his reputation because he is a perfectionist and he gets rid of people if they don't live up to his expectations. He said there are an awful lot of millionaires walking around the street today that he made millionaires, and you never hear from *them*. Which was true.

"But then," says the woo-ee, "he began rambling around the subject and—you know, he's always an hour late, and we didn't meet at The Four Seasons until ten. The restaurant closed at one, but he got up and tipped somebody to keep the place open—the kitchen and everything—and we must have sat there until at least three o'clock talking, and he was still answering that question. He's very defensive on it.

"Charles and I and his personnel man, Jay Bennet, are at one table; his wife Lyn and, I think, their friend Jerry Zipkin at another. And Charles says: 'Now, as to this thing about owning people, that's bullshit. I don't own my people. Why, I just hired a guy—fantastic, a real professional manager, just came in a few months ago. I don't follow him at all—I don't even know what he did last week. I don't own him. Jay, call Harry [not his real name] and have him get his ass on down here.'

"So Jay gets up and calls Harry, who lives out in Connecticut, and wakes him up. And he drives in, sleep in his eyes—it must be three A.M. by now—and Charles says, 'Kiddie, tell him I don't own you.'

"I broke up. I was thinking: 'You're not ruthless, you're crazy!' I think he saw the humor in the situation, but he didn't say anything."

They left the restaurant, finally, and walked over to one of Revson's favorite all-night drugstores. "This is where the hookers hang out," he told the woo-ee. "You learn a lot from what they buy."

The woo-ee joined Revlon at a high level and does not regret it. The man from Connecticut, though he harbors no ill will, left Revlon the day his contract was up. He recalls this meeting, but denies it took place so late. He would never have driven to New York that late, he says. Yet in another context he acknowledged that his Revson meetings would sometimes last nearly till dawn.

(XI)

The $64,000,000 Quiz Show

I venture to say that I don't know where we would have
been without that show.
—Martin Revson

It seemed like a good idea. Chrysler is supposed to have
turned it down because they were afraid of labor problems: how would it look to their rank-and-file to be giving
away huge sums of money on the air while fighting
pennies-an-hour increases at the bargaining table? Madame
Rubinstein turned it down because, not then owning a
television herself, she thought "only poor people watch
those awful machines." The Lewyt Vacuum Cleaner
Company turned it down because Alex Lewyt felt the
mass appeal of television was better suited to selling
inexpensive impulse items than $79 vacuum cleaners—
why not show it to Charlie Revson? But Revson, too, had
supposedly passed on it the first time around. He was
getting awfully tired of investing in one "stiff" of a TV
series after the next. He had a natural bias against tele-

vision advertising anyway. It was black and white, and he was selling colors. Nor could he control TV ads the way he could control print. This new medium was not his dish of wax, as he would say. Yet Hazel Bishop had been murdering Revlon's lipstick business with its sponsorship of *This Is Your Life*, and Revson was not about to lose a competitive battle. So with a good deal of prodding from Walter Craig, of Norman, Craig & Kummel, Charles agreed to sponsor a new show, to be called *The $64,000 Question*. He insisted, however, on the unusual right to pull out of the show after thirteen weeks if it proved a dud.

After the first night, Charles, Martin, and Norman retreated to Charles's table at Billy Reed's Little Club, the first table on the right past the bar. Charles was morose. It was another goddamn dog, and he wanted out.

Of course, Charles was by nature morose. As he had said once in another context: "If it wasn't terrible, it wouldn't be my life." (The yacht he had chartered didn't have gold cutlery or modern stabilizers—wasn't even air-conditioned!—and that was his comment upon returning: "Well, if it wasn't terrible, it wouldn't be my life.") So he may not really have wanted to dump the show without giving it more of a try. But Norman and Martin had to stay up with him late into the night defending the show's potential. "I think he thought it was a long way from cosmetics and wasn't conducive to the emotional aura and surroundings in which he'd like to see his products," says Norman. He was proved wrong.

First aired June 7, 1955, within four weeks *The $64,000 Question* was number one in the ratings. Some of the products featured on the show were experiencing 300 percent and 500 percent sales increases. One lipstick shade sold out in ten days. What was advertised on Tuesday night was sold out Wednesday morning. "We could have sold urine in a bag," admits Jay Bennett.

Charles was not about to sell urine in a bag, however. Or even, for that matter, perfectly good powder in Love Pat compacts. He had a roomful of back orders for those compacts, but held up production for months until Sol Levine could devise techniques to make the tortoiseshell

156

look more nearly real and to make the gold stamping on the compact even more impervious to wear. Levine was running around the country like mad, commandeering plants in what was almost a war effort to meet demand and to launch a dozen new products (Living Lipstick, Satin Set hairspray, Futurama lipstick cases, Silicare medicated lotion, Clean & Clear, Sun Bath, and more) ... and at the same time Charles refused to cut even the most trivial corners.

On an average Tuesday night at ten, nearly twice as many people—55,000,000—were watching Revlon's ads as had watched Nixon's "Checkers" speech. At its peak an unbelievable 82 percent of the television sets switched on around the country were tuned to emcee Hal March, the famous "isolation booth," Revlon spokeswoman Barbara Britton, and the latest Revlon promotion. Movie theaters complained of sparse attendance on Tuesday nights. Restaurant business was off.

The ten-thirty to eleven time slot following *The $64,000 Question* suddenly became very valuable. General Motors won out in the bidding for it, and Edward R. Murrow's *See It Now*, which had occupied the time, was forced to move to make way for a more commercial show. Imagine —General Motors bidding to capitalize on Charlie Revson's success! It would have swelled his chest with pride ... if only he had taken credit for having discovered, or at least not bad-mouthed, the show. Instead, it rankled him—which may have been the underlying reason for his dumping Norman, Craig & Kummel in 1956 despite the fact that Revlon's sales and profits were exploding as a direct result of NC&K's having brought in *The $64,000 Question*. (Dumping the agency at such a time did little for the Revson reputation on Madison Avenue.)

Soon Revlon had captured Sunday night audiences with a spin-off, *The $64,000 Challenge*. And in an effort to make it a triple sweep—Sunday, Monday, and Tuesday— it was announced that *The Most Beautiful Girl in the World* would debut at 9 P.M. Eastern Daylight Time, October 22, 1956. The show was to be a sort of weekly Miss America pageant, with $250,000 thrown in as top prize to keep the contestants smiling. Revson set as criteria for contestants that they be beautiful, talented, and intelligent. After screening hundreds of potential contestants, the last of a string of producers assigned to create a pilot went to Charles: "Would you say Judy Garland is talented?" Of course. "Intelligent?" Yeah. "Beautiful?" No. He then proposed Hedy Lamarr, whom Charles faulted on a different count. "Well," concluded the producer, "how do you expect us to come up with three contestants a week if Judy Garland and Hedy Lamarr wouldn't qualify?" The show never made it to the air.

It may be argued that *The $64,000 Question* was the difference between Revson's becoming just another successful businessman and his becoming a superstar. Up until this time, Revlon had risen to the level of its competitors, but did not dominate the field, except in nail polish. It had to fight costly battles with competitors. It did not have huge advantages of scale. Profits were modest. The company was not home free. There was no IBM-versus-everybody-else relationship here.

The Question raised Revlon sales, profits, and consumer awareness so dramatically as to put it miles ahead of its competitors. And that sort of edge tends to be self-perpetuating, or even self-expanding. The rich get richer. The companies with the most resources, other things being equal (not better, just equal), can swamp the competition.

Sales, which had been growing at from 10 to 20 percent a year in the first half of the fifties, suddenly shot up 54 percent in 1955—even though *The Question* was only on the air for the second half of the year. Profits tripled. It was a fine way to kick off Revlon's public stock offering.

The next year, sales were up yet another 66 percent, to $85 million, and profits better than doubled. The pretax profit on every sales dollar had widened from eight cents in 1954 to twenty cents. Helena Rubinstein, Max Factor, Coty, and Hazel Bishop, which had all been at least within striking distance of Revlon before *The Question* went on the air, were left bitterly in the dust. Revlon was number one in lipstick, number one in hair spray, number one in nail products, and number one in makeup. The chairman of Hazel Bishop had to report a surprising

$460,000 loss for 1955, "due to circumstances beyond our control," as he put it. Hazel Bishop had been swamped by Revlon.

By 1957, a spate of competitive quiz shows, most notably *Twenty-One*, with its Charles Van Doren, had begun to cut into *The Question* craze, and Revlon found itself doing things like upping the top prize money from $64,000 to $256,000. (Ten-year-old Robert Strom, who had just collected $64,000 for his store of scientific knowledge, was given the first crack at the extra prize money and took home $192,000.) And a year later quiz shows had become old hat—the subject of a budding national scandal. *The $64,000 Question* was quietly folded. But not before it had lifted Revlon sales by about $64,000,000.

Revlon's weekly cost of producing *The $64,000 Question*, including prize money, which averaged a mere $14,000 per show, was $27,800—about half what it cost Hazel Bishop to produce *This Is Your Life*. Another $40,000 went for each half hour of network broadcast time. In total, Revlon got more than three minutes of national attention for less than $70,000 a week. By contrast, three minutes of commercial time when *The Godfather* was shown on TV in 1974 cost a sponsor $675,000.

But it was better than that. *The Godfather* dragged on for hours, with countless sponsors, one after another. People were riveted to *The $64,000 Question*, for which there was only one sponsor. Identification of Revlon with *The Question* was very close; Charles himself appeared to present the first $64,000 check (to a U.S. marine who knew all about food). The commercials were all done live. The studio audience oohed and aahed at Revlon's extravaganzas just as they sat in tense silence during the show's most suspenseful moments. Barbara Britton was almost as much a part of the show as Hal March. The electricity was shared. Constant national publicity mentioned Revlon again and again.

Doing the commercials live had a number of advantages, not least of which was that it allowed Revlon to steal television time. Each of Revlon's three commercials per show was supposed to run one minute. Few, if any, ran less, and a great many ran longer. Says a key figure from that period, still with Revlon: "We would run 'sixty-second' commercials for *three minutes* and there was nothing they could do to stop us because we were live. What were they going to do? Run to the middle of the stage and yell, 'Stop!'? So there were times when we were literally running three-minute one-minute commercials. I think we ran over three minutes once."

CBS naturally screamed its head off—but only so loud. This was a very hot property they had, and they didn't want to see it moved to NBC. That network had quickly tried to lure the show away, offering, it was widely reported, $2 million of free midday commercial time. Revlon ultimately decided to stick with CBS, but not before *Variety* had summed up the battle as "the most extravagant power play in TV's annals." Agencies and sponsors, *Variety* wrote, "are even yet salving wounded feelings as they recapitulate the most fantastic crisscross pattern and chain reaction of events that transcends anything that vets in the business can recall." As Daniel Seligman concluded his profile of Revlon in the April 1956 *Fortune*—even before the quiz scandal erupted or Martin sued Charles—"The company is what might be called controversy-prone. It will bear plenty of watching."

Another reason Charles insisted on live commercials (which were not unusual in those days) was the flexibility it gave him in deciding almost up to the last minute what to pitch and how. He could drive everybody crazy, and did.

"All during *The $64,000 Question* and *The Challenge*," a veteran of these wars remembers, "he would never start a script until maybe a week before air, which made life impossible. You would get approval—alleged approval—generally no more than forty-eight hours before air. You'd be at rehearsal at six o'clock for the first run-through. Mandel would walk in with a long face. 'Bad news.' 'What's the matter?' 'Charles hates it.'* Then you'd re-

---

* I asked Mandel whether there were any commercials Charles particularly loved or hated. "He hated them all," Mandel said.

160

write, starting at six-thirty, seven o'clock, and you'd have a whole [tele-] prompter crew there to redo the prompter. Go and dress at nine; on the air at ten. Charles felt there was greater spontaneity by doing that.

"Each one of these things was like a little Broadway production. The first one I did, I remember we had dry-ice fog and willow trees and slaves all over the floor. We did three live commercials a week on each of three different shows. We broke every union rule in the book. They just learned to accept it because if we had had their people doing it, we would have killed them. So they let us kill ourselves, instead. The guy who made it work, in my opinion, was our crazy art director, Ben Colarossi."

Colarossi talks of the difficulty of running ads for color promotions in black and white. You had to be dramatic, he says, to create an image. Plumes, smoke bombs, waterfalls, flaming goblets—all live. You also had to be nimble to satisfy Revlon's last-minute changes of heart. New supers—black cards with white lettering that would be superimposed on the screen—would be ordered up minutes before air time, and there was no way, according to union procedure, they could be done in time. Colarossi would dash downstairs to the men's room, lock himself in a booth so the union couldn't see him, sit down, dip his brush into the bowl between his knees, and letter the new super.

A lot went on in that men's room, actually. One evening the producer from the ad agency showed up in work clothes. Charles had made it clear that anyone associated with Revlon was to dress properly, but Charles almost never came to rehearsals. In comes The Black Specter. Black overcoat, silver tie, neat black pants, black shoes. The producer took one look at him and ran for the men's room. They had to run a monitor down there, and a phone. And he stayed down there until nearly eleven o'clock—Charles didn't leave that night until after the show.

A lot had to go right when you were doing live commercials, and it generally did. Barbara Britton couldn't come down with the flu or get stuck in traffic. The jewel lady had to show up each night without getting mugged.

161

This Ruth Buzzi-like lady would ferry maybe $100,000 worth of jewels to and from VanCleef & Arpels in her handbag each night for Revlon's models to wear. No one would have guessed from her appearance what she was carrying.

Of course, you couldn't expect *everything* to go smoothly on a live show. The gaze of millions of viewers suddenly panned up in an arc one night, from the isolation booth to the rafters. Some nut had walked in off the street and knifed—killed—the first man who caught his eye, a CBS cameraman. On another evening, a Hungarian freedom fighter walked out on stage with Hal March. "I really want to thank you for coming tonight, sir," March said, putting his arm around the man's shoulders. "Come over here and let me put you on the other camera." Whereupon he was grabbed from the wings.

Miraculously, nothing so dramatic went wrong with any of Revlon's productions. Models were given few lines to say, so there was little they could flub. One model was charged with looking up indignantly at the camera and saying "Soap on my face? Never!"—in connection with an ad for Clean & Clear. This very sexy model studied and studied her line, and when the great moment came she looked up indignantly at America and said, "Face on my soap? Never!"

And of course there were the ducks. The idea was to have a baby duckling swim over to a model, who would pick it up and cuddle it by her cheek. An ad for Love Pat. Chateau Theatrical Animals, Inc., was engaged to provide a dozen baby ducklings and a duck handler. You had to have a lot of back-up ducklings because they have a tendency to doze off. Anyway, the moment comes and the ducklings swim the wrong way, off camera. If they had known Charles Revson, they would never have dared to do it, but they didn't, and they did. Bill Mandel, hysterical in the control booth, is yelling, "Cue the ducks! Cue the ducks!" Eventually the model managed to grab one and finish the commercial, but it was not Revlon's finest hour.

Says one agency man connected with the show: "The next day was a bad day at Revlon. Charles very seldom

162

said something to us about anything he didn't like. You'd go in and he'd just sit there and shake his head. He'd summon fourteen people into the conference room and just sit there for ten minutes with his head in his hands, staring, without saying a word. I went to two meetings where that's all there was. He'd just sit there and stare around the room, and you could just feel the hate. He'd give it to you, then the next guy, then the next, and then he'd say: 'Shit.' And walk out." There were gargoyles under the lighting fixtures all around the conference room at 666 Fifth Avenue; at times like this they all looked like Charles.

Working on the Revlon account was like riding in a rodeo. It was a challenge, you could win some money, and the ride generally ended fairly quickly anyway. From 1944 to 1957 Revlon used nine separate ad agencies. "Revlon's then small $600,000 account," *Time* reported, "was first snagged by McCann-Erickson's John McCarthy —who lasted a stormy six months with Revlon. The two men finally fell out over McCarthy's dirty fingernails. When Revson needled him McCarthy snapped: 'What do you want me to do, use nail polish?' Revson laughed —and ordered McCarthy thrown off the account." Reportedly, sixteen or seventeen other top account men followed McCarthy until, in 1948, the account moved to the William Weintraub agency. There it was handled by Norman B. Norman, who later formed Norman, Craig & Kummel. Norman managed to work with Charles for seven years. He, too, was a "street fighter" not universally loved. He drove a white Silver Cloud with NBN plates, dressed like Charles, acted like Charles, and came from much the same mold. He was, however, taller, more articulate, and able to work for someone else, which Charles would undoubtedly have found extraordinarily difficult. After seven years he was canned.

Norman attributed his downfall to George Abrams, a Revlon V.P. he felt was out to get him—and on whom, accordingly, he placed a private detective. Norman, as I say, was a street fighter. Maybe he got the idea from Mickey Soroko. Or maybe he was inspired by the Revlon wiretapping revelations that had been made not long before, and to which we will return in a subsequent chapter. In any case, despite the detective, Abrams stayed on and Norman was out. The specific cause, Norman told the press, was a fight over Revlon's failure to pay agency commissions that were due. Revlon attributed it, rather, to "neglect of service." Martin told *Time:* "Norman is just a mere infant, that's all. He should shut up." Norman managed to get in a quote about having had to put out the *Fire and Ice* promotion over Charles's dead body, "even though it was the best ad he ever had." (A statement totally at odds with Kay Daly's recollection, recounted earlier.) Like many a Revson controversy, this one sheds little light on what actually happened, but a good bit on the atmosphere that surrounded the man and his company. Batten, Barton, Durstine & Osborn inherited the Revlon account from Norman, Craig & Kummel—and lost it the following year.

George Abrams, the advertising V.P. Norman paid to have investigated, was propped up at Revlon by Mandel, whom he had brought over from his former company, Block Drug, as his assistant. After a while, Mandel decided to let George fend for himself, and that was the end of George. Of course, Abrams doesn't see it that way. A tireless and widely disregarded self-promoter, who credits himself with, among much else, the invention of the chocolate chip cookie, he confides that "Mandel turned out to be a barracuda of the worst kind." Abrams was not alone in this opinion, but Mandel says that he "only killed when attacked." And Mandel was so shocked by the stories he found out George had been telling Charles —stories that far exceeded for venom and malice the bounds of even Revlon office politics, he said—that he made me turn off my tape recorder even to tell me that he wouldn't tell me what they were.

Abrams left Revlon and Mandel quickly became the most important man in the company after Charles. (For a fuller account of George Abrams's brilliance, read *How I Made a Million Dollars With Ideas*, by George Abrams. Playboy Press, 1972.) It was Mandel, largely, who presented the marketing side of Revlon to Wall Street security analysts; Mandel who developed much of the heming for Revlon campaigns; Mandel who would battle with Charles over the proper positioning of new products and the proper strategy for the company as a whole. He filled the gap left by Martin Revson's departure, and he served as the interface between Charles and the rest of the marketing and agency people. He would take their work and sell it to Charles. The underlying logic of this arrangement was simply that in a group Charles would bully people, whereas one-on-one he was not bad. He was reasonable. The agency, Grey Advertising this time, managed to steer clear of Revson for so long—years— that one day Charles looked up, as if struck by a sudden thought, and asked Mandel: "Where's Grey?" Structured his way, Grey has managed to keep the account for seventeen years.

Similarly, Mandel never showed Charles TV advertising in advance—"because we would never have gotten it on the air." Charles had mixed feelings about TV commercials, anyway, even though they had contributed so directly to his success. When he once asked to see a review of all the advertising that had been done in the prior six months—"everything"—Kay Daly, Mandel, and Sandy Buchsbaum organized it and decided to start with the most recent commercials. Charles arrived, impatient as always—"Come on, come on"—and they started to run the commercials. Charles said: "I didn't want to see television, I told you I wanted to see *advertising*."

Print would hold still and he could perfect it. It was a permanent statement. A TV commercial, good or bad, evaporated. It was more important to him to get the ad for the Sunday *Times* perfect, even if it reached fewer people, because (a) they were the people he cared about; and (b) an imperfection would not evaporate—it would just sit there and embarrass him.

There's hardly a veteran ad man in New York who hasn't had some kind of contact with Revlon. What follows are the impressions of just one advertising man who worked on the account through the quiz show years and on into the early sixties.

165

The Ad Man

When I first went to work on the Revlon account they were in the Squibb Building. Then they went to 666 Fifth Avenue. ["Sick-sick-sick," as Revlon executives used to refer to their madhouse.] Charles despised 666. He leased the space before it was finished, and when he looked at it, he threw a tantrum. The building has metal bumps up and down the sides, like pimples. He tried to have them redo the side of the building. He also hated the elevators, which were too slow.

I first met him when Mandel took me in to show him a carbro—a very expensive type of proof they don't have anymore. He looked at the art and he didn't like the eyes and he picked up a ballpoint pen and he's about to destroy . . . I just couldn't stand to see him do it, so I grabbed the pen. And his hand went down empty and he turned around and his eyes are cutting me to shreds. I handed him the pen like a waiter, across my left forearm, and I said: "Mr. Revson, I just saved you ten thousand dollars. Would you mind making your corrections in the margin?" Which he did, but he didn't say another word to me. As I went out the door, he says to Mandel: "Who's the clown with the moustache?" Mandel told him. He said: "Keep him around, he's got balls." That's an insight into Charles. The only thing he respected was spunk.

The second time I went to see him, I was wearing a brown Glen plaid suit, perfectly matched. He said: "Kiddie, you know what brown's the color of? Get out." I had to dress like a Mafia member from then on. Gray was as flamboyant as he would go.

He had a miraculous hand lotion called Silicare. Fantastic. It was discovered during the First World War, for its healing powers. But he was never able to decide whether it was a drug or a cosmetic. The minute he would lean toward cosmetic, you'd come in with a campaign and he'd scream that you hadn't captured the healing powers, and vice versa. One of the account men had the disastrously bad taste to tell him that the problem with Silicare was that it looked like mucous. He was taken off the account that afternoon.

Charles never innovated anything but color. He stole everything. He had a lab up in the Bronx with a spectroscope that would make the CIA jealous.* And what he did was to wait until some small innovator would come out with something . . . he had a fantastic intelligence network . . . and if it was moving, *zap*—up to the lab, analyzed, copied, and out on the market with packaging and advertising before the little guy knew what had happened.

There was a small French outfit that came in with a multiplicity of pastel colors, not just one. It was moving like hell, so we put together a shade promotion called *Colors Unlimited* and it was out within six weeks.

Eterna 27 was a weirdie. [One important product Revlon did innovate was Eterna 27.] We were going to launch it on *The Ed Sullivan Show* with a ninety-second commercial. Whereupon word is sent over from Sullivan that he will not do the commercial until it was proved to him that the claims for the product were true. Sullivan didn't like Revson and, in truth, Sullivan was a very anti-Semitic guy. So they send me [a Gentile] over to sell Sullivan. Charles gives me more books than I can carry with clinical data on Eterna 27. The tests were done at a women's prison, ending up with one side of the woman's face looking great and the other side looking awful. The tests were overwhelming. I walked in to see

* A roomful of them, in fact: an infrared spectrophotometer, an ultraviolet spectrophotometer, an atomic absorption spectrophotometer, and a thin-layer chromotography plate-reader, for starters. Also, on other floors: a guillotine-like "bottle drop," used to drop bottles to see if they break; a spice rack-like perfumery, with vials of such ingredients as Bulgarian Rose Otto, at $4,000 the pound; and a rabbit/rodent ranch where the rabbits, the day I saw them, wore mascara, and the rats were being force-fed Head & Shoulders, a Proctor & Gamble product, to see how much it would take to kill them. (One more reason to be a rabbit and not a rat.)

Sullivan and sat and sat. The great man was busy. Finally he gets through taping and I'm taken into his dressing room and I start showing him the materials. He turns around and grabs me by the arm and says: "I've got one question. Does this stuff work on guys?" I said: "Ed, honestly I don't know." I went back and Charles said, yes, it would. Sullivan had a case sent over that afternoon and went ahead with the commercial.

I wrote Revson's speech for a UJA appeal. I did a lot of research on it and I really did write a heartbreaking speech about the kid with a rifle going hands and knees across the Gaza Strip and can you let him do it all? This kind of thing. Charles didn't rehearse the speech and he blew it badly. He was so mad when he got off the podium, he comes down and he's walking past a table, and there's a very well-dressed woman there, with a beautiful silver fox stole . . . I don't think he even knew this woman . . . but as he walked by her table he snatched the stole off her back and threw it on the floor and said: "Fox is for whores." She looked at him incredulously, she started to cry . . . and he stormed out of the room. He has a list of things that offend him and fox is one of them, just like brown suits. [Mandel confirms Charles's hatred of fox, but doubts Charles could have acted as described.]

I went to a stockholders' meeting. Five seats in front of me was a little guy with a stack of law books with place marks in them. And he finally gets up and says: "I have some questions." And he starts quoting *Business Law* and all kinds of jazz. He goes on and on but he's really well-informed and his complaints are exceedingly specific.

All of a sudden this Valkyrie comes screaming down from the back of the room . . . it's Ancky. She can't get to him because he's in about four seats from the aisle and she's screaming at the top of her lungs—"What have you ever given to this company? What have you ever done? I have given it my husband. I have given it my life. My children have no father so he should run the company right. You stand there with your books

. . . I'll buy your stock right now at ten dollars over market." She opens her bag and is waving this money around, and they had to take her out. Charles is up there on the podium, dying.*

[Even under ordinary circumstances, Charles found stockholders' meetings trying:

"I'm Mrs. Shapiro. Will you please tell me one thing? You have painted a wonderful picture for us. But when I bought your Revlon it was at eighty-six. Now it's thirty-eight and you're doing wonderfully. Where are the profits? You're such a big company and you can't afford to give anything more?" (In past years a package of Revlon products had been given to each attendee.) "Why shouldn't we get a little something more? You don't serve anything here and there are no microphones and . . . Well, this is the dullest meeting I ever attended. I go to Pfizer and a lot of others, and I certainly get much more. At least if I lose with them, I enjoy losing."

"Madam," Revson began his reply, "sometimes you talk as though you were a competitor." But it was true: Revlon had cut out giving away free cosmetics at its annual meetings to discourage women from coming, and had purposely neglected to provide microphones to put a damper on the question-and-answer period. Thank God these things happened only once a year.]

Charles's office looked like the lobby of a French bordello. His main executive office was exceedingly masculine . . . paneling and all that, dark wood desk. But he spent a great deal of time in a series of rooms that ran down from his office, off of which were other executive offices and a sort of showroom. It was all very pastelly, French-bordello.

[*Fortune* was more generous: "Among recently designed presidential suites, perhaps the most spectacular deviation from the antiseptic norm, and surely the most fanciful, is the suite occupied by Charles Revson. The visitor approaches by way of a corridor labeled Fifth

---

* Ancky recalls the incident well, but says it was Martin's wife, Julie, not she, who caused the scene.

Avenue, lined on one side with lighted display windows and on the other with white-marble intaglios representing big Fifth Avenue stores. The floors are of unpolished terrazzo, meant to suggest a sidewalk, with a strip of red carpet somewhat incongruously running down the middle. ... A corridor called Pomander Walk ... is decorated with murals depicting formal eighteenth-century English gardens. At intervals there are trees made of green glass. The presidential suite is at the end of this corridor, just past a mosaic fountain.

"Revson's conference room ... has white-leather walls and a twelve-foot ebony table, also covered with white leather. In addition he has a formal, or ceremonial, office; a big corner room paneled in Brazilian rosewood. (The aluminum window sashes have been painted and grained to match.) The formal office contains, among other things, a huge walnut and rosewood desk, a Tiffany-glass ceiling lamp, a reproduction of a glass-fronted bookcase once owned by Samuel Pepys, and two electronic consoles— one by Revson's desk and the other in the conversation area—which permit him, by punching the right button, to get through to any one of twenty-five subordinates. Revson's suite includes three other rooms: an informal sitting room furnished like the sitting room of an English country house; a massage room with a rubbing table and a sun lamp; and a bathroom with a marble-topped wash-basin and gold-plated fixtures."]

George Beck was one of Charles's personal aides. An ex-navy pilot, aide to Admiral Halsey, and a big ladies' man. And there was an account man at Grey, a very nice guy, who was running around with one of Charles's girls. Only this guy didn't know she was Charles's girl friend when he started seeing her. So George Beck arrives at his apartment one night and he says: "David, are you in good health?" He says: "As far as I know." Beck says: "It could be very temporary." David says: "What do you mean?" Beck says: "If you ever see whatever-her-name-was again, it would be bad health. If you see her twice, you probably won't survive." He took Beck seriously; he never saw her again. He told me this himself. [In an unrelated incident, Beck and his fifth wife were found murdered on board a houseboat anchored off Ft. Lauderdale, in 1971.]

I was in Mandel's office one time when Charles called him from Greece. They were on the speaker box. "You know the trouble with this place, Bill?" "No, Charles, what is it?" "They got no goddamn pastrami. Tell Beck to bring me some pastrami." So George Beck went over to the Stage Delicatessen to buy ten pounds of pastrami and flew it to Greece that night. That's the truth.

(XII)

Heartburn

He was a rather unusual patient. If you told him to do something, he'd do it twice as well. He realized that in order to make Revlon great, he had to live.

—Dr. Alfred Steiner

Revson buffs will immediately question the validity of the ten pounds of pastrami flown to Greece on the preceding page, because it was not long after the debut of *The $64,000 Question*, and not long before the public offering of Revlon stock—in June and December 1955, respectively—that Charles had a mild heart attack. As a result, he quit smoking and embarked on a fanatically strict low-cholesterol diet. Is there such a thing as fat-free pastrami? From the Stage Delicatessen?

The only thing Charles Revson took more seriously than his business was his health. Compulsive about his products, he was an out-and-out nut about his health. "He swallowed every fucking pill in the world," says Irving Botwin. "The guy was a walking drugstore." His doctor objects to use of the term "hypochondriac," on the grounds that any man who has survived two heart attacks has reason for concern. But the intensity of his concern far exceeded the severity of his attacks. They were so mild his ex-wife doesn't even believe he ever had them.

He had a variety of digestive complaints throughout his life, including at one time a small ulcer; and also a variety of attempted cures, many of them self-devised. In the early forties he went on a baby-food diet. Around the same time, he consumed great quantities of halvah. At Billy Reed's Little Club he would order Bumble Bee salmon and baked beans (neither was on the menu); and if the beans were not kept properly separate from the salmon, he would send the plate back to the kitchen to be rearranged. He didn't want salmon juice mixing with his beans. For many years he would pour a gloopy white liquid into a glass of water before every meal and gobble a fistful of antacid pills after, leaving the corners of his mouth chalky white. It was for his stomach, also, that he gave up hard liquor.

And it was for his heart that he gave up everything else. "He never had any heart attack," scoffs Ancky, who was married to him when both were alleged to have occurred. "He had two," says Dr. Steiner, much of whose livelihood lo these thirty-six years was derived from Revson and Revlon. Katie Lowery, attempting to reconcile these seemingly contradictory views, suggests Charles may have talked Steiner into agreeing that his minor heart problems were "attacks." After all, beyond a point what purpose is served by arguing with your patient? Particularly when he has you on retainer and is helping to fund your research. If he wants to exaggerate his brush with death, why aggravate him by insisting on a less dramatic interpretation?

It is fair to conclude that Charles had at least two mild cardiac episodes—call them what you will; that one occurred in late 1955, so as to land him in the hospital the day his stock went public and to require a longer than usual stay in Arthur Godfrey's suite at the Kenilworth Hotel in Miami to recuperate; that at the same time as he may have been exaggerating their importance

173

in his own mind, he was simultaneously doing his best to conceal them from the public; and that mild as they may have been, they scared the shit out of him.

Accordingly, he brought extraordinary self-discipline to the task of caring for his heart. To begin with, he gave up smoking. The three to five packs of Phillip Morris regulars he smoked each day were cut, immediately, to nil. Cigars were likewise discarded. To ease his withdrawal he placed jars of hard candy all over his office. And from time to time he would dangle an unlit cigarillo from his lips. Naturally, the uninformed were forever lunging to light it and had constantly to be fought off.

Having achieved such remarkable reform in his life, he ever after attempted to reform everyone else. He offered Ancky ten dollars for each of her normal twenty cigarettes she didn't smoke. The first day she didn't smoke at all and got her $200. The next day, $180. "And before you know it," she recalls, cigarette in hand, "I smoke just as much as before. I tried to stop, but I just couldn't." He offered Jack Friedman, his close friend in later years, $10,000 to quit, with no better success.

On instruction from Dr. Steiner, he also swore off cholesterol. These days such a diet (less stringently observed) has gained wide acceptance. In those days people thought he was crazy. Always a picky eater, he now became impossible. He shunned eggs and dairy products, of course, and was buying margarine in the days when it was still sold in tins at the drugstore. He developed the habit of running his finger over his steak and his vegetables and then sniffing it to be sure the chef or hostess had followed his butter-free instructions. He would seat himself, when possible, with a view of the kitchen to watch his food being prepared. It would be ridiculous to suggest that he thought people were trying to poison him—but neither did he trust them. Even at home he would suspect that contraband had been slipped into a particular dish.

He would pull up to Les Ambassadeurs, in London, in a chauffeur-driven Rolls, carrying a bottle of corn oil in a paper bag. And then call the chef out to instruct him on its use. He would leave frantic messages for a vice president who was joining him abroad—"Call Mr. Revson *immediately*." When the vice president called, he would ask, "Kiddie, you got the marge in the fridge?" He wanted to be sure the man had remembered to bring his margarine. On flights abroad he sometimes carried a soft athletic bag with two of his specially trimmed steaks and two bottles of Dom Perignon, to be sure of truly first-class treatment. In his last year on earth he had his meals chauffeured all the way up to the hospital in the Bronx from his apartment on Sixty-fifth Street. (One can never be too careful of that rich, spicy hospital food.)

His steaks had to be broiled from the top only, to let the fat run off, and they had to be charred dry. "He was not an adventurer in food," Irving Botwin admits. "Never. He ate enough tuna fish [packed in water; opened in front of him, like wine, so he could check the label] to start his own tuna factory. He loved meat loaf, steak . . ."

And yet in a way he *was* an adventurer—adhering to an untested diet and devising his own cholesterol-free recipes. Stuart Levin, former owner of Pavillon, credits him with "some marvelous ideas in cooking—really terrific." He would have breast of chicken with the skin and all the fat removed, dipped in beaten egg whites and then fresh bread crumbs and sauteed in Mazola corn oil. "It just never occurred to me to do it that way," Levin says, "and it was delicious!" Nothing was ever sent back to the kitchen, he explained, because both he and the chefs knew exactly how their "cherished client"—Levin's phrase—wanted things. Few restaurateurs were so talented or fortunate.

Much of the Revson legend, in fact, stems from quirks in the way he took care of himself. One could paint quite a sad picture of a man with grave health problems whom others unfeelingly ridiculed. Imagine his embarrassment at having to ask for special treatment in a restaurant! At having to have a special plate at a party! Except his health problems weren't grave; and if he felt embarrassment over his special requirements, he never showed it. Nor were they truly necessary. He feared cholesterol as the Wicked Witch of the West feared water, but without the justification. He acted as though a pat of butter would cripple him, and a second pat do him in. "He thought," says an executive at U.S.V. Pharmaceutical, "that if his cholesterol count could be reduced to zero he would live forever. Of course, if your cholesterol count is zero you're dead."

As a result of his regimen, Revson's cholesterol level declined from around 300, the upper limit of normality among American males (and considered by many doctors to be substantially too high), to under 200. To be on the safe side, however, he would frequently take his own pulse; he kept electrocardiographs in the city, the country, and on his yacht; he had electrocardiograms taken daily when he traveled (a doctor was always aboard the yacht); and to remain fit, he exercised six mornings a week for twenty years with his private trainer/masseur/ chiropractor, Dr. Mac—a Jewish ex-fight-trainer and semipro football player from Rumania.

His exercise room at 625 Park Avenue was small but elegant, with naked Greeks cavorting on red wallpaper. Dr. Mac would in later years arrive from Levittown every morning a little past nine. Charles was usually on the phone by then or, occasionally, asleep. A quick shower was followed by ten or fifteen minutes on the Mr. Jogger Cadette, twenty or thirty minutes on the electric bike, a minute or two under the sun lamp, and twenty minutes of exercise with tension cables. Mac was careful not to have Charles work up a heavy sweat. "But sometimes he'd give a sneeze or two and say, 'Gee, I think I'm catching a cold.' And I'd say, 'You don't have a cold.' And he'd say, 'Well, I'll go and see Dr. Steiner anyway.' Each time I'd bet him a dime he didn't have a cold—and I won myself quite a pile of dimes."

After the exercises, a massage. Not like one sees in the movies, but a gentle rubbing/kneading "treatment." Then he would shower or bathe and pick out one of his hundred or so Fioravanti suits that all looked the same, anyway (so much so that the butler had to number them to be sure which jacket went with which trousers), and have breakfast. Saturdays, this routine would be conducted up in the country. Sundays, Mac's day off, Charles would go through it alone.

Mac says that when he first met Charles, "he was a

176

very stiff man." (In his demeanor, that is, not his musculature.) Gradually, he loosened up. "I kept horsing around and kidding with him, and little by little he'd smile. He liked to hear a little joke, and I'd tell him one almost every day." Pressed for an example, Mac tells the good news/bad news doctor checkup joke. (The good news is that the patient's peter is going to grow six inches longer; the bad news is it's malignant.)

Once at work there was another routine. "Charles had the most routinized life of any man I've ever met," says a man who got a call from him every Sunday night in the middle of *Mission: Impossible*.

He paced himself. His anger, for example, was always *controlled*. He would never leap out of his chair and start shouting. He would uncoil himself slowly, like a rattler, if he rose from his seat at all. There would be a slight tremble to his lower lip, which could curl up over his upper lip. His eyes drilled you. And if he was really furious, a little foam might show through his lips. But that's all. Never any quick or violent movement.

During his daily marathon lunch meeting, he would rest his head in his hands or on the table. He had the habit, too, of closing his eyes—you could never tell whether he was with you or not. But the sleepy look was deceptive. Watch out.

After the marathon lunch, a nap. Years ago they were working on lipstick cabinets. The supplier was there and the buyer, and they were all fighting like mad. All of a sudden Charles goes over to the side of the room, stretches out on the sofa, and says: "Wake me up in half an hour. I'm going to sleep now."

By five or six in the afternoon he would be just beginning to catch his stride. His creative people, who arrived earlier and took no naps, were beginning to flag. Meetings would last another couple of hours, after which he would walk the few blocks to his apartment, shower, take another nap, dine, and around half past ten he would be ready, at last, for the meat of the day, the things he really wanted to do. "I had some fascinating evenings with him," one former associate says, "but they would most of the time run well past midnight. Charles was

177

really a very lonely person who wanted company, and I guess the night was the loneliest period. He found it difficult to sleep. He was very much a night person."

With all the time he spent worrying about his heart, one marvels that he still found time to worry about other parts of his body. He would run up to Dr. Stovin, his ear, nose, and throat man of forty years, at the slightest provocation—often accompanied by executives so he could work on the way up and back. He suffered from allergies, was given to fairly frequent nosebleeds, and liked to have his sinuses X-rayed periodically. (Also his stomach, kidneys, and bladder.)

He was concerned with his skin. He used Eterna 27, his wondrous wrinkle remover, every night. (He also ordered the tip of his nose and the tips of his "devil's ears" airbrushed out of all photos.) He would "collect" his blackheads, and the bumps that come with old age, and every couple of months have Revlon's staff dermatologist remove them. "I would send all my tools down to his office by messenger," says Dr. Brauer, "and then at the end of the day, when everyone had left, he would show me the areas and I would remove them. He was aware of every square of his body, including his back."

For all this (and I have spared you his opththalmologist, his throat specialist, and whoever else)—for all this the man was hardly sick, *really* sick, a day in his life. He almost never missed a day's work. Which proves either that his elaborate self-attentiveness paid off or that it was unnecessary.

He was nearly as concerned with the health of those around him as he was with his own. With a few prominent exceptions, he wouldn't hire fat men. Mandel, being a marketing genius, he would tolerate, even though he periodically blew up like a little Buddha. Sheldon Feinberg squeezed by on his financial acumen. One Revlon president took to carrying around a note from Dr. Steiner testifying to his unusually low cholesterol level, so that he could order dessert.

People talk of Revson's inviting them up to his home

in Premium Point during the Lyn era for his famous Saturday night double-feature movies (the perfect non-social social evening), during which the butler would serve popcorn in a golden bowl and Charles would berate his guests for eating it.

"Where are you going, Mildred?" he asked pointedly of Mildred Custin, past president of Bonwit Teller, from across the room at one of his informal dinners. He was in the midst of another conversation, but he never missed a thing. He could see where she was headed. "I'm going to take another piece of angelfood cake," Mildred admitted. "Take the fruit, Mildred—the fruit."

At a large and serious marketing meeting, Charles suddenly broke off in midsentence. "Stop eating those cookies!" he ordered vice president John Revson. "You've been eating them all day and that's enough, already. Joey," he said to another young whiz, Joe Spellman, "take those cookies away from Johnny and don't let him have any more." And then he finished his sentence.

At a lunch in his suite at Claridge's—the Royal Suite —he ordered cold chicken for everyone, minus any kind of dressing. When they had finished, the maitre d' popped his head in: "Sir, would you care for some cheese?" "Okay," Charles asks, "who's stupid enough to have some cheese?"

He loved to diagnose the conditions of those around him and to prescribe cures. For a layman, he knew a great deal about medicine. He was forever arranging for people to see Dr. Steiner, or to be treated by prominent specialists whom they would otherwise have had to wait months to get in to see. (Dr. Wilbur Gould, who treats all the opera stars for throat problems, Dr. James Nicholas, who handles Joe Namath, for bones, etc.) He often paid the bills himself.

"What are you eating eggs for?" Charles once asked Eli Tarplin, alarmed. (In his mind, eggs and death walked hand in hand.) "I went to the doctor and he thinks I have an ulcer," Tarplin replied. Charles stops the meeting and calls Dr. Steiner. "Al," he says, "Eli Tarplin is here with me and I think they're killing him. Okay. Good-bye." He tells Tarplin to meet Steiner at Columbia

Presbyterian Hospital at two o'clock. (The hospital fed Tarplin milk and eggs for a week and the incipient ulcer disappeared.)

This was the one area—people's health—where he couldn't possibly have been more considerate. It was almost as if he had found in this hobby an acceptable outlet for his otherwise repressed warmth, a way of saying, "See, I'm not such a bad guy; when it comes to something really important, I'm the nicest guy in the world." Or it may have been his need to control people or, as with paying huge salaries, his way of making them feel forever beholden to him. No doubt it was also in part an extension of his own hypochondria. But the fact remains that Charles Revson did wonderful things for people around him who were injured or sick.

Suzanne Grayson's nine-year-old daughter was hit in the head by a golf ball, fracturing her skull in three places. Charles immediately arranged to have the head of neurosurgery at Lenox Hill Hospital break up his July 4 weekend to drive out to the rural Pennsylvania hospital.

Jerome Zipkin, full-time social person and walking laugh-riot, says if Charles hadn't gotten him down to Dr. Gould when he did, a tumor that was forming would have killed him.

Not to mention all the lives Revson saved indirectly. Myron Blumenfeld, Bloomingdale's cosmetics buyer, first met Revson in a hotel elevator after a Revlon sales presentation. "You work for me, don't you, young man?" Charles asked. "Thank God I don't," Blumenfeld replied. Some years later, he had a kidney disorder and, for the first time in his life, had to go into the hospital. "As I was going in," he says, "I looked up and saw that I was entering the Revson Diagnostic Center of the Albert Einstein College Hospital—that it had been given by him. I remember writing a thank-you note."

Stanley Kohlenberg, on the other hand, was suffering from no more than a mole on his forehead when he met Revson for the first time, newly recruited as marketing director of the Ultima line. (He subsequently left to become president of Coty, and was then lured back to Revlon.)

"The first time, in 1968," he says, "I had never met Charles, but had heard about him, and I was obviously afraid of him, as most people are when they first meet him. I was here two weeks, in the product-training class downstairs [through which all executives go], and I get a call: 'You have to attend a Charles meeting as an observer because it's a meeting on your line and we want you there. All you do is go to the room, be very quiet, and leave when everybody else leaves. That's all we want. Nobody is going to ask you any questions, because you're brand-new . . .'

"I entered the room and there's a certain little ritual that goes on at these meetings. Charles sits in a certain chair and eventually everyone knows where they are to sit, in order of importance. I went all the way down to the other end of the table, sat down quietly, the meeting went on, I took some notes, nobody asked me any questions. However, as part of this same ritual, everybody gets up and leaves quickly when the meeting is over and Charles waits for the next group to come in.

"I turned around and everybody was gone. And there is Charles at one of the table and me all the way down at the other end . . . just the two of us. Charles is basically a very shy man and terribly introverted . . . which is why he has built this whole little world around him as opposed to going out. That's why he eats inside every day and brings people to him, where he's comfortable. Even traveling, Charles has to bring his own environment with him—which drives everybody else crazy—because he feels confident then. I can understand it because he's shy.

"Anyway, here we are alone together in the room. He doesn't even know who I am . . . I could be from the outside . . . and I was petrified of him. I couldn't talk. So I figure I've got to brazen it out and walk past him and get out of the room. I get up, gather up my papers, and start to walk—smiling nicely to Charles as I go because there was nothing else I could do. As I start to walk by he says, 'You sit down.' So I do. And he says, 'Who are you?' And I say, 'Stanley Kohlenberg, Mr. Revson. I'm the new marketing director on Ultima.' He

181

says, 'Oh, yes, I've heard about you.' Then there's a big silence.

"Now, the next thing Charles does, which is what he does to everybody he meets: he looks them over. He doesn't care how long it takes or what you're doing while he's doing it; he starts at your shoes and actually goes right up your body. You feel yourself being undressed. It seemed like hours, but it must have been a minute, or even less. I had a birthmark on my head, about the size of a dime . . . a black mole, which I don't have now. He looked at me directly, which he will always do to anyone, and says, 'What's that on your head?' I almost fainted because I thought something must have been crawling—when you're born with a birthmark you don't even know it's there, because it is part of you. I said, 'What? Where?' I started to look around and he said, 'No, the thing on your head.' I said, 'My mother calls it a beauty mark, but I think it's a mole.' I felt like a little jerk. He said, 'It's no good for you. Take it off.'

" 'Take it off?' He said, 'Yes, get rid of it because you will get sick from it.' I said, 'Mr. Revson, I've been to doctors for examinations and they said as long as it doesn't get bigger, or change color, it's okay.' He said, 'Those things are never good. Call Dr. Brauer [the staff dermatologist] and tell him to take it off your head.' I thought he was kidding, but he was worried about cancer. [And maybe he didn't like looking at it. Dr. Brauer thinks it was probably more the latter than the former.]

"I thought he was kidding, so I ignored it. I figured he'd never remember that. Two weeks later I'm sitting in a meeting and he turns to me and says: 'You didn't do it yet, did you?' I knew what he was talking about and I said, 'Well, I just started, Mr. Revson, and I have to—' He says 'Do it.' So he had told me again. And I put it off again. Next meeting with him—about a week later, I'm sitting on one side of him and Norman Greif, head of the research center, on the other, and he's fed up with me now and he turns to Norman and he says: 'Call Brauer and get that thing off his head.' Now he's got me to the point where I'm so aware of it that I'm looking in the mirror all the time.

"I go back to my office and there are several anxious calls from Dr. Brauer, who doesn't even know me. I call him and he says, 'Stan, I understand you're joining us and you have something on your head. Come up here quick and we'll take it off.' And by 'quick' he meant the next morning. So the next morning I go up to the lab, in the Bronx, where Brauer has his office. He sits me down in the chair, examines it, and says, 'I can't do it. It's too close to your eyebrow, and if I stitch it, it's liable to raise your eyebrow, permanently.' I'd look pleasantly surprised for the rest of my life. So I said, 'Okay, fine. Let's forget it.'

" 'Oh, no,' he says, 'Charles wants it off. We'll make an appointment with a plastic surgeon, Dr. Rees.'

"I go back to the office and who do I bump into but Charles. 'You didn't do it. How come you didn't do it? I sent you up there—why didn't you do it?' So I explained the situation to him and exaggerated a little and told him that Dr. Rees was going to operate on my head. 'He's going to operate on your head?' 'Yes,' I said, 'he's going to operate, take the whole thing out.' Charles said, 'You're not going to lose any time, are you?' You see, now he's drawn between two considerations. He wants it off my head, but he doesn't want me missing work. So I said, 'Don't worry, I'll do it at night and come in the next day.' It was just an office procedure, anyway. Charles went off on his annual August cruise, and by the time he came back Dr. Rees had removed the mole and, sure enough, the next day I was at work."

Postscript. "Charles comes back from the Mediterranean and now he doesn't notice I had it done. Finally we were in a meeting and Charles says, 'There is a plastic surgeon I know who uses a particular night cream, which he feels is very good as an emollient. We ought to find out what it is and maybe we can incorporate it into one of our lines. Who knows Dr. Rees?' So I raised my hand. That was the guy who operated on my head.

"Charles looks at me and says, 'How would you know Dr. Rees?' I said, 'Charles, he's the man who operated on my head. You sent me to him.' He said, 'No, I didn't.

Dr. Brauer sent you to him.' [Charles did not like to be bested in even the most trivial exchange.]

"He never said another word about it again . . . not 'Good that you got it off,' or anything. But the basis for the whole thing was that Charles had accepted me as one of the family. I was going to work on his favorite line, Ultima, which was the line he most associated himself with, and to which he would soon be attaching his name. And it was important to him that I shouldn't get sick. What if this thing grew or became cancerous? [Or if he had to look at it every time they had a meeting?] Therefore, correct it.

"And once Charles makes a decision, it just has to be done. What do you mean, wait two or three weeks? Go tomorrow and get it done. Charles is black and white. There are no gray areas. It's right or it's wrong. If it's wrong, you get rid of it."

(XIII)

Who—Me?

Defendant Charles Revson engaged in a practice of mistreating executives and abusing them personally to such extent that men of proven capacity who held high positions in nationally known corporations before and after their employment by Revlon, Inc. suffered humiliation and impaired efficiency during said employment and left Revlon, Inc. to escape mistreatment; these practices of defendant Charles Revson reduced working conditions for executives at Revlon, Inc. to a state of widespread ill-repute and ridicule until by 1957 the recruitment and replacement of executives at Revlon, Inc. had become extraordinarily difficult; the rate of turnover of Revlon executives became a subject of ribald humor . . .

—Martin Revson,
plaintiff

The headlines were extraordinary. This whole quiz show mania, touched off by *The $64,000 Question* and gripping the country for three years, had turned out to be a fraud. The front page, eight-column headline of *The Washington Post*, November 5, 1959, ran: EX-REVLON AIDE ADMITS TV FIX. This referred to an affidavit sent down to the congressional hearings by George Abrams, who invented the chocolate chip cookie, and it came at an embarrassing moment for the Revsons, each of whom was testifying that they had been flabbergasted—just flabbergasted—to learn that their shows, *The $64,000 Question* and *The $64,000 Challenge*, had been rigged. Meanwhile, the producers of the shows, who actually did the rigging, were blaming the Revsons, Martin in particular, for pulling the strings. President Eisenhower likened "this whole mess" to the Chicago Black Sox scandal of 1919 and said nobody would be satisfied until it was cleared up. Dave Garroway broke into tears on the *Today* show and had to leave the show half an hour early when his cohost, former quiz-show star Charles Van Doren, was dismissed from NBC for his role in the scandal. Revlon stock fell five points in one day.

Revlon loyalists will tell you it was *Twenty-One*, a rival show, and not *The Question* that was fixed. They will tell you, with a note of resignation at having been unfairly wronged, that most people think Charles Van Doren was on *The Question*, when in fact he was on *Twenty-One*. Dig a little deeper and you arrive at this somewhat subtle distinction: *Twenty-One* was fixed; *The Question* and *The Challenge* were "controlled." Charles Van Doren and others on *Twenty-One* were actually given answers before the show, and were taught to stammer and stutter for dramatic effect. ("Let's skip that part of the question till later, please.") The air conditioning in the isolation booth was purposely left off so that contestants would sweat under the hot lights, as if from tension. Contestants on *The Question* were *not* handed answers; instead the producers ascertained in advance just what they did and did not know and devised their questions accordingly. It amounted to much the same thing.

Xavier Cugat testified that each time before he was to appear on *The Challenge* he would be visited at his apartment by a man from the show who would ask him a series of questions and provide answers to those that stumped him. The same questions would later be asked on the show itself, and Cugat managed to win $16,000. He told the House subcommittee, as if right out of *Peter Pan:* "I know that as an entertainer I am called upon all the time to make believe, to help make a good show. I suppose the producers of *The $64,000 Challenge* also wanted to make a better show, and so they made believe, too. If there was too much make believe, I wish you could do something about it without giving entertainment too much of a black eye."

John Ross, manager of twelve-year-old actress Patty Duke, testified that she had been fed questions right before going on the air to compete with twelve-year-old actor Eddie Hodges, with whom she tied and split $64,000.

The *Daily News* headline of November 5, 1959, read like a parody of a *Daily News* headline: HAD BANK VAULT KEY, SAYS GIRL TV FIXER. The girl TV fixer (not a TV repairwoman, you understand) was none other than thirty-six-year-old Shirley Bernstein, Leonard's sister. (The Bernsteins' father, coincidentally, was a Revlon jobber in Boston.) Ms. Bernstein was associate producer of *The Challenge*. She was in reality the producer, she testified, only Revlon "felt very strongly that a woman should not get the producer credit." Her statement was taken by Richard N. Goodwin, an ambitious House subcommittee staffer one year out of Harvard Law School (first in his class) out to make a name for himself.

Ms. Bernstein would have extensive discussions with the contestants to find out the range of their knowledge, she said, "so that in writing the questions I could, with some degree of success, prognosticate the outcome of the match." She would ask questions almost identical to those that were to be asked on the show when Revlon requested a particular outcome.

Goodwin: Was this request made of you?

Bernstein: Not directly, but through Mr. Carlin [the executive producer].

Goodwin: Was it your complete understanding from the start that you were receiving instructions from the sponsor as to how a match should come out?

187

Bernstein: Yes, completely. There were many meetings with the sponsor where Mr. Carlin would come back white with anger.

Goodwin: Did Mr. Carlin ever tell you directly that the sponsor had requested a particular outcome to a match?

Bernstein: Yes.

Goodwin: With what degree of accuracy would you control the outcome of a match?

Bernstein: At the peak of my efficiency, about 80 percent.

Ms. Bernstein said that both she and her assistant had keys to the famous Manufacturers Hanover Trust vault (Revlon's bank of long standing), and that they would go in and get the questions at any time.

No one disputed that there had been weekly meetings between the producers, the agency people, and Revlon, chaired by Martin. Yet Charles and Martin denied any knowledge of the controls. PROBERS SEE PERJURY OVER $64,000 "FIX" ran the *Herald Tribune* headline, with the subhead: Revsons Deny Ordering Rigging; Producers Swore Sponsor Did.

Charles would attend the meetings only infrequently, usually at the tail end just to express his general dissatisfaction. (Weekly meetings with a sponsor were unheard of in the TV business, but Revlon was a uniquely demanding sponsor—and had a lot at stake.)

Martin admitted that he would voice opinions at these meetings as to which contestants had audience appeal and which he hoped would lose. He admitted that his opinions could be forcefully stated. But he claimed to have *no idea* that his wishes would be taken as orders, or that the producers had some way of carrying them out. Neither was he apparently surprised to notice, as the weeks and months went on, the remarkable consistency with which his idle wishes, expressed innocently at these meetings, seemed to be fulfilled.

Mr. Carlin, executive producer of the show, told the subcommittee they would discuss "every possible phase of the show . . . in the minutest detail." Martin admitted that, but testified he "never once suggested that a con-

188

testant win or lose." Carlin said Martin made "urgent suggestions that certain contestants leave the show." (One contestant they tried—and failed—to dump was Dr. Joyce Brothers, the lady boxing expert. It was thought she had a grating personality that turned off the viewers.)

Martin went so far as to say that *had* he ever known that the shows he sponsored were controlled in any way —he would have dropped them ... even though they were catapulting his company's sales and profits beyond even his wildest hopes.

George Abrams, who attended the weekly meetings with Martin, testified that "we understood ... the technique used for controlling the destiny of a contestant." It's true that George would do almost anything for a headline—but would he lie to make himself look bad?

"Somebody is not telling the truth here," concluded Congressman Steven B. Derounian of New York.

Charles, meanwhile, had all but escaped coming under this embarrassing congressional spotlight. Subcommittee staffers had sifted through a great deal of material and decided it was not necessary to call him to testify. At the last minute, he sent a telegram to the committee *insisting* on his right to do so. It was not the smartest thing Charles Revson ever did. In his defense, it should be said that he sent the telegram on advice of a public-relations expert. The thought was that all the other witnesses would doubtless try to shift the blame onto Revlon, so Charles should have a chance to defend the company's good name. It's quite possible Charles really didn't know the extent of Revlon's implication in the controlling of the shows, and accordingly feared less than he should have.

One problem was that the congressmen assumed Charles knew what Martin knew—that if one brother was fibbing, the other was, too. Charles couldn't come right out and tell the congressmen that he and Martin had not been on speaking terms for some time—that they would pass each other at these very congressional hearings without so much as a nod. That would have been embarrassing. At one point it was Martin's turn to resume his testimony. The chair asked Charles if he knew the whereabouts of his absent brother, and he had to admit he did not. It became a bit awkward, Bill Mandel recalls. When Martin did show up—late for his own testimony at a congressional hearing—he was apologetic: "May I say, Mr. Chairman, I am sorry I was late. I was at the Hotel Statler. One rest room was busy and I went to the other, and it was busy and I went upstairs."

Charles spent three days at the hearings waiting to be called. Mandel, who was with him, says he was magnificent in a crisis. "He taught me not to panic." His first reaction upon hearing of the brewing quiz scandal, Mandel says, months before the hearings, had been to go over to see Bill Paley at CBS. Paley was another egotistical entrepreneur whose Russian-Jewish emigrant father had been in the cigar business—only Paley's father *owned* the cigar business. According to Mandel, Revson told him there was only one thing for CBS to do and that was to appoint a TV-industry "czar" to investigate all questions of quiz-show propriety and oversee such problems in the future. In other words, head Congress off at the pass. "Charles was right," says Mandel, "and they wouldn't listen to him."

So he is now at a hotel in Washington, scheduled to testify at ten A.M., to be accompanied by no less an attorney than Clark M. Clifford. Mandel wakes him at eight, which is early for Charles, and hands him a copy of the final draft of his statement. Carl Erbe is about to take the statement up to the Hill to have it mimeographed and distributed, to make the afternoon papers. Charles says: "Wait a minute; I haven't read it yet." Mandel says: "We've been on this thing for two days now; you've changed it eighteen times; if we don't get it up to the press it doesn't make the papers; and if it doesn't make the papers, our side never gets heard."

"Okay," says Charles, getting out of bed, getting a fountain pen, and getting back into bed. He is scheduled to testify at ten, remember. "We sit there from nine to nine-thirty . . . to ten . . . ten-thirty," says Mandel, "and he's rewriting his statement. My stomach is going through the roof and I keep telling him he'll be in contempt and all that stuff. He doesn't care. He's as calm as can be.

Finally, he's satisfied with it, so I rush it over and Carl has it retyped and mimeographed... we finally got up to the Hill, I don't know what time it was, and they don't call him until four o'clock. This man has never been on time for anything in his life and he's never suffered for it. I don't know why."

He did fail to get his side of the story to the press in time, however, prompting Mandel to comment: "He was calm, but I don't know if it was worthwhile. Maybe it would have been better to get excited and get our stuff to the papers. That's a microcosm of my dealings with Charles; his lack of priorities, his sense of proportion."

Charles was simply not one to be rushed. In this respect he could not have been less like the high-strung, nail-chewing, instant-retort Mandel. He would not make snap decisions—he chewed his cud. He would not walk fast—perhaps out of fear for his heart. He never wolfed down his food. He didn't talk fast. "He could destroy an airline by getting to a plane just as the doors were closing," says Irving Botwin—and he wouldn't be running down the ramp, either. He was even late for his son John's wedding (as was John).

When it finally did come time for Charles to testify, he said that he never missed watching *The Question* if he could possibly help it. He would walk out of a theater in the middle of a play just to watch the show on Tuesday nights to see whether the Italian shoemaker would win $32,000 by answering a question on Italian opera. "Sure, I was the sponsor," he said, "but I was just like the rest of the millions of Americans caught up in the drama of this program. If I had known that these shows were fixed, crooked, rigged, do you think for one minute that I would have watched or bothered this way?" A cynic might point out that watching the shows was the only way Revson could see his own live commercials, which may have been of more interest to him than the questions and answers; and that even people who fix prize-fights generally turn out to watch the contest.

Revson concluded his statement deftly: "Remember that [the producers] admitted to this committee yesterday that they also rigged *The Big Surprise*... [That show

191

and ours] had only one thing in common. It was not the sponsor, it was the producer. This producer would have you believe that sponsor pressure from Revlon drove him to do what he did on our show. Then what caused him to rig *The Big Surprise?*"

It was a neat twist—but not enough to appease the congressmen, who were by this time in the hearings feeling their self-righteous oats.

Mr. Rogers: You made a lot more [from these shows] than any of the contestants or all the contestants put together, didn't you?

Mr. Revson: . . . Yes, we did.

Mr. Rogers: Since you have branded these as deceitful practices, have you made any efforts or thought of any way to make restitution of that money to the American people?

Mr. Revson: I would not truthfully know how to answer that question, sir.

Mr. Rogers: I don't either, Mr. Revson.

Mr. Revson: Pardon me?

Mr. Rogers: I would not know how to answer it either. I just wonder—you and your brother come up here and say you were victims of fraud, too, but you were the kind of victims of the fraud that some of the winners on these contests were—that is, you profited very well by being a victim. You brand these other people as deceitful, and I agree with you, they were deceitful; but you are the one who profited the most by the deceitful practices that were played upon the American people. I am wondering what is in your mind and the mind of the Revlon Company, to try to make restitution or correction of a wrong which you admit occurred.

Mr. Revson: We have never given any thought to that.

Mr. Rogers: Apparently, some of the contestants had not given any thought to giving their money back, either . . .

Mr. Revson: In view of the circumstances, we went along for the several years in sponsoring the show. We did not realize what it was. It is the same as any other commercial company that would earn something because of something—a network or producer or contestant, and so forth. I don't know how to answer it. It is something that is past. It is part of a business experience.

Mr. Rogers: Yes, sir. You are not planning on giving the money back or making restitution, are you, Mr. Revson?

Mr. Revson: I had not even discussed it or thought about anything in that vein. I think, in turn, by virtue of the fact that it was done yesterday, I don't think there is a basis for it.

Mr. Rogers: You don't think there is a basis for it when someone obtains something by false pretenses that they ought not to make restitution? Is that your statement?

Mr. Revson: No, but see, we paid for the show. We paid for the time. We paid for the contestants, sir. So, therefore, in turn, we made a profit on it. I don't follow you there. I am not trying to be cute.

Mr. Rogers: I don't follow *you.* You have branded this, you and your brother both branded this as a deceitful practice and a reprehensible practice. Yet you are willing to accept the profits from it and let the contestants take all of the blame. Both of you said you had nothing to do with the running of it. The most you did was to make suggestions, isn't that correct?

Mr. Revson: Yes, sir.

Mr. Rogers: Were those suggestions subtle suggestions, Mr. Revson?

Mr. Revson: The suggestions made as far as I am concerned had no relativity to that.

Mr. Rogers: You mean they were about as subtle as a blow by a baseball bat?

Mr. Revson: I certainly do not.

Mr. Rogers: That is what the evidence would indicate, as you know. You heard the testimony.

Mr. Revson: I heard it, yes.

Mr. Rogers: It would indicate [that] when . . . Mr. Martin Revson made a suggestion, there was not any question in his mind or anyone else's mind as to what he meant and what he intended to have.

Mr. Revson: That is correct.

Mr. Rogers: That is actually what happened. A suggestion was made and you expected it to be carried out?

Mr. Revson: Pardon me?

Mr. Rogers: A suggestion that was made in one of these meetings you expected to be carried out, didn't you?

Mr. Revson: I didn't get the first part, then. I thought I got it.

Mr. Rogers: I say, that in these meetings you had, when you made a suggestion, which you claim you had the right to do under your contract, you expected that suggestion to be carried out, didn't you?

Mr. Revson: The few infrequent times that I was there, I don't remember discussing anything about a contestant or anything like that. The times that I would be in there would have relation to the format of the show, or possibly a change in the plateau aspects of the money part, or the show could be more interesting, or something such as that.

Throughout the congressional massacre, which covers a full thirty pages in the printed manuscript, Clark Clifford sat slouched deeply in his chair, perhaps sorry he ever got into this mess in the first place. For his afternoon's efforts he sent Charles a bill for $25,000. "When Revson gets the bill," Clifford said, "he'll cuss and call me a son of a bitch and the whole business. But he'll pay it. And next year, when he's down in Miami Beach playing gin rummy with his buddies, he'll talk about 'his friend Clark Clifford,' and how much the so-and-so charged him—and it'll be worth twenty-five thousand dollars to him."

Clifford may have believed Revson was innocent of wrong-doing in connection with *The $64,000 Question*, but apparently Charles was not "his kind of guy" and he felt no compunction about screwing him.

As if the congressional hearings hadn't been bad enough, they were followed only four months later, in March 1960, by an even more embarrassing controversy. Brother Martin, by now two years gone from the company, was suing brother Charles for fraud, seeking $601,460.80, and alleging (rather irrelevantly), that Charles "humiliated," "mistreated," and "abused" executives to the point that working conditions at Revlon had become the subject of "widespread ill-repute and ridicule."

A tenet of Charles's existence was to avoid embarrassment, let alone ridicule, and this suit dished up both. He managed to have the most offensive paragraph struck from the complaint, on the basis of its irrelevance—but not before it had been brought to the attention of the national press.*

Ordinarily, Charles went out of his way to avoid legal problems. Revlon attorneys were faced with the fact that their star witness simply refused to go into court or even to give a deposition. "He had a fear of the law and certainly a fear of being a witness—he was almost paranoid in this respect," says one of the lawyers who was instructed to settle out of court many cases that could easily have been won. He may have been afraid of being tied up in knots by a Perry Mason-type cross examination; he may have feared probes into some of Revlon's dicier activities from the distant past; he did not enjoy confrontations of any sort (in the old days, he would take the elevator up an extra flight in the Squibb Building and then walk down the back stairs to his office to avoid running into insiders or outsiders who might have been lying in wait for him). Yet in the case of Martin's suit—although it eventually *was* settled out of court—pride for a while got the better of paranoia.

Martin's attorney, William G. Mulligan, professed "amazement and dismay" that the suit had hit the papers, and swore that he and his client had "maintained absolute silence." In the then prevailing atmosphere, however, one must assume that Martin was more pleased than mortified to see his charges widely quoted, and that Charles was more mortified than pleased. Charles would state only that the suit was without merit, and that he regretted it. "It is unfortunate," he said, "that the language of the complaint contains the kind of emotional statements which sometimes characterize suits involving members of the same family."

---

* The full text of the deleted paragraph may be found at the head of this chapter.

(To try to bolster the generally disastrous public image Charles was building on what seemed an almost month-to-month basis, Bill Mandel arranged to have him retain a distinguished old-line public-relations firm. He set up a meeting at Charles's suite at the Pierre so that the P.R. experts could assess Revson and decide whether to take him on as a client. As Bill and Charles were sitting there, laying on the charm—the pushy but sincere Jewish kids trying to develop a rapport with the Ivy Leaguers—Bill Heller walked in with the night's entertainment . . . a woman whom, all things considered, it would be best not to have join the conversation. Mandel frantically shunted Heller and guest off into another room; Charles was taken on as a client; it did no appreciable good.*)

The suit was an offshoot of Martin's leaving the firm. Doubtless it could have been settled amicably had Martin left on amicable terms but, as will be further noted, such was not the case. The suit concerned 231,000 shares of Revlon stock which Martin owned, but which he had assigned to the famous "voting trust." Martin owned the stock, but Charles, as sole trustee, controlled it.

Martin wanted to remove his stock from the trust; Charles was in no hurry. He didn't want Martin to be in a position to dump a lot of stock on the market and thereby depress the value of Revlon shares; and, more importantly, he was determined to keep at least 51 percent of the company under his own control. With Martin's 231,000 shares in the trust, Charles controlled about 55 percent of the stock. Without it, he would have controlled less than half.

As a practical matter, Charles would have had effective control of the company with less than a majority of the stock. However, Charles's "neurotic anxieties" on this point—as Martin's lawyers referred to his concern—may have stemmed from the frustrating years when Revlon was still a private company and Charles had to submit

---

* Mandel does not remember the Heller aspect of the meeting but does not deny its plausibility.

decisions to Lachman for approval. Or perhaps they stemmed simply from Charles's general paranoia.

Nonetheless, control over a majority of Revlon stock could hardly hurt, and Charles was determined to have it. Martin came up with a possible solution: 131,000 of his shares would be released to him, which would still leave Charles control over a majority of Revlon stock. The remaining 100,000 shares would be sold back to Revlon itself in exchange for stock in Schering Corporation, a pharmaceutical company Revlon had for a time been trying to acquire.

Charles decided this wasn't such a bad idea . . . only he wanted Martin to agree to give up $6 a share in figuring the value of his Revlon stock. In other words, for Revlon stock that was selling at $35 a share in the open market, Martin would be given only $29 worth of Schering stock. Charles offered Martin three reasons, Martin alleged, to accept such a deal. First, he claimed to have inside information that Schering stock would very likely do better than Revlon stock over the coming year, so Martin would come out ahead. Second, if Schering did outperform Revlon—what would Revlon's other shareholders think if Charles had made an even swap? Mightn't they accuse him of giving his brother a sweet deal? Charles claimed he had been advised by his lawyers that he *couldn't* make an even swap of the Revlon and Schering stock without inviting lawsuits. (But, Martin alleged, no such legal opinion had in fact ever been rendered.) Third, Martin could not get the full $35 a share if he tried to sell his shares on the open market, because a block of stock that large would knock down the market price. So it would only be fair to accept a discount in this deal, also.

Martin said a $6 discount was too much; Charles agreed to cut it to $4. Martin said a $4 discount was too much; Charles agreed to cut it to $3. What's more, according to Martin, Charles promised that in the unlikely event Schering stock did *not* outperform Revlon over the following year, he would see to it that Martin got the extra Schering stock he was forfeiting by accepting the $3 discount.

197

As it turned out, Schering stock appreciated a stunning 71 percent over the designated time period (August 15, 1958 to July 15, 1959). Only, Revlon stock appreciated even a bit more—by 75 percent. And Martin, notwithstanding his $2 million profit on the Schering stock, expected Charles to stick to what he understood their agreement to be: namely, to deliver the Schering stock Martin had forfeited by accepting the $3 discount on his Revlon shares. He demanded either 7,518 Schering shares or $601,460.80 in cash. (The amount to which those shares would have appreciated by the time the suit was filed.)

Charles claimed he had never made any such promise. "Show it to me in writing," was the essence of his position, and Martin had nothing to show.

After a modest amount of backing and forthing, barking and frothing, they settled out of court. Charles paid Martin $300,000 out of his own pocket.

The suit itself was really just a battle in a larger war between the brothers. Many said that the provocateur of this war had been Julie Revson, Martin's wife. Julie knew both men well, and it was her opinion, no doubt biased as a consequence of her marriage, that Martin should be running the show. She wanted him at least to be president, with Charles kicked upstairs to the chairman's seat. After some pressure Charles had actually agreed to such a change in titles, to go into effect by 1959, but Martin did not stay around that long. He explains why:

"I'm not going to tell you all the inner feelings that I had, because I don't want to reveal them. I'll give you a general answer. While he and I got along very well when it came to merchandising and products . . . we didn't always agree on finances. My compensation. Also, while I had tremendous latitude, certain things still had to be cleared to his opinion. And sometimes, whether it was the name of a product or something like that, it became kind of sticky. I felt, after we had so many meetings, if he said, 'No' and 'Why don't you fellows go back and look at it again?'—it became a little irritating. Things like that.

198

"Those are the two factors, I think. And the other things had nothing to do with my wife, although he thought they did. We never discussed this, really, but he thought, I think, that if I hadn't been married to her it would have been different. I assure you it wouldn't. I assure you that the main reason is the certain individuality some of us have—I like to think I have it—and because of that individuality I've contributed to the company. I don't know what people on the outside think, but I know what I contributed—it's been large. Things he may not have seen because he wasn't close enough to it.

"So this is what looms large in my mind—that my contribution was great to the company. While it was recognized by him, I'm sure, it wasn't always said. And little things took place and grew into large things. Then there became little personal things which I don't want to go into. Human relations, etcetera. Our relationship had deteriorated . . .

"Our problems stemmed from—part of it was wives, that was true . . . he didn't want to take Ancky to the convention, so my wife couldn't go to the convention—things like that—and part of it was inside the business. A different philosophy about certain things in the business—personalities, people, their actions, what makes an executive . . . I think a lot of things stemmed from that. His viewpoint and mine differed on many people.

"I irritated him and he irritated me on certain things. The point is, I wasn't going to let him . . . It wasn't a point of wanting to run the company myself or supersede him or kick him out of the business. I never thought of that. I always knew his value . . . I felt that these personal irritants had grown to such a degree it would be better for us to go our separate ways . . .

"So I made my decision in February [1958]. When Charles and I sat down on a Monday morning I opened the meeting by saying: 'I have it in mind of leaving.' He asked why. I said: 'It's got to the point where our views are different. There's no sense in going through any details—why don't I leave amicably?' If he was surprised, he didn't indicate it. He was calm through

199

the whole matter, which he had a way of being during matters like this."

They agreed that Martin would stay until a replacement could be found. When Charles kept stalling on the question of releasing Martin's stock from the voting trust, Martin told him, "I'm not discussing anything else until we settle this matter." He collected a few papers and never appeared in the office again. But because his resignation was in a sort of limbo, his office at 666 Fifth Avenue—never occupied—was kept empty, but fully furnished and dusted daily, in case he should one day show up back on the job.

It took thirteen years for the fraternal rift to mend. During those years Charles was nothing short of frigid on the subject of his brother. "What brother?" he once said. "I don't have a brother." What made this state of affairs bizarre was that the two Revson families remained in close proximity. Their sons went to each other's houses, went riding together; Charles and Martin could be sitting close to each other at a horse show at Konrad Fischer's Kenilworth stables and they wouldn't even say hello.

Charles blamed wives; Martin, as quoted, maintains this was not so. But he does credit wives—a new set— with bringing about the reconciliation. "That's the happy thing, that we got back together," he says. "I think Lyn was an important instrument in getting us back together. She and Eleanor [Martin's second wife] got along fine. I think she convinced Charles; and Eleanor convinced me."

(XIV)

"Women Are Liars
and Cheats"

When you own a $2 million apartment at the Pierre and you close the door behind you and you're alone—you are alone.

—Dave Kreloff,
Revlon veteran

Beset by deep-seated insecurities, Revson was a different man in many respects from the image he chose to project. Manly, stern, tough, crude—much of this was a front. He had an almost pathetic yearning at times to be a warmer, more accepted person. When Lester Herzog was dying of cancer and someone reminded Charles how much it would mean to him if he would only call or visit, he replied, in the most touching way, "Joe, I know. I just can't." He bought Ancky a "beautiful, gorgeous diamond bracelet" (as she described it); but rather than present it to her directly, he turned and handed it to Helen Meresman. "Do you think Ancky will like this?" he asked. He was embarrassed by his own warmth. He once did manage to compliment an executive on a job well done—jaws dropped—then said: "There. I did it. Now don't ask me to do it again."

His emotional straitjacket, like his extraordinary drive, stemmed from insecurities the basis of which are not hard to imagine. His size, his lack of athletic prowess, the femininity of the products he always seemed to be selling (ladies' shoes, dresses, cosmetics), the nail enamel he wore, his self-styled "sensitivity," his hypochondria—reasons aplenty to have to prove oneself a man.* Then there were his growing up Jewish among Gentiles, his lack of education or polish, his tenement upbringing, the narrowness of his interests—added to whatever less obvious reasons he may have had to feel insecure, it was a lot for a man on the forty-ninth floor of New York's General Motors Building to cope with. (He would have been on the top—the fiftieth—floor had not the hum of rooftop air conditioners led him completely to revise the corporate floor plan midway through construction.) He was even insecure about his breath, gargling Cepacol by the gallon. And he would do anything to avoid embarrassment. He drove all over Manhattan before a formal dinner once to find Mandel proper shoes to go with his tuxedo—not because he was a perfectionist or because he felt badly for Mandel (who had thought black loafers would suffice), but because *he* didn't want to be embarrassed by Mandel's gaffe.

His insecurities fell roughly into two sets: those that led to the striving for manliness and those that led to a striving for class. He would be rough and crude to be one of the boys; proper and genteel to be classy. The friction between these not entirely compatible sets of insecurities must have generated some psychological heat. And sometimes the wrong set got the upper hand. At a small luncheon in his honor in Chicago, which included Mayor Daley, top financiers and retailers, a leading clergyman

---

* As for the *classic* cause of male insecurity, however, Charles felt so secure he was able to joke about it. A magnifying mirror was affixed to the toilet in the guest men's room of his Park Avenue triplex, such that anyone relieving himself would come away with greatly renewed self-esteem.

and the publisher of the *Chicago American*, he discarded the well-chosen words that had been prepared for him and—perhaps taking his cue from Daley's own tough-guy image or from the all-male composition of the group—launched into a fond reminiscence of his early days in Chicago. What Charles remembered best about Chicago, he said, was Carrie Finnell, who, he needn't have reminded his audience (but did, at length), could twirl her betassled bazooms in opposite directions simultaneously. (Much harder than walking and chewing gum.) He also remembered the Windy City beauticians he had bedded in the course of his work.

It was a disaster, this speech, and from the same man who had what Mandel called "a mortal fear of embarrassment."

(In another speech once he was doing beautifully until he got onto the idea of how he wished he could be nine people instead of just one, and thereby get involved with even more of the goings on of the company. That started him musing about what it would be like to have nine penises, and it was all downhill from there.)

Insecure, Revson hid behind his business in a world he created for himself, venturing outside only with trepidation, sticking closely to established routines and familiar places and, as far as possible, taking his environment with him. Riding down in the office elevator he seemed almost to shrink into himself. Up there, he was king of the mountain. Outside, he was alone.

He was lonely because he couldn't open up; he couldn't open up because he didn't trust people; and he didn't trust people because he wouldn't believe they liked him—or even could like him.

He felt eternally ill at ease, with strangers especially. Arriving, alone, at Kay Daly's for a party, he sent his driver in to ask: "Is this a good time for Mr. Revson to arrive?" He was nervous, unsure he was really wanted and anxious to have a familiar face greet him at the door. (It was his way, also, of demanding special attention.)

The years between his estrangement from Ancky and his marriage to Lyn were, with the year of his death, the loneliest. "I don't know how many times I walked the streets and had dinner with him because he had no place to go," Mandel says. But even married he was a lonely man. His wives did not share his life—his life was his business, and they were carefully excluded. He had never learned to make friends with women—they served a different purpose. He married three times. Lester Herzog, Bill Heller, and Jack Friedman, one after the other, were the people he was closest to. (Mandel's was strictly a business relationship, and a competitive one at that.)

He would become comfortable by establishing himself in a dominant position. A straightforward, giving, peer relationship was very difficult. "He didn't know how to love," governess Katie Lowery believes. His love, like the rest of his life, was reduced to routine. For months he would call Boochie at Deerfield every night at exactly 10:15 (until Boochie finally asked him not to call so much and, wounded, he stopped calling altogether). He went about lovemaking, women who slept with him said, as though he were going through an exercise class: ten minutes of this, fifteen of that, five of the other, orgasm, no repeats, off to the showers. Whether this was true where his wives were concerned, one has not the temerity to ask. But it would not have been out of character. "Everybody should pace themselves," he believed of intercourse as of everything else. He was a man of control, not passion. In his youth, embarrassed by his sexual naïveté, he told one woman, he had paid a professional to help him improve his technique. He was so . . . *practical.* "Marry a Eurasian," he advised an associate. "They make the best wives." "Any man can wear out three wives in a lifetime," he told another. When Eugenia Sheppard asked him at dinner one evening on the yacht what he thought of women, he said: "I think they're all liars and cheats." "It's not one of my favorite anecdotes," Ms. Sheppard says, "because I liked him very much. But I think it was an insight to his character."

His view of women and wives was at best utilitarian. Under the slogan, "You don't hire a man, you hire a family," Revlon wives in the fifties were summoned to special "wives clinics," at which they were told of their husbands: "If he doesn't feel like playing bridge or is too tired to go to the movies, you get your bridge-playing and movie-seeing in during the afternoons. If he gets home most nights too late to see the children, let them stay up now and then and make it up with longer naps in the afternoon—it won't kill them. If he has a lot of paperwork to do, learn to type if you don't know how, and then give him a hand with the reports if he wants the help."

"Woman in the abstract he idolized," an associate from the forties feels certain. "He put her on a pedestal and paid tribute. But individually, women were to be trampled on and cast away like you would a cigarette." He had, incidentally, the unusual habit of calling women —and referring to them—by their last names. Even those he knew well.

Writing of blue-collar workers in *The New York Times Book Review,* a Boston psychiatrist said: "They hate Jews and blacks and homosexuals and people on welfare. They hate protesters and do-gooders and outsiders. But more than anyone or anything else, what they really hate most is women. They spend much of their time pursuing women, but in their heart of hearts there is a dim rage at the claims of lust on their emotional freedom . . ."* Charles did not come from a typically blue-collar background—he certainly did not hate Jews—but the essence of the statement seems to apply. "I don't know," says Mandel, "but guys who like whores have an unconscious hatred of women." Why else would he, upon finishing with two women at the Beverly Hills Hotel, throw their money on the floor?

At Old Oaks Country Club one afternoon, two competent women golfers, mother and daughter, happened to arrive at the first tee at the same time as Revson, the pro, Harry Meresman, and Victor Barnett. Because any golfer knows that two women play faster than four men, the younger woman naturally quickened her pace to tee off first and get out of the foursome's way. Revson,

* Matthew P. Dumont, May 18, 1975, on *Blue Collar Aristocrats* by E. E. LeMasters.

enraged, said, "What do you think you're doing?" "I'm teeing off as quickly as possible to get out of your way," she said. "No, you're not," Revson snapped, and proceeded to tee off ahead of her, followed by his three partners. As he started off down the fairway, he turned back to the woman and snarled: "This club is for men, you know."

His definition of the male and female roles was exceedingly rigid, even by pre-lib standards. He, Ancky, and the omnipresent Lester Herzog were taking John out in his carriage. Charles, to be chivalrous, was helping Ancky push. But when Ancky and Lester gradually fell behind, as a joke, and Charles realized that he was pushing the pram all by himself, he flushed with embarrassment. "What are you *doing* to me?" he whined. Thirty years later, when the ladies on the *Ultima II* asked that some romantic titles be included in the fare of nightly films shown on board, he overruled them. His taste ran strictly to good guy/bad guy shoot-'em-ups. Among the paperbacks in the *Ultima II* library were *Trail Smoke* ("No man is bigger than a .45 slug"), *Law Man* ("A blood-mad town and a condemned law man"), and *The Texan* ("When they took away his badge, they enforced the law—with blazing sixguns").

With his parents both long gone, Joseph and Martin out of the company, the boys off at Deerfield, Lester married and Ancky actually going through with the divorce, in the spring of 1960 Charles relied for companionship most heavily on Bill Heller and then George Beck.

Heller first showed up at Revlon in 1948, in a powder-blue suit and light suede shoes. His hair was solidly greased and he sported a thin mustache. He looked a little shady, and people described him as "crude," but he had a mind for figures and a great desire to get ahead. Soon the powder blues had been mothballed and Heller was going to the same tailor as Charles, the same shirtmaker, the same accountant, the same lawyer, the same doctor, the same dentist, and eventually to the same Rolls-Royce dealer. (He got a sizable chunk of Revlon stock at the public offering.) To make the transformation complete, and to please Charles, he divorced his first wife and moved into Manhattan. ("Careful, Bill," Charles would occasionally say, in front of others, "the Brooklyn's showing.")

As Lester had, Heller would eagerly do anything for Charles. He waited around the office every day until "C. R." was ready to leave, often went out to eat with him, served as his "beard" (so Charles could pass off as Heller's the girl he was with), ran out for sandwiches, carried the money and the margarine, secured and paid off women, took the wiretapping rap, wrote Johnny's term papers for Deerfield—anything. If he wasn't as altruistic in his devotion to Charles as Lester had been, Charles didn't seem to notice. Heller became his closest companion— not to mention secretary/treasurer of Revlon, and then head of its international operations. It was not your standard intercorporate relationship, as might prevail between the chairman and the international vice president of General Motors or Xerox, but neither was Revlon your standard corporation.

For ten years Heller's life was simple. Then in 1959 he met Iris Segal. They fell in love. Suddenly Heller found himself torn between two much stronger, more talented people, each vying mightily for his devotion. It took him all of three years to collapse and die under the strain.

Heller was forty-seven when he met Iris, then vice president and director of Seligman & Latz, the leading beauty salon operator (headquartered, like Revlon, at 666 Fifth Avenue). Charles had known Iris from that day in 1933 he had come to Seligman & Latz looking for his $48. He respected her success and ability; but because he didn't want her breaking up his relationship with Bill, he was given to making derogatory remarks behind her back. He told several of his executives to try to discourage Heller from seeing her.

Bill, for his part, was so terrified of displeasing Charles —and, incidentally, jeopardizing his chances for the top spot in Revlon's international division—that he underplayed considerably the love he felt for Iris. He didn't mention, for example, that they had gone off and gotten married.

They had done this secretly in a town that did not require that legal notice be published in the papers. Bill pretended he was still just dating Iris as Charles enumerated all the reasons he shouldn't marry her. He hadn't the nerve to come to his wife's defense. Months later, after the international job was his, Heller announced the second, public ceremony. Rather than face Charles directly with the news, however, he wrote him a letter and ran off on a business trip.

"Charles called me up to the office," Sid Fread, who was financial vice president at the time, remembers, "and he acted like he had gotten a Dear John letter. It was the most amazing thing I had seen in my life. He turned to Jerry Juliber and said: 'It isn't that he couldn't tell me himself—he has to write me a *letter*, like he don't *know* me. He writes me a *letter!* Look at this! Look! Go find me a new head of international.' "

Eventually, Charles cooled off. Bill was kept on as head of international and as Charles's very close friend. Charles was even best man at the (second) wedding. But now things were more complicated. Even bizarre. At the wedding, for example, in front of the ark at Central Synagogue in New York, Rabbi Seligson performed a standard Jewish ceremony in which the bride and groom each take a sip of wine. At the conclusion of the ceremony, as they were preparing to leave the chapel, Charles leaned over and drank the rest of the wine. "Evidently he was thirsty," Iris says. "The fact that it was a ceremonial glass deterred him not one whit. And I looked at the rabbi and he said to me—he was a very funny man—he said, 'Do you, Iris, take thee, Bill and Charles . . .' Because he had never seen them apart."

After the wedding, Charles may not have demanded from Bill more than his standard measure of fanatical devotion, but it seemed for all the world to the newly betrothed Mrs. Heller that her old friend Charles was doing his best to break up her marriage. (As he had, for example, broken up Lester's first marriage.) "Charles," she even claims to have confronted him once, "are you trying to break up our marriage?" "Yes," he replied.

He was forever calling Bill at home—"the call of the

wild," the Hellers used to call it—and, naturally, whenever Charles went abroad, he expected the head of his international operation to come with him. Not for business reasons so much as to keep him company. They enjoyed gambling and kept joint safe-deposit boxes in some of Europe's finest hotels. Bill would do much of the betting, with Charles looking on, under an arrangement whereby he would get to keep 20 percent of their winnings but sustain none of the losses. Winnings were left abroad to avoid taxes.

They were given to other vices as well, which led Iris to place detectives on Bill's trail, and then to write poison pen letters to a number of Left Bank bar girls. "Iris was a brilliant woman," a contemporary notes, "but rough—rougher than the Revsons." Charles later assigned one of his own vice presidents to track down and retrieve some of the letters.

It was a highly charged situation, and it took its toll.

"I was married twenty-five years the first time," Iris recalls, "and only twenty-five months the second time. [To Bill.] It was a rather tempestuous marriage. Bill would get calls from Charles at two in the morning asking him to come down to his apartment. He used to tell me it was because Charles wanted to discuss something, but later he admitted that Charles used to get midnight frights." Iris says Bill would sometimes sleep with Charles in his huge bed—a matter not of sex but of loneliness. On such occasions Bill would come home with a little 'chr' monogram on his shirt instead of the 'wdh' he had left with. (Their shirts were in other respects identical.) Charles's loneliness could be acute. "One night he called from Premium Point," Iris says, "and I heard his voice. It was a strange kind of—almost a sob-resentment thing in his voice about being alone. My Bill had a cold . . . the snow was up to your navel . . . Charles didn't know we were married at the time. I'll give him that. Anyway, I drove up there with Bill and then I drove back. The last thing I could see was Bill trudging in that snow up the hill to the house to be with Charles, and that was one of the nights he came back with another shirt. It was pathetic."

Iris's memory may be colored by her readily acknowledged hatred of Charles Revson—mellowed though it has been by a dozen years and by their earlier long-standing friendship. But the gist of her story is entirely consistent with those told by others who were intensely loyal.

The upshot of all Bill's trudging and traveling and trying to keep Charles happy and trying to keep Iris happy was a massive coronary. He had recently returned from a trip to the Orient with Charles, then flew off for Mexico and Chicago with Iris. He was going to Chicago for a job interview. He had decided, with a good deal of prodding, to abandon the Revlon life-style—it was killing him. Their plane was due back around seven, but the weather caused delays. Charles called Bill's number-two man in the international division, Sid Stricker: "Where's Bill?" Stricker told him that Bill was on his way back from Chicago. "*Chicago?* What the hell's he doing in *Chicago?* He told me he was going for a weekend in Acapulco." When Bill finally did get in, around midnight, he phoned Stricker and told him he felt "tired, real tired," but that he'd be in the next morning for their eleven o'clock meeting.

"That night, when he got into bed," Iris remembers, "he expressed exhaustion and I said, 'Promise me that you won't go in tomorrow—at least not until the hour that Charles goes in.'" But it didn't do any good. Bill apparently was terrified not to make an appearance and to say he was tired—at forty-nine you do not say you're tired, you just march on. When he got to the office that morning, he was feeling pain in his back. He called Steiner, who instructed him to come to his office. "I hooked him up to the electrocardiogram machine," Steiner says, "and saw right away he had had a heart attack. While he was here in the office, he went into what we call ventricular fibrillation." Steiner didn't have the equipment to shock the heart back into action. Within minutes Heller was dead.

Charles was distraught. Iris was disconsolate—and very bitter. She was accusing him of killing Bill—of knowing about but concealing Bill's heart condition, and of driving him mercilessly until he dropped. Charles was saying that Heller killed himself running around the country trying to meet Iris. But he was shaken. He ordered Mandel to arrange a meeting with the rabbi who was to perform the funeral service. In his paranoia, according to Mandel, Charles was afraid Iris would get to the rabbi first and persuade him to say that Charles had murdered Bill. "We talked for twenty or thirty minutes," Mandel says, "and Charles was nervous. He fiddled with his glasses and his knuckles were white on the armrest. We went through this whole thing about how wonderful his relationship with Bill was and about Bill's value as a person and so on, and when the rabbi left I said to Charles, 'Well, I've never done that before.' He said, 'What?' I said, 'I never fixed a funeral.' "

And now life was lonelier than ever. Fortunately, there was George Beck to help fill the void. George was a swinger among swingers. He was married five times. Indeed, he was married to his second and third wives contemporaneously. One lived in Long Island, the other in town, and neither knew about the other for nearly eight years. (There may even have been *another* wife at this time also—no one knows for sure.) Beck divorced his third wife and then his second, in that order, to marry his fourth, who thought she was only his second. John Revson was best man at that fourth wedding, in 1964; Charles Revson gave away the bride and sponsored a champagne-and-caviar reception. The marriage lasted until 1969. It was nine weeks after marrying his fifth wife on Christmas day, 1970, that he (fifty-one) and she (thirty-one) were murdered in the nude aboard Beck's fifty-seven-foot houseboat, the *Bachaven* (short for "Bachelor's Haven"). Some of his children met each other at his funeral for the first time. Even as this is written, wife number four and one of Beck's former mistresses work in the same department at Revlon. Their relationship is not warm.

(The murder remains unsolved. The sleeping couple were bludgeoned and stabbed so violently that blood hit the ceiling. Valuables were left untouched. A team

211

of detectives, perhaps overwhelmed by the size of Beck's "little black book," got nowhere. A psychic of sorts did appear after some months to announce that a civil servant named Charles B. Stackhouse, whom he had never met, was their man. "Don't ask me how," the psychic explained, "I just know these things." An investigation proved this accusation to be totally groundless. But in the meantime it so badly shook Stackhouse that he committed suicide.)

Beck's remarkable life-style was facilitated by his good looks—"the blond Adonis," he was called, though his hair would go gray around the roots from time to time; by his access to a twin-engine Beechcraft QueenAir that each financial official in turn tried to persuade Charles to unload, but which George always managed to persuade him to retain; and by his influence over Charles himself, the basis of which was a source of considerable rumor-mongering.

He had joined the navy at seventeen and become a crack pilot. Tiring of the discipline to which pilots had to conform, he attained a succession of highly social and comfortable assignments, and after twenty years, aged only thirty-seven, was able to retire. Admiral Halsey, retired also, took him on as his aide. It was when Charles met the Admiral on the golf course that he met George Beck as well. The chemistry, apparently, was excellent. George was one of those tuned in to Charles's wave-length. And being as calculating as he was outgoing, George knew a good thing when he saw one. He was soon working for Revlon. Just what he was doing for the company could not always be defined (any more than just what he had been doing for the navy), but his services were valued highly and he had himself a marvelous time.

Revson was drawn to Beck for his youth and good looks, his intelligence, his war record, his self-confidence, his zest, his women, and his ability to get things done. Others in the company were not nearly so enthusiastic. He and Mickey became great buddies—they were in much the same line of work, as it turned out. (A photo of George, Mickey, and James L. Goddard, then chairman of the Food and Drug Administration, hangs in

Mickey's office.) But others resented his instant success and influence.

In the summer of 1960, when Charles first purchased his home in Premium Point (Ancky having gotten the house in Rye as part of her settlement), he decided to commuted to work by seaplane. George was Charles's chief pilot. Charles persuaded his neighbor, Alfred Perlman, then head of the New York Central Railroad, to allow him to establish runners for his seaplane from the water up onto his beach. He saved twenty minutes' commuting time in each direction—and it was *different* (or ridiculous, depending on your point of view). Charles was not one to do things like everybody else. When the copilot crashed the plane into the East River on a practice flight one day, Revson reverted to his chauffeured Rolls-Royce. But George still had the much more substantial Beechcraft QueenAir to fly around in. (It was this plane he used each weekend to fly down to the houseboat in which he was killed.)

Technically, George should not have been flying at all. He was a diabetic. But he had apparently learned, through a balance of insulin and a certain pill, to arrive at a doctor's office symptomless. Or else it may have been the financing he helped one of his doctors obtain.

On a strictly business level, Beck was soon running a sales program to the military and was later given charge over certain department stores. But George Beck's importance to Charles lay elsewhere. One of his first assignments concerned Ancky. The Revsons had agreed on their divorce settlement, but they remained on reasonably good terms. Charles was still asking Ancky to reconsider; she would later say it was a case of "loving a person but not being able to live with him." Anyway, she had agreed to wait a while before actually considering the divorce final. It was Easter weekend, and Charles had asked Bill Heller to have a special arrangement of flowers delivered to Ancky; it was very important to make just the right impression. Word soon came that the florist had been unable to deliver the flowers—Mrs. Revson was not there to receive them. And the next evening, according to Iris Heller, "We were all at dinner

213

at his apartment in the Pierre and the phone rang. It was Ancky. Charles went out to take the call and when he returned he was in a blithering fury. Apparently, Ancky had asked him if he would like to buy a set of Royal Doulton china with the letter 'R' and a set of crystal with the letter 'R' and some monogrammed silver—and Charles, falling for it, said, 'Why?' and Ancky said, 'Because I now have a crest. I am the Baroness Van Boythan, and he is younger than you are.'"

Whatever the exact dialogue, the baron was real enough —well, he was a fake, actually, but Ancky had really gone out and married him. And this is where George Beck comes in. Concerned that Ancky had rushed into something without knowing what she was doing (which she had), concerned for his two boys and, one can only assume, spiteful—as Ancky must have been to marry this man in the first place—Charles set George about investigating the baron. By flying to Austria, wandering through graveyards and photographing nursing homes, he was able to compile an extensive report.

Stephan Van Boythan, Beck found, had been born Otto Feldmann on April 2, 1907 (which made him a mere six months Charles's junior), in Vienna. He had come to the United States in May 1941, enlisted in the air corps, and was honorably discharged as a private first-class on December 21, 1944. "Service record," Beck's report read, "reveals no disciplinary action and entries are routine. A national agency check is essentially negative. Subject . . . pays a monthly rent of $400. He previously was employed by Harry Winston, Inc. as a jewelry salesman, however he currently is unemployed." There followed his passport number, his bank balance, and a photograph of his mother, whom Beck had found in the Altersheim der Israelitischen Kultusgemeinde, a charitably supported Jewish home for the aged. The "baron," Beck reported, had been unwilling to provide the $100 a month in support the charitable home had requested, but had agreed to contribute $38 a month. Neither his deceased father, Jacob Jack Feldmann, nor his mother, the Czech-born Ernestine Bentum, made any claims to royalty.

The baron, according to one Beck intimate, was paid

off to bug off. It was a very brief marriage which Ancky makes no effort to conceal or defend.

George was too good at his work to leave many traces, but a reliable source states categorically that he arranged, on Charles's behalf, for scores of bugs and wiretaps, both in the office ("every major executive was tapped"), at homes, and at various apartments Revlon executives had occasion to frequent. He would not actually place most of the bugs himself; he would direct one of Revlon's security men to do the work. "There is no question about it," this source states.

It was Beck, too, who helped mastermind the capture in midindiscretion of the third Mrs. Revson . . . but that came later. For the moment, Charles was very much a bachelor, and George helped keep him company and keep him entertained. He channeled a great many attractive women Charles's way. One was Cristina Austin, whom Beck was hoping might become Cristina Revson but who became Cristina Ford (Henry's wife) instead. They did date for a while and spent at least one weekend up at Premium Point. One of Charles's closest associates at the time double-dated with them a couple of times, and says that "she was the first woman who gave him a hard time. This was a woman with tremendous class and elegance . . . she was so unlike Charles. She was the ultimate in refinement and she wouldn't give him the time of day. I think that's what intrigued him about her."

Earlier, he had been intrigued by another sensational woman, Eartha Kitt. If Charles was not in the forefront of equal-opportunity employers—and he wasn't ("He was terribly prejudiced," says one current, white Revlon executive)—he was nonetheless exceedingly turned on to Ms. Kitt. London, Puerto Rico, the Plaza—the sets for their rendezvous were as glamorous as the lady herself. But for fear of endangering Revlon's image, especially with distributors in the South, the relationship was kept as quiet as possible and terminated perhaps as much for business reasons as any other. One evidence of his regard for the lady was a $28,000 diamond watch he had Bill Heller buy for her.

What George or Bill Heller couldn't come up with—

most of it much less glamorous and sophisticated—Billy Reed did. Billy Reed's Little Club was by far Charles's favorite hangout when he outgrew Bill's Gay Nineties. It was described by one occasional patron as "a high-class pimping academy."

It was only with his marriage to Lyn, in 1964, that his day as ladies'-man-about-town came to an end. In the meantime, his most intense emotional relationships were probably with his executives.

(XV)

Dividing and Conquering

He's a great leader of people, a great stimulator. He inspires people to do much more than they thought they were capable of.
—Victor Barnett,
former Revlon executive vice president

"Nobody gets along around here," says one current Revlon vice president. "Bergerac is trying to change that, but if you took Kalish, Bennett, Woolard, Armstrong, Barnett, Bottner, and all these other executives and put them in the same room, nobody would be left alive. Under stress conditions, they dislike each other sometimes to the point of embarrassment."

How can a company run like that?

"With a whip and a chair and Charles as the lion tamer. Each is very strong in what he does, each jealous of his prerogatives, and each goaded on by Charles, to a degree, to get the other."

About the only time they would really work together

217

was when a threat loomed from outside. An Irishman came to Revlon from Colgate once, in the fifties. He got everyone in a room and told them he was a barracuda —that he wasn't going to take any crap from them. He lasted three months. Before an important meeting, he asked the guys: "Think Charles is going to go for this?" "He'll *love* it!" everybody lied. There was an inside group that sort of respected each other, one of its number explains, "but we were rough on outsiders. New people had to fight their way in. There were people like Bill Mandel who were able to take it and manage very well without any problem. He became the biggest barracuda of all."

There was a sameness among the executives who lasted at Revlon. "Even those of us who weren't Jewish were alike," says Eli Tarplin, who was. The New York Telephone Company is Irish-Catholic, Marriott Corporation is Mormon, the Mafia is Sicilian, Morgan Guaranty is blue-blood, and Revlon was tough, unpolished Jewish. These were the people Revson could relate to: resourceful guys who knew how to survive. "Oh, Lord," Charles often said, "give me a bastard with talent."

"If you go down the list," says Mandel, ". . . let's leave out the word 'killer,' but they're all dark, kinky-haired guys . . . Kalish, Levine, Herzog in his day, Heller in his . . . Shelley Feinberg, who was the same kind of killer I was, a killer when he had to be . . . Jay Bennett, who learned how to be a killer . . . all these guys have the same oily, sinister approach. Irving Bottner is of the same ilk. Soroko. Soroko's legal assistant. Juliber. Victor Barnett . . ."

"Diamonds in the rough," one rare Harvard M.B.A. who worked with these men recalls, "and the roughest was Mandel."

(Picture one of these men sitting, self-confident and bored, as Charles rambles on. For amusement, he catches the eye of someone for whom he has special contempt and flicks a piece of dirt from his nose at him.)

The fear and even hatred that was engendered in some Revlon executives, both of Revson himself and of the men he pitted them against, led to the expenditure of great effort on Revlon's behalf, and to constant self-evaluation. Am I doing this right? Where could I be criticized? How can I do it better?

Certainly such an atmosphere led as well to ulcers and unhappiness and to the famous rate of executive turnover. But the system seemed to work and it weeded out the "soft sisters." Furthermore, the cause of the turnover —having two bodies for each job—was also its solution. Someone was always panting to take over where whoever-it-was left off. Revson ran a heavy inventory of executive talent, but there wasn't as much duplication as there seemed: in his mind one group was earmarked as coming, the other as going.

Sandy Buchsbaum, who somehow survived without being much of a barracuda himself, came to Revlon as an associate ad director, responsible for all TV commercials. But there was also a fellow in charge of TV production, the man in the green velvet suit, Mort Green. "They never told him I was coming, and they never told me he was there."

Soon you had the relatively conservative Buchsbaum saying of a certain commercial, "This is the way it's going to be"; the flamboyant Green saying, "Over my dead body"; Buchsbaum saying, "Well, I'm sorry, but that's just the way it's going to be"; Green screaming, "I'm going to throw you out of here bodily"; Sandy suggesting that Mort was acting "like a child"; and Mort, as Sandy recollects the exchange, saying, "I *command* you to leave this room!"

"I must truthfully say," says Dr. Harvey Sadow, formerly of U.S.V. Pharmaceuticals, "that the most unsavory human relations evolved in the Revson/Revlon organization, largely because of the conditions created by Charles's driving need for total acknowledgment. It was almost divide and conquer rather than unify and succeed. This is my singular criticism of the man."

He would be meeting with one of his executives and then buzz a third man on his squawk-box intercom. Without telling the third man that the second man was listening, he would ask what he thought of the second man's idea. Or he might say, "I have so-and-so here and

219

he says such-and-such, but you told me this-and-that. Now which is it?"

"Charles was a stirrer-upper," one ex-president says. And a needler.

For mental stress, Revlon's corporate jungle must have been the match of any ongoing nonpenal institution in the western world. If the hours didn't kill you, the blood pressure might. Take the classic tension between the marketing department and the lab—between Ray Stetzer and Bill Mandel. Both men strong, brilliant, blunt, egotistical. Charles had Mandel sample opinions on a proposed new product. The opinions were unfavorable. On Tuesday—lab day—Revson asks Stetzer: "Raymond, what do you think of this product?" Stetzer thinks it's fine. Charles says, "Bill, tell Raymond what you found out with your testing." Mandel reports the comments he's gotten, and Stetzer gets out of his chair and goes wild. "He claimed I had made up all the comments and hadn't really done the testing—that he had had a report from someone downtown that I hadn't really done it . . . He went wild. That's what killed him. Five or ten years later he went wild in a meeting and died that night."

(It should be noted that Charles was always solicitous of Stetzer's health and that in later years Stetzer had been reduced to a three-day workweek. Far from "hating" Revson for "killing" her husband, as I was told she did, Stetzer's widow was in fact warm and positive in her remembrance. The question rears, *Equus*-like: would it have been better for Ray Stetzer to have lived longer, but without the tremendous passion he felt about his work?)

Even Mandel did not escape unscathed. Revlon took a terrible toll on his fingernails, and worse. A man who radiates loads of energy but very little warmth, Mandel would start shaking Sunday afternoon in preparation for Monday morning management meetings. He actually *passed out* at one such meeting, it became so heated. He had to be carried out. He was rushed to Doctors Hospital, all of thirty-four years old.

Mandel also took to seeing a psychiatrist, although

not as a direct result of his job. Knowing that Charles would look with disfavor on the "weakness" psychiatric help implied—and the time it took away from business— he would leave Westchester shortly after sunrise for his two or three appointments a week, and get into the office as early as usual so no one would be the wiser. Not unlike Katie Lowery taking the boys off to Sunday School while the chairman of the board was still in bed. On one occasion, he told his doctor about a dream he had had where Charles got killed, eliciting "the only comment I can recall that shrink saying to me in two years: 'Well,' he said, 'you sure polished him off in that one!'"

Just as the jitters started for Mandel Sunday afternoon, so Suzanne Grayson remembers her Friday nights for the feeling of relief they brought her. She and her husband never scheduled social engagements for Friday night, because she was just too wrecked from the week to go out and face the world. One Friday night, however, they did go out with friends. All of a sudden, in the middle of a restaurant and with reference to nothing, she just burst into tears.

It was only nail polish and hair sprays, just as football and chess are only games, but when you get into the big leagues, you are not just playing. If you can't measure up, as inevitably many people at Revlon couldn't, the toll on your self-esteem can be brutal.

Peter Revson, quoting from a French writer, once defined "a gentleman" as one who never undermined the self-respect of another. "That's as good a definition as I've ever heard," said Peter.

Picture Charles in a meeting with Bea Castle—with others present as well—saying in reaction to something of hers he didn't like, in his needling whine: "What's the matter with you, Beatie—are you getting old and soft in the head?" It was the cruelest thing he could have said, and to a woman who would gladly have walked out a window for him. Bea just blanched.

Picture a Revlon president on his way out, working off his contract, sitting in a marketing meeting with the Revlon pros, saying of a certain product, "I gave it to my wife and it's my opinion that—" and Charles interrupts: "What would *you* know about it?"

Picture a man presenting a new product idea he has been working on, a translucent soap on the order of Neutrogena. This man is not one of the stars in the company; he is not used to dealing with Charles; the opportunity is very important to him; and it is apparent to every one else in the room but him that the presentation is not going well. Yet Charles, uncharacteristically, does not interrupt. He even allows a faint smile to cross his lips. ("When he smiles," an ad man once said, "you know you're gone.") On and on this presentation goes until finally it is over. Charles fixes the man with his eyes and says calmly: "You stupid fucking idiot." And then, rephrasing that thought in a variety of ways, manages to intersperse two others: First, soap is a commodity (which is not altogether true), and he hates commodities. But worse, *this* soap you've been presenting has square corners. Do you think people want to wash their crotches and their armpits with soap that has *square corners?* And on and on. It's true that a soap with square corners is not a well-thought-out soap. It's also true that it would have been no problem whatever to round the corners, so the whole idea need not necessarily be discarded on this basis alone. And it's supposedly true that the man broke down in tears under Charles's attack.

It was, of course, precisely the toughness, seriousness, and brutality of Revlon that made it so satisfying to those who could cope. (Also the money.) To some of them, Revson was a father figure. To others, he was the unsympathetic mirror of their own inadequacy.

At the behest of his board of directors, Revson hired three presidents before Bergerac. "It was impossible to work for him," says one, "because you had no role." Charles was everywhere—and not about to share either credit or control. The president-as-office-boy was how Charles conceived of the job.

The marketing people, by contrast, were responsible for . . . everything. Advertising, selling, packaging—but production, too, because how can you make a profit if your goods cost too much to make, or if they aren't shipped out in time for Christmas?

The controller was also responsible for everything. *Controller*—that word was simple enough. If anything was out of control, Charles explained to each new one in turn, that meant the controller was screwing up.

Mickey Soroko, in his day, was responsible for everything—or at least for anything that needed special handling. Bill Mandel was certainly responsible for everything. Victor Barnett was responsible for everything but marketing. Eli Tarplin, once upon a time, was responsible for everything, too.

From the fifties on, perhaps most heavily relied on of all was the personnel chief—first Juliber, then Bennett. Besides having to attract new talent fast enough to replace the old and to keep pace with expansion, they were key advisers and also Revson's very own secret police.

"Charles was by nature a suspicious person," says Juliber. "He had confidence in just two people after Martin left: Bill Heller and me." Not the ideal choices, some said.

Because personnel was separate from the marketing battleground, Charles looked on these men not as his competitors but as his coconspirators. Together they would assess the various players, their loyalty, their output, their frame of mind, and act accordingly. Bill Mandel thought Charles didn't know about his early morning visits to the shrink? Charles knew, Jay Bennett assured me. Charles knew.

The power Juliber and Bennett wielded was clear to everyone; they never knew for sure what reports Charles was being fed behind closed doors. The personnel department not only initiated contact with prospective employees, it negotiated compensation, monitored office politics, checked to see who was coming in on time, communicated Charles's wishes and, when the day came, did the firing as well. If you were on Jerry Juliber's shit list, you were in big trouble.

Revson thrived on innuendo, gossip, and infighting, so that's what he got. He paid more attention to whispers in the ear than to factual memoranda. He delighted in calling the head of the plant and making him squirm: "I hear the Aquamarine lotion isn't being filled to the top," he would say. "How come?"

"I don't know anything about that, Mr. Revson. I'll investigate right away."

"I don't know," Charles would moan. "I sit here on Fifth Avenue and I know about it and you don't? Maybe we should trade places."

One such plant man in the days when Revlon was still a private company found these conversations so debilitating that he placed a mirror on his desk to strengthen his resolve. A somewhat savvier Revlon executive took pity on him once and offered to help rub out at least one snitcher. They got the paperwork on a big order that had been shipped out to the Pennsylvania Drug Company, and the savvy executive (by his own account) went down to the factory floor and started spreading a rumor that the order had never been shipped. Then he ran like hell back up to the office to wait for the phone to ring. It soon did.

"Do yŏu know that we're breaking with advertising in *Life* and *Vogue* and *Mademoiselle*," Charles asks indignantly, "and we are killing ourselves to get these orders, and you can't even ship the merchandise?" Why am I always surrounded by incompetents? Why do they screw up everything I try to do? Why is my life so lousy?

"I don't know what you mean, Charles."

"You haven't even shipped the Pennsylvania Drug order, *have* you?"

"Why, yes," the plant man says, grinning at himself in the mirror, with all the documentation in front of him: "We shipped twenty-two hundred dozen of such-and-such and forty-two hundred dozen of so-and-so, via XYZ Trucking Company on the fourteenth. The bill of lading number was 367009-Y, and ..."

Just how much internal spying there was at Revlon is hard to assess. Bugging rumors ran rife, and when the company moved out of 666 Fifth Avenue, a network of wires was discovered in the walls—installed, the story ran, for an intercom system that was never hooked up. After the 1955 New York State wiretap hearings, one good-humored executive took to cupping his hand over his mouth and leaning down into the space beneath his desk: "You hear that, Charles?" he would ask.

But it was not entirely a laughing matter. In November 1955, Bill Heller testified that for five or six years Revlon, with the cooperation of the phone company, had been monitoring conversations of certain of its employees to be sure they were handling calls properly—a practice, he said, which resulted in better service to the public and "higher morale" among Revlon employees. Furthermore, he testified, on one occasion he and Jerry Juliber arranged to have the Madison detective agency hook up a tape recorder, kept locked in his closet, that would automatically record the conversations of a certain executive without his knowledge.

A dozen years later, Revlon's president, Dan Rodgers, noticed some clicking sounds on his phone and asked his secretary to ring the phone company and have it fixed. Jokingly he suggested that his line was tapped. Indeed it was, the phone company discovered. Soon there were six men from the phone company and an assistant district attorney in the basement of Revlon's building, tracing the tap from there on up to—well, what do you know?— the floor Bill Tracy, Revlon's security chief, had his office on. Tracy, an ex-FBI man, worked for Jerry Juliber.

The investigators asked to be admitted to Tracy's office, but he said no, not until he had a chance to consult the company counsel. The company counsel wanted to take a day to think about it, then said okay. The investigators found a little hole and some wood shavings down in the back of a credenza, but no wires or recording equipment. A cynic might suggest that during the day's delay such embarrassments had been removed, but Tracy explained to the grand jury that he had made the hole to plug in a radio so he could listen to the World Series. Witnesses claimed to have seen Tracy puttering around down in the basement; but Tracy explained that he was merely doing that in his capacity as security officer, checking to see that Revlon's lines weren't tapped.

There is no question that Rodgers' phone was tapped, that the tap led to Tracy's floor at Revlon, or that Tracy denied the investigators entry. (Tracy, moreover, has told friends after a drink or two that he had tapped "hundreds" of phones in his day.) But as there was no conclusive proof, the grand jury was persuaded not to indict anyone, which would only have hurt Revlon's innocent shareholders. How would it look to Wall Street to suggest that the chairman of the board had been tapping the president's phone? Surely Tracy wouldn't have been doing this work, if he did it, without instructions from *someone*. Revson may or may not have ordered the tap, but it was he who set the tone of his administration. "We don't have any friends," Nixon told his closest aides soon after being elected by one of the largest majorities on record. Revson, too, never knew whether people were really on his side, which he doubted, or whether they merely wanted something from him. Revlon executives were nicknamed "the Jewish Mafia" by one of their number; Charles was the Godfather. As anyone who goes to the movies knows, a Godfather can never be too careful.

Like the Godfather, he had a certain presence. Short and lean, more head than shoulders, "lovely nails," "amazing eyes," hairy arms, skinny legs, he was voted one of America's ten best-groomed men and featured in full-page, full-color ads as a Calvert Man of Distinction. He was not handsome so much as he was arresting. A 135-pound presence. When he was introduced to a two-star admiral, it was the admiral, not Charles, who was a bit awed.

Like the Godfather, he was hard to read. Martin was a reactor; Charles was impassive. Except for those occasional thin smiles, signaling trouble, you never knew for sure what he was thinking.

Like the Godfather, he was hard to fool. He could walk into a room and tell immediately who was prepared and who wasn't, who believed in his convictions and who didn't. Those who tried to tell him what they thought he wanted to hear got burned. "Don't try to second-guess me," he warned associates, who kept trying anyway. It's true that he had his penchant for yes-men—Lester Herzog and others—but from most of his executives he expected strong opinions and a good fight. Then, rather than saying, simply, "Well, I've listened carefully to what you all have to say and weighed both sides and decided to do it my way . . ." he would keep at the argument and keep at it and keep at it, relentlessly, until he either wore them down into submission or persuaded them of his position. More than wanting them to carry out his bidding, it seemed, he wanted them to acknowledge he was right. In this respect, he was less like the Godfather and more like *der Führer*. Sidney Stricker, an architect of Revlon International, remembers a case in point.

Sidney Stricker

He and I and Bob Armstrong, and Lyn Revson, and his man in France in charge of fragrances, and a woman named Princess Rachevsky [formerly Vera Pratt] were all having lunch at the Plaza-Athénée. It was a Saturday —I well remember it. He was going around the table to each of us—"What's doing here? What's doing there? He got to the fragrance guy and he wanted to know why Intimate wasn't in the show windows in the Hotel de Paris down in Monte Carlo. And this fellow, very honestly and in his very broken English—he speaks very beautiful French—said, "Charles, eets not the exqueesite chic perfume like Joy or Chanel." Charles went through the roof. He wanted to fire the guy right on the spot. He couldn't understand a guy who could tell him this. He swings around to me: "How's our nail enamel selling?"

"Lousy."

"What do you *mean*, 'lousy'? What's wrong with it? Who's the big one?"

"Dior."

"Why's Dior so big?"

"Dior's big because we have a problem and I've tried to tell the problem to the lab but nobody would listen."

"*I'm* listening to you," he said. He was beginning to get pretty mad because he didn't like to think that occasionally he had quality problems with his products—and it was only on occasion, because he made fantastic products. I said, "Well, ours is all settling on the bottom."

And he said, "Well, what the hell—we give them a stick with it. They can stir it up."

"But they don't, Charles, they take the stick and throw it away."

"Well, what does Dior do?"

"They've got two little steel bee-bees, two little balls in there, and the women can shake it up."

He looks at me and he says "You don't know your *business, do* you?" I said, "Of course, I do." And he says, "They only have it in the frosted, not in the creme." I said, "No, Charles, they've got it in both." Well, that started it. Bob Armstrong, president of International, is looking out the window and his face is white. Everybody else starts to move away, and there the two of us are pitted. And he says, "You don't know your business. I tell you it's only in the frosted!" I said, "No, Charles, it's in both!" And he looks at me and he says, "You know, we were all supposed to go out and see the new plant today." I said, "I know." And he says, "Well, you ride with someone else. You don't have to ride with me." He and I were very good buddies at this point; we went out at night and everything else. I said, "Well, that's all right, Charles, I'll ride with somebody else." I'd spent fourteen years working for Lew Rosenstiel at Schenley, so I didn't scare easily. When I got out to the plant he already had the plant manager by the throat. "Come up here," he says to me. "All right," he says to the plant manager, "tell him." "Sid, I hate to tell you this," he says, "but the bee-bees are only in the frosted." I said, "Okay, Charles, so I made a mistake." "Not a mistake Mr. Marketing Man, a *major error*," . . . and his lower lip was quivering. ["Hitler was triumphant. Once again he had proved that he was right and the generals wrong."] And he said, "You better go learn your business, Mr. Marketing Man, and you better give me another reason why our nail enamel isn't selling in France!" With that, he said, "Let's all go to town. I don't care how *you* get there." So I hopped into another guy's car, and he drove me to a great big drugstore in Paris which has since burned down. I went in and bought two bottles of Christian Dior frosted and two bottles of creme.

I brought them out to the car and I opened them up and they all had steel balls in them. So now this other guy says, "I don't want to be around you, what are you going to do?" I said, "I'm going to go and show them to him." So I walked down the Avenue George V and into his hotel. I sat in the lobby for four hours, waiting for him. He finally walks in with Princess Rachevsky and Lyn, their arms loaded with shoes from Christian Dior. They must have bought a pair for every week of the year. He sees me sitting there. "What do *you* want?" I said, "I want to show you something." "What do you want to show me?" I said, "Well, don't shout, we're in the lobby." "Well, what is it?" I said, "Here. Here are two bottles of Christian Dior frosted and two bottles of creme, unopened." And he looks at them, and shakes them up, and then he looks at me and he says, "Well, why aren't *we* doing this?" He starts across the lobby and he turns around and yells over his shoulder, "I was wrong, Sid."

[More often than not, though, he was right:

He was with Iris and Bill Heller at the Beverly Hills Hotel (in Bungalow #3—he always insisted on that one), and over dinner asked Iris what kind of mascara she was using. "Rimmel," she replied truthfully (to Bill's dismay), a foreign brand. "Why do you use it?" Charles asked—not angry, just doing his market research. "It applies easier and it makes my lashes look longer, and I just like it," Iris answered. "But it's not waterproof," Charles said. Iris allowed as how she didn't think *any* mascara was really waterproof when you came right down to it and Charles told her that for a bright girl she really had "bats in her belfry."

The next day sitting around the pool Iris went for a swim. She was careful to keep her head out of the water to protect her makeup. As she was climbing out, Charles said: "Hey, you're a pretty good swimmer. Bill tells me you can dive, too." Iris, falling for it, dove gracefully off the board. And came up screaming for help. "The Rimmel *burned*, as if there were lye in my eyes or something,"

229

she remembers. And there were big black blotches all over her face and on her light-colored Bonwit's/New York bathing suit. She got out of the pool, a tearful mess, and Charles, mimicking her, said: " 'It doesn't matter if it's waterproof. None of them are waterproof."

But then, having proven his point, he became most apologetic. Without having to ask Iris, he was able to describe the exact style and size of her bathing suit, and had a new one flown out the next day. Then he bought her a purse, a sweater—he kept buying her things by way of apology.]

Like any dictator, Charles had occasionally to put down a coup. Mandel all but left for the top spot at Helena Rubinstein at the end of 1966, and key marketing people were ready to leave as well, when Charles and Jay Bennett lured him down to the Bahamas for a week-long negotiation that was concluded on New Year's Eve. "How could you *do* this to me?" Charles wanted to know. He was always good at playing the victim—clutching his heart in mock pain at the obstinacy or stupidity of those around him. But on this score with Mandel he was quite serious: he didn't want to lose him; he considered it an act of great disloyalty; and he was afraid of all the "secrets" Mandel would be taking with him.

Mandel agreed to cancel his contract with Rubinstein in return for greater authority within Revlon (plus a handsome compensation package). But the authority didn't last long, and soon Mandel, passed over for the presidency he so badly wanted, was working part-time as a consultant to the company, and then not at all.

And then there was the famous facial hair conspiracy: While Charles was on his August cruise one year, in 1969, Norman Greif, Stan Kohlenberg, Bill Mandel, Larry Wechsler, and Joe Freedman all grew beards. Just to see what would happen. Charles returned and called a lunch meeting. His secretary, in an inspired moment, had seated all the beards on one side of the table, all the nonbeards on the other. Charles walks in without so much as a double take or a smile and proceeds to rip everyone apart for four hours . . . never mentioning beards.

The next day each man received a rare C.R. memo. "I would appreciate it," he wrote, "if you would test the enclosed product as soon as possible." Enclosed was one can of Braggi shave cream. Off came the beards. (Except for Greif's—a Van Dyke was deemed acceptable for the head of the lab—and Mandel's. He was already in a state of semi-retirement from the company, and Charles thought it best not to start up with him.)

Somewhat more serious was the mutiny two summers later, again conceived during Charles's August cruise, as though only then could the executives summon the required nerve and only then manage to work together. A committee of Revlon's six top executives flew to Ashdod, Israel, to confront the chairman on his yacht. "We just can't keep running things this way," was the gist of their message. The committee consisted of Paul Woolard, its chairman, who was head of Revlon domestic; Victor Barnett; Jay Bennett; Bob Armstrong; Sol Levine; and Joe Anderer. Bennett was delegated by the group to arrive at the yacht early, to prepare Charles for the meeting to follow. His version: "We were all at different hotels in Tel Aviv, and I was supposed to get to the boat at noon. The meeting was set for one. We had flown all night and I slept through my wake-up call. I woke up at twelve-thirty, and you never saw a man dress so fast. I tore downstairs and got a cab and said, 'Look, how long will it take to drive to Ashdod?' He said, 'Three-quarters of an hour.' I said, 'I'll give you a hundred dollars if you get me there in twenty minutes.' The guy sat up and we tore off. I'm sitting in the front with the driver, thinking that the guys will be on the boat before I get there. What an embarrassing, lousy thing to have happen. But we were tear-assing through the desert and suddenly I see a cab up ahead and it's our guys. I slouch down so they won't see me and we zoom by them. I arrived on the boat a few minutes before they did. But as it turned out, Charles still hadn't gotten up, so it didn't make that much difference, after all."

Everyone else's version: "We get to the boat around twelve-thirty and there's no Jay Bennett. Did he zoom past us in his cab? Hell, we called him at his goddamned hotel!"

Whoever arrived first, once the conference convened, it lasted two or three days. "In retrospect," says Woolard, "I think the committee was well-intentioned, somewhat immature in its attitudes, and expecting more than was feasible. These were men who were themselves fathers and mature in their own right—but with Charles somewhat immature. Looking back on it, Charles held all the cards. Not because he wanted anybody on the committee to leave the company, or that he could have lived without the services of anybody on the committee, but *emotionally* he held all the cards. The people at Revlon are very emotionally involved with the company and with Charles himself."

While Israeli coastguardsmen were exploding depth charges in the harbor to jar alien frogmen, Charles was telling his children: You want to form a management committee? Terrific idea! By all means! Notify the press! (Which they did.) ... And within days of his return he had everyone back at each other's throats and business as usual.

"While Charles was away," one of the committee members says, "considerable momentum and enthusiasm were built up. I think Charles found this unity among his people very disconcerting. Things fell apart pretty fast when he got back."

In most growing companies (or cities, or economies generally), success tends to smooth over many a potential personnel problem. But not at Revlon. Conversely, continuous internal strife tends to erode long-term success. But not at Revlon. For at least thirty years, Revlon employee relations (as distinguished from its pay scales) may well have been the worst, over a protracted period of time, of any modern American "growth" company. How could Revlon get away with this? First, the very top of its management structure—Revson—was deeply entrenched and highly competent in many key respects. Second, Revlon had very little professionally managed competition. (The only reason Madame Rubenstein's

232

management stayed as constant as it did is that many of her people were family she felt she *couldn't* fire, bumblers though some of them were.) Third, this was a business with high margins for waste, human or otherwise. Still, had people like Bill Mandel, domestically, and Robert Armstrong, overseas, not acted as buffers of a sort, and had the company not been subject to the restraining influence of public scrutiny after 1955, it is entirely possible that with time Revson might have substantially wrecked his own organization.

(XVI)

A Touch of Class
(But Just a Touch)

I attended a marvelous dinner party before the Versailles Ball in Paris in 1973. It was lobster in lobster in something else—wonderful. Charles, at the head of the table, was given a hamburger and soda water, and then he asked for ketchup. The butler went mad.

— Patrick O'Higgins,
man about town

Where others collected money and hoarded it, Revson collected it to spend. He had to have the biggest and the best, tip the most, and pick up every check. It was very important to him to have a "good table" in a restaurant. When the Lazaruses, who run Federated Department Stores, passed his table on their way out of Côte Basque, he greeted them and asked where they had been sitting. They pointed to a table in the rear. Revson snapped his fingers at the captain. "Whenever a Lazarus comes in here from Cincinnati," he told him, "put him up front." He thought that would impress them.

His taste was so quiet it screamed, people said—the mark of an insecure man. But his consumption was so monumental it also screamed. The quiet taste reflected that yearning for "class"; the big spending, the need to prove he was a "big man." He paid cash wherever he went, gangster style, rolling out the fifties and hundreds. He kept piles of both in a safe in his office. What drove him to work so hard after he amassed his first million around 1941? He needed the money! He could go through $1,000,000 the way another man would go through $10,000.

"This is what most people didn't understand, in my opinion, about his success and his money," Martin reflects. "Most people who make money spend below what they make. Then you have people like him or me who live up to it or a little bit beyond. They have to work like a son of a bitch."

Revson purchased his first yacht for $1 million, spent another $700,000 fixing it up—and within a year decided he didn't like it. Too small. (One hundred fifty feet.) So he laid out a couple million more for the *Ultima II* and owned *two* yachts for a while. When the first was finally sold, he recouped none of the money he had sunk into improvements.

"He used a word a great deal: 'chintzy,'" says Irving Botwin, who saw mainly his personal side. "He didn't like chintzy people and he was not chintzy himself." Yet he also had a thrifty streak—a touch of Joe Revson, a touch of the Depression—that could leave him upset about a ten-dollar doctor's bill in the late thirties (he thought it should have been five); about the two-cent deposits on pop bottles people were tossing off an acquaintance's boat in the fifties ("What are you *doing?*" he said, truly alarmed. "There's two cents on those bottles!"); or about the hefty Xeroxing bill Revlon was running up in the late sixties. This last involved the business, of course, and there he was particularly careful. "Two dollars was a lot of money to him," Irving Bottner, president of the salon division, says. "He looked at each item above the bottom line looking for ways to trim it." He insisted that pencils not be thrown out until fully used.

Where the business was concerned, he had the not inconsiderable facility to adapt his spending all the way from parsimony to reckless abandon as he felt circumstances warranted. When he noticed copper quotations falling in *The Wall Street Journal*, he got on the line to a lipstick-case supplier to squeeze a few pennies out of their contract. But when he took it into his head to open up The House of Revlon—a beauty salon to end all beauty salons he hoped would guarantee Revlon a place alongside Rolls-Royce, Patek Philippe, and Chivas Regal —he spent money like a sheik in heat.

The salon was begun in 1959 and for a dozen years its true cost and losses were hidden from the shareholders. It was a pet project, a fantasy made real and, in some respects, a sort of multimillion-dollar bad joke. It occupied the second floor of the Gotham Hotel, on Fifty-fifth Street at Fifth Avenue. A Fred Astaire dance studio occupies the space now.

The $64,000 Question had diverted Revson from class to mass. The House of Revlon was his way of getting back on the track. (When Madame Rubinstein returned from a European sojourn and saw it from the window of her limousine, she said to her companion, Patrick O'Higgins: "Why, Patrick, you naughty boy. You didn't tell me the nail man had erected his own mausoleum.")

A woman would arrive at the salon's big glass doors (too big, as it turned out, for many women to open, forcing management to engage a doorman); pass through an oh-so-elegant Revlon boutique that featured a 2,000-piece crystal chandelier and a marble sales counter supported by gilded swans; and ride the luxuriously upholstered, freshly flowered elevator one flight up to the salon. Installing the elevator was a problem because the third floor, to which it ordinarily would have been anchored, was off-limits to Revlon, and that meant breaking down the wall into the Gotham Hotel kitchen. (There was also the problem that the second floor of the Gotham was not strong enough to support the salon and had to be reinforced.) Anyway, having arrived in a reception area befitting a princess—and more than one of the salon's clients *was* a princess—she was served coffee in cups and saucers so lovely that "women would slip them into their handbags and we could hear them rattle," one ex-manager remembers. "We would go to women and say, 'Please, did you misplace your cup and saucer?' And they'd say, 'Bill me'—or just walk out in a huff." (Women even came with wrenches to remove the gold faucets and fixtures.)

From the reception area a woman was sent into a spacious dressing room, where she was given a Pierre Balmain-designed robe and plastic gold slippers and sent off to be made beautiful. There were eight hair stylists in suits and ties (not smocks), each one a star, each temperamental—and Revson managed to antagonize them all.

Special gold-plated hair driers (brass, actually, but they called it gold) descended from recessed nests in the ceiling at the push of a button. In practice, there was the problem of keeping the patroness positioned so that the descending drier would encompass, not cleave, her head. The driers were left down most of the time.

A sunken Pompeiian marble whirlpool bath was so large it took twenty minutes and 196 gallons of sea water, scented water, sulfur water, or milk to fill. Naturally, it had to be drained and cleaned after each use, so only six or seven baths could be performed in one day. When it became apparent that a woman could fall asleep and drown in such restful surroundings, a maid had to be hired to lifeguard. She would also dry the patroness with enormous prewarmed, triangular terry-cloth towels.

There was, too, a long, shallow "antisepticized" pedicure pool, with a fountain at one end, a blue, star-studded "sky" above, and fresh lilies every day, in which one woman actually did try to end her life. A more glamorous setting she could hardly have found, and her chances of success were reassuringly remote.

Telephone jacks were everywhere; movie people were forever on the (gold) phone to California—Ingrid Bergman, Eva or Zsa Zsa Gabor . . . Meals were sent up from the Gotham kitchen; drinks (lots of them) from the bar.

A limousine was on call to return clients to their apartments. There was a kennel, with two maids from the adjoining dressing room in attendance, but dogs were always a problem. People would trip over them. Some of the stylists would even kick them.

Little dark-wood wicker thrones covered the standard white toilet bowls, just as in Charles's office and at his apartment. Not everyone, apparently, understood exactly how they worked. Dress-designer Pauline Trigère came out of the ladies' room one day looking for a maid to mop up. Someone apparently had forgotten to lift the wicker seat. "I knew this place was elegant," Ms. Trigère is supposed to have said, "but I didn't know they even strained the urine."

Customers tended to be temperamental; so was the staff. Stylists would be invited to Bermuda for a long weekend and simply take off, leaving the salon manager with their full book of appointments to cancel or reschedule. When Judy Garland demanded that her stylist accompany her on a tour, what could management do but accede and lose all his bookings? The manager had also not infrequently to mediate between the client, who thought her hair had been disastrously misunderstood, and the artist, who knew it was only madam's lack of refinement that kept her from appreciating his work.

There were problems collecting bills. If the alimony checks did not come through, the salon did not get paid. Jack Paar gave an allowance of $35 to women who were to appear on his show to get fixed up. They'd beautify themselves to the tune of $70 or $80, then say—"Bill the difference to the Jack Paar show."

Three months before all this magnificence was to open, Charles—who had endlessly scrutinized every detail down to the last gilded swan—came through to inspect. Construction was all but complete, the network of complicated pipes and wires and ducts painstakingly hidden in beautifully molded and finished walls. He decided some of the work areas were too small—move the walls. Never mind that walls connect with ceilings, and that moving them even an inch required ripping everything apart.

Working nights and weekends for three months, they

238

managed to open on time. The publicity was fabulous. Beauty editors could not help being dazzled by the sumptuous elegance, the extravagant gold-and-white Barbara Dorn decor, and the lighting design of Abe Feder (who has also done Washington's Kennedy Center and New York's Philharmonic Hall).

Charles had been so worried about what people would think, and was now so pleased, that he told Jerry Levitan, who had coordinated the project, to take a few days in Florida. "In those days," Levitan explains, "his idea of 'getting away from it all' was Thursday through Monday at the Fountainbleu." Levitan, however, had already made arrangements for two weeks in Italy. Upon arrival, he gets a call from Jerry Juliber: "What are you doing in Rome? Charles is looking for you." So he cancels the second week of his itinerary. The next night, another call: "Charles says, 'You're over there, you might as well stay.'" So he and his wife go on to Venice, check into a hotel, and at three in the morning are awakened by another call. There's been a catastrophe. New York is in the middle of a heat wave, and the strain of the air-conditioning system has burned out the salon's custom-built generator. No water is running. They had to take water from the pedicure pool to rinse the suds out of their clients' hair, and then send them home in mid-beautification. Where, they wanted Levitan to tell them, could they get another generator? (Charles finally had one flown in from Detroit.)

And so it went, crisis after crisis, for nearly a dozen years. The premium prices Revlon could charge, about 20 percent above the competition, did not begin to compensate for the deluxe service or for the deluge of headaches, large and small.

Irving Botwin had responsibility for the salon for a while. Years earlier he had run an exclusive men's health spa in the same hotel. Before Irving was thrown into the breach, the salon was put under the supervision of Billy Reed, whose Little Club had gone under in part because Charles had managed to instill in him the ambition to expand and upgrade his operation, without having managed to instill in him the ability required to do so.

239

A manager he tried, but failed, to recruit for the salon was Elsa Sieff. A tall and slender woman then about fifty, Elsa Sieff was an executive with Seligman & Latz. English accents always impressed Charles, and she had one. After Jay Bennett had failed to make headway in interesting her in the job, Charles himself called her and "made it a much more personal thing." He invited her to lunch at the office, then for drinks that evening at the Pierre. "He wanted to put it on a much more personal basis," she says, "which I refused. He then called constantly and did the craziest things. I was in Dallas and he was in Europe and he would call me. I don't know how he knew I was there and ever found me." This went on for some time. "Then one evening he called me from the Little Club [then still in existence] and asked if he could come over and have a bottle of champagne with me. I lived just a few blocks away." He came over with the champagne and tried to sweep this woman off her feet. She would not be swept. She did like him very much, however. "I found him to be a very human man. The cutest remark he made to me was, 'You know, Elsa, you can have anything you want. Ask for it and you may have it. The only thing I cannot do is marry you.'"

Perhaps if Charles had gone the extra mile and offered to marry Elsa Sieff, he would have gotten her to manage the salon, which then might somehow have been made to stop losing money. Instead, he married Lyn, and things at the salon got worse and worse until in 1972—shortly after signing a long-term lease renewal—he lost interest altogether and washed his hands of the whole thing.

(XVII)

Empire Building

In negotiations with us he couldn't have been more of a gentleman. As for working for him, I think I'd rather clean streets.

—A former Revlon acquiree

The standard ways to build business into an empire are to acquire other companies and to set up operations abroad. Revson did both. Armed with a high multiple of earnings and the conviction that he could run any business there was, he acquired more than a score of them. And believing that "if it's good enough for America, it's good enough for Japan," he launched operations in ninety-seven countries.

His first major acquisition came as the result of an office-warming he and Martin attended in the fall of 1957 at the new digs of one of Revlon's smaller ad agencies. The agency had thought to invite all its clients to one big party, but remembering the last such affair, when Barney Pressman (of Barney's, a huge men's clothing store) had grabbed Emanuel Ronzoni ("*sono buoni*") by his unfashionable lapel and jokingly called him "an old spaghetti bender"—a joke that had somehow come off flat—they had decided to hold a series of small luncheons instead. This turned out to be not such a great idea, either.

At lunch with the Revsons were Sam and Al Abrams, founder/owners of Knomark, Inc., which made Esquire shoe polish. Charles quickly assessed their business and told them they should be selling their shoe polish for fifty cents, not fifteen, the same way he had entered the nail polish market. Three weeks later, to the dismay of the ad agency—which suddenly found an even larger proportion of its business subject to the whim of Charles Revson—Revlon bought Knomark. (One can just hear the boys clustered around the Dow Jones ticker: "Nail polish . . . shoe polish . . . it's a fit!") With some $15 million in sales, it was Revlon's first major acquisition. Supposedly, one of Revson's first questions upon buying the business was "How long have you had your agency?" From the beginning, they said. Eighteen years. "That's much too long," Revson said. Before too long the agency found itself with neither account.

Revson put Irving Bottner, his treasurer/controller, in charge of Esquire. (That's Bott*ner*—Bot*win* you've already met.) The Abrams brothers, despite huge salaries, soon quit. It was the basic acquisition syndrome: You buy a small company that depends on the energy and expertise of a couple of highly motivated people. You make them millionaires, which kills much of their motivation. And you meddle in their business, which drives them up a wall—or out the door.

What Irving Bottner wanted to do, in accordance with Revson's vision, was "to take shoe polish out of the kitchen and put it into the bedroom." Make it a class product, in other words, just as Revson had done with nail enamel. Change its image and double its price. However, this proved difficult. It was hard to sell a sexy, romantic, glamorous shoe polish.

Lady Color was introduced in the hope that women

would paint their shoes to match their attire. Instant Patent Leather and an application that made leather look like alligator skin were also introduced. But none of these products revolutionized the instep.

Estimates of Revlon's lack of success with Esquire vary, but it was enough that Revson decided eventually to get rid of the business. As he told *Forbes* in May 1969, several months after disposing of it and a couple of other acquisitions: "We've had it ... We're not running a hospital [for ailing businesses] here." He had bought Knomark for $6 million-plus, and hoped his financial people could recoup the investment. To do so, they prevailed on him to pick up yet another product—Ty-D-Bowl—to make a more attractive package. Needless to say, it pained Charles to spend a million dollars to enter the toilet cleanser business, but he went along. The package went for $12 million in cash—much more than he had expected.

Bill Mandel says there was no reason to get rid of Esquire. "It could have been built," he says. He assesses Charles's motivation as "trying to screw" his then president "and make him look dumb."

Looking not at all dumb, but perhaps relieved to be out of Revlon, that former president says Revson wanted to ditch Esquire because he had failed to turn it into a class operation. Shoe polish was still under the bathroom sink where it had always been. "Charles was never confused by dollar profits," this man explains, "although he was certainly aware of them. You may have heard him say that one of the greatest mistakes of his life was *The $64,000 Question*, because it directed his business away from where he wanted it to be—away from Bonwits and into Walgreens. He would rather have been the most important supplier to Saks than Safeway. You are dealing with the basic ego and philosophy of the man: he would rather have owned the Pavillon, and served fifty customers a night, than McDonald's, serving millions."

It may have been more trouble than it was worth, but Esquire was by no means a disaster. Evan-Picone, a sports wear manufacturer, was. Acquired in 1962 for $12 million as it rode the crest of popularity for its women's slacks, it was sold back to one of the original partners (Picone) for $1 million four years later. The $11 million difference, plus operating losses along the way, retarded Revlon's growth. Women who felt they "had" to have the latest Revlon lipstick did not feel the same about Evan-Picone's fashions. Even Revson, had he devoted his full attention to this business, might not have been able to make every season click. He foresaw the sportswear boom, but was wrong to think he could capitalize on it with Evan-Picone. "This will be my first failure," he said when he agreed to take his losses and get out.

Then there was an importer of silk dresses, a plastic molder, a large investment in Schick shavers, an artificial flower importer—and others, most of which proved that businessmen should stick to the businesses they know best.

It has been said of William Paley's disastrous acquisitions at CBS that broadcasting is such a lucrative business his mistakes were smothered in profits. Much the same was true of Revson's acquisitions and the cosmetics industry. It is the seller, not the buyer, who generally holds most of the cards in this game. He knows exactly what he's selling and is not likely to undervalue it. Revson paid very full prices for his acquisitions. He was not bargain hunting; he wanted businesses that returned at least 16 percent pretax profit on each dollar of sales— businesses with margins like his own. Financial pros look at return on *investment*, not sales, but Charles was a merchant by instinct and a financial man only by the accident of his success.

Where he did shine was in his determination to buy U.S. Vitamin and Pharmaceuticals Corporation, in 1966. Attracted by the profit margins and by his own hypochondria, he had long been after a drug company. He had found the industry closed to him, however, not least because of his religion. U.S. Vitamin was one of the few Jewish drug companies around—and even at that he had to pay $67 million for a lackluster company with a mere $20 million in sales. But pay it he did, and in nine years U.S.V. grew nearly tenfold

The big break came in 1971, when Ciba-Geigy, the multi-billion-dollar Swiss pharmaceutical combine, was being forced by antitrust regulators to dispose of a grab bag of products. U.S.V., by contrast, had most of its chips riding on a single oral antidiabetic drug, DBI. Although DBI was doing very well, there was always the fear that it could be made obsolete, or that it could prove to have harmful side effects. U.S.V. hit on the idea of *trading* DBI for the Ciba-Geigy products. A startling idea at first—it meant disposing of the major portion of U.S.V.'s business—but a good one whose advantages Charles quickly grasped.

Just as negotiations were being concluded, a comprehensive study was published that cast doubt on the life-lengthening properties of DBI. It suggested that DBI might actually have life-shortening effects, instead. Suddenly the deal was almost dead. At the very least, Ciba wanted a lot more cash along with DBI than had been originally proposed.

Charles was reached in London and asked if he wouldn't lend his weight to concluding the negotiations. So he and Lyn, a product manager assigned to carry Lyn's jewels, Revlon's general counsel, and a team of U.S.V. executives all hot-footed it to Basel, Switzerland.

Charles was enormously impressed by the Ciba operation. A thousand marketing people! Scientists all over the place! It made his pride and joy in the Bronx look awfully modest. As the Revlon/U.S.V. forces were huddling on the way into the negotiations, he told them: "This is a fucking white shoe operation." Pardon? "A fucking white shoe operation," he repeated, as though that would make his meaning clear, "so I don't want any swearing or shouting in there. I don't want these guys to think we're a bunch of bums." He assigned the head of U.S.V. to be the group spokesman and asked how much the deal was worth. "Well, we've gone up to ten million dollars so far," came the reply; "I think we could go to twenty million, but I wouldn't go any higher than that." "Okay," Charles said, "let's go."

In the conference room a team of Ciba professionals proceeded to assault the blackboard with numbers, relative values, best- and worst-case growth projections, probabilities, present values, cash flows . . . they're drawing analogies with Brazilian growth rates . . . From their point of view, a couple hours of analysis is not unreasonable when millions of dollars are up for grabs.

Charles, on the other hand, is sinking deeper and deeper into his chair. He is not used to sitting silently while someone else lectures. His hemorrhoids are bothering him. There is a draft in the room. Lyn is back at the hotel. Basel is not the kind of city you want to stay in, if you are a jet-setter, any longer than you have to. Finally, he can restrain himself no longer. He flings his arms out, Christ-like, and says—"Fuck! How much do you guys *want* for this fucking deal?"

The Ciba spokesman, startled, fumbled about for a few moments and said, "Twenty million dollars."

"*Done*," says Revson, who gets up, shakes hands, and walks out.

Revlon's overseas distribution was first handled by the United States Government. During World War II, post exchanges all over the world carried Revlon products. At least one GI would give his local ladies Revlon lipstick cases, promising the lipstick itself if the relationship . . . matured. Thus the gospel spread. American cosmetics—many of them Revlon's—became the envy of the rest of the world. As Inez Robb wrote in a syndicated column (March 15, 1952)—that Carl Erbe, Revlon's brilliant, roughhewn publicist, no doubt planted: "What Scotland is to tweeds and tipple, Ireland to linen and blarney, France to perfumes and Switzerland to cheese and chimes: that is what America is to cosmetics in the eyes of the world and his wife, particularly the little woman." ("The little woman"—how times have changed!) She went on to say that "only a few months ago Revlon received a letter from Prague from a woman who enclosed a big, old-fashioned dollar bill. She explained that it had been left to her by her father, and would Revlon send her a shade of lipstick, which, incidentally, the factory had ceased to make years ago." Not to mention a request from Agah Aksel, Turkish minister to Budapest, who ordered "six pieces of lipstick and six pieces of nail lacquer to match," or requests from Ethiopia, Patagonia . . .

Beyond the PXs, however, sales abroad were slight. Revlon had operations only in Mexico and England at first, and in other areas merely exported goods to distributors over whom it exercised little or no control. Bill Heller was put in charge of selling Revlon to the world in 1960, but at the time of his death, in 1962, the world had yet to catch fire. Foreign sales were then running around $20 million. A dozen years later, they would be ten times as great.

The international division, after Heller, went to Robert Armstrong. Later, in keeping with Charles's management style, Armstrong was given Sam Kalish as his second-in-command. Where Armstrong was a tall, Gentile, easygoing diplomat, Kalish was the typical Revlon killer. They were like a nice-guy/tough-guy team of cops, only they weren't just playacting to get a suspect to talk. They hated each other. Kalish reported directly to Armstrong, who theoretically could have fired him. But he also reported, unofficially, to Charles, so Armstrong was stuck with him.

Except for translating ad copy, it was Revson's idea to sell abroad exactly as he was selling at home. American cosmetics, like American denims and soft drinks, were in great demand. Eventually, he came to allow each foreign subsidiary enough independence to adapt their marketing to their market. But to a large extent, what worked in the U.S. was equally successful abroad. One much noted TV commercial, for example, included in its sixty-second message a silent, forty-seven-second kiss. The ad was for Intimate perfume; the message universal.

Still, each country had its quirks. The Spanish would not allow such a kiss to violate the pureness of their airwaves. In Italy, at least in 1960, commercials had to run two minutes—but only twenty seconds of that time could be devoted to "the sell." The rest had to be entertainment of some kind. In Venezuela, the announcer had to be a Venezuelan national, which meant recording everything. In Germany, it would have been inappropriate to call Revlon's men's fragrance "Pub," because it was too close to the German slang for "fart."

247

In Mexico, the 64,000 peso show went off without a hitch. But in England, in accordance with a parliamentary white paper governing commercial TV, Revlon could only sponsor—not own—*The 64,000 Shilling Show*. Moreover, the order of appearance of commercials had to be determined by lot. Revlon could not even be sure of appearing first. Martin flew over to watch the debut, broadcast live from the Palladium. Sitting with Lew Grade on his left and Armstrong on his right, Martin saw, at the first commercial break, an ad for Max Factor. "Livid" would hardly have described his reaction. As Armstrong recalls the exchange:

"I don't understand this," Martin spluttered.

"Martin, the white paper . . ." Armstrong began.

"Screw the white paper," Martin said.

". . . from Parliament . . ." Armstrong offered weakly.

"Look, there's a way to do everything. Put the fix in if you have to," Martin said.

"Put the fix in—to *Parliament?*" Sir Lew asked.

"Well, you've got to do *some*thing," Martin said.

It was one of the few times Max Factor outfoxed Revlon. Years later, Factor went to great expense to co-host the Versailles Ball in Paris—but Revlon stole the show with free gift packages at every table. The industry tittered for months. When Revlon went into Japan, the largest cosmetics market in the world after the U.S., Revlon decided to stick not only with his western products, but with his western ads, western product names, and western models. Only the ad copy was translated. Factor, already well established in Japan, quickly countered with a "Japanese cosmetics for Japanese women" campaign—but Revlon sales took off. Eventually, Factor had to switch to the same Americanized strategy.

Revlon's success in Japan was doubly remarkable—exactly double—by virtue of the fact that the operation was 100 percent Revlon-owned. From 1950 to 1967 there was a rule that American companies had to obtain Japanese partners if they wished to set up shop. Revson had been planning to go fifty-fifty with a wealthy Japanese named Takara, who flew all the way from Tokyo to strike the deal. When he and his interpreter arrived in Revson's

248

office, Sid Stricker introduced them and briefly reviewed the purpose of the meeting. Revson asked to be excused a moment. Stricker was then asked to step outside, too. "Get rid of that Chinaman," Revson told him. But why, Charles? "I don't like his gold tooth." Stricker spent the weekend showing Takara around New York and then bid him farewell.

If there was more to Revson's ditching Takara than his gold tooth, it was not that he had figured some brilliant way to go it alone in Japan. This was the achievement of some of his brash and resourceful lieutenants. "We just went ahead and did it," one of them explains. "No one stopped us."

(Similarly in 1944, when shipments to Italy were nearly impossible, one of the play-it-by-ear Revlon types contrived to ship merchandise through the Vatican. He had a *Yiddishe kopf* and Catholic connections.)

Charles visited the fledgling Japanese operation in 1962 with Ruth Harvey, Bill Heller, George Beck, and his two boys. The trip included a ride up into the provinces in a private railroad car, complete with geisha girls. Revson was quick to grasp that the geishas were among the country's most avid and affluent cosmetics buyers, and fashion-setters to boot. Accordingly, he spent considerable time studying them and urged his marketing people to do likewise.

Sailing from Capri to the Holy Land aboard his 257-foot yacht, with thirty-one in help and cases of Dom Perignon in the hold, finding his products regally displayed in every port along the way, and telephoning instructions to his generals back in New York, Charles Revson in his later years was indeed an emperor. And self-made at that. An odd sort of emperor when you looked beneath the robes—but what emperor wasn't?

Twice a year, beginning in the late sixties, Revlon would gather its international executives for a three- or four-day dog and pony show. One of the meetings was generally scheduled during Revson's annual month-long Mediterranean cruise, in the fervent hope that he would not break up his vacation to attend. He invariably did.

It wasn't that he lacked valuable experience to impart to the international staff, it was just the way he imparted it. The executives from New York who were used to him could ignore the profanity, follow the analogies and endure the digressions. Not so the hundred-odd international managers, sales managers, and chief beauty consultants. It was like listening to a verbal Jackson Pollack.

Charles would sit with a box of Kleenex beside him, periodically clearing his throat; push his glasses up onto his head and rest his elbows on the table, supporting his temples with the heels of his palms; look out over his audience of stuffy Englishmen, genteel Frenchmen, stilted Germans, exceedingly well-mannered Latin Americans and Japanese—well, *any* American entrepreneur would likely come off as something of a cowboy before such a group . . . and he would proceed to talk. And talk. And talk. No prepared text, a few key words on a napkin. He always believed that a man who could not speak extemporaneously was not worth much. (His boyhood "ambition," as given in the yearbook, was "to be an orator.")

One talk ran five hours. During a break, Bob Armstrong and Joe Anderer pulled him off to a corner and tried to get him to tone down his language. Charles returned to the group fuming. "They tell me," he said, "that some of you are offended by my language. Well, goddamn it, this is *my* fucking company, and if I want to say 'fuck,' I'll *say* 'fuck!' Anybody object to that? . . . Nobody? . . . Good."

Says one Revlon big-wig: "These were the most rambling, unstructured, give-'em-hell, cover-the-waterfront, crude speeches you can imagine. Regardless of whether the audience was ninety percent men, entirely men, or what, it was an entirely unnecessary display of who was boss. I don't know how much damage they did, but I'm sure Bob Armstrong spent the next six months picking up the pieces." Wasn't Revson aware of the impression he was making? "Yes, I'm sure he was." Then why did he do it? "I think Charles still thought in many ways that he was just a poor boy from Manchester, dealing with polished foreign talent. He felt very much at a disadvantage and had to gain control of the situation. The

250

only way he could do it was to shock them, to embarrass them—to show that he was the boss and could get away with it."

But he was also trying to teach them. He once spent forty-five minutes in front of a seminar of his international marketing executives having a dialogue with a glass of water. He was trying to teach these people the meaning of product differentiation, and the water glass caught his eye. He picked it up, held it out in front of him, and said, in his friendliest way, "Hello, glass. What makes you different? You're not crystal. You're a plain glass. You're not empty, you're not full . . ." and then he began telling the glass how it could be made special . . . by changing the design, changing the color of the water, giving it a stem, and so on. Sam Kalish was so bowled over by this performance, he says, that at the end he went up to Revson and asked him to do the same thing for another group upstairs. "C'mon—I can't do that," Revson said. They went upstairs. "You know," he began, "I was just talking with Sam Kalish and he wants me to show you what I did downstairs, how I grabbed a glass and started talking to it, 'Hello, glass . . .'"—and he did it all over again. Kalish acknowledges the performance was "probably over the heads of eighty percent of the people there," but he thought it was great nonetheless.

Perhaps the fundamental skill Revson tried to impart in his long-winded lectures was simplicity of thinking. "The funny part of it is that we get so smart, we get so educated, we get so intelligent, that we forget the simple things of the A, B, C, D, and E are the only ones that matter. All the rest of them just don't matter a goddamn bit," he said. Take a watch, for example. "The first thing I must understand about a watch is that it is a timepiece. Regardless of how beautiful it is, regardless of how expensive it is, that the purpose of this watch is to tell time. Is that correct? Now the minute I forget that this watch is a timepiece I'm a horse's whatever it is. Is that correct? And we get so smart, sometimes, that we want to take a watch and make it into an alarm clock. And we keep forgetting that this is only a watch. The next thing that a watch has to be after it keeps time . . . now, there's such a thing as keeping time, and there's such as keeping perfect time. And there's such a thing as not winding it —that's a great help, too. Then there's such a thing as being most beautiful—then there's such a thing you don't have to repair it for five years. Then it is in solid gold. Then it's this and then it's that and it has a great name. That's a watch."

One reason Charles's ramblings were hard to follow was his unfamiliar use of language. Revsonisms: "Stop beating around the rosary bush." "I want it done one, two, six." "Asshole to asshole." (Like peas in a pod.) "What you guys have to do is reupholster your thinking." "Remember the dumb lady." (The typical consumer— things must be kept *simple*.) "It should be *at least* twenty-four-karat gold." "Mediocrity." "Don't answer that— that's a historical question." "Who hit Annie in the fanny with a flounder?" (Who started it?) "I'm the kind of a guy who burns his graves behind him." "There are lots of slips between the cups and saucers." "Five-hundred-dollar millionaires." (Little guys who thought a Rolls-Royce and $1 million made them Big Men.) "It's too Jewish." (Said of a packaging design—too gaudy.) "Is it clearer than mud?" (Perfectly clear?) "It's as plain as the five fingers on your face." "That's not my dish of wax." "Don't make a case celerb out of it."

Norman Norman, rather than being confused or put off by Charles's endless malapropisms, says he found them "enduring." (Endearing.)

Charles was an inadvertent master of non-sequitur. "If you had all the money in the world," he counseled once, "whatever it may be, you can't have it all. You can't have all the window displays and all the advertising you want, and all this and so forth. It's impossible. And so therefore, you must find out what are the most important things that you need, and what are the winning numbers. What are those numbers that pay off the best? [I.e., the most profitable marketing formula.] Is it seven? Is it eleven? Or is it three? Or whatever it may be. *Because what do we want fundamentally?* [Profit? Share of market?] We want the least amount of turnover as far as people is concerned . . ."

A handwritten note: "Birthdays couldn't happen to a nicer guy. So just keep on having more of the same, and the same is good enough."

After viewing the results of a decision he himself had made, he would say, "How could you let me do this to myself?"

Launching into one topic, but wanting first to cover another, he began: "Might I say before I say what I am about to say . . ."

He would say: "The first thing is that the color must be right, and the second thing—which is really the first thing—the texture must be right." He tried to crowd everything up into the number-one position. *Everything* had to be right, so *everything* was number one. The idea of ranking bothered him because he didn't want to accept a lipstick, even if it had great luster, if it didn't have great wear. The two are somewhat incompatible and he had a tough time making a choice—so he put them both first.

"The reason I am opening my talk this morning of marketing," he said once, about a thousand words along in his preface, "is because I think it is one of the key—that does not mean and I don't wish to infer that operations are not important. They are. Administration is important and it is. But it does mean that you can have great administration and great operations, but if you don't have great marketing, you will not make it. You do have some chance with great marketing and mediocre administration and mediocre operations to make it, but vice versa, you will not make it . . ."

As Mandel says, he had a hard time setting priorities. Paul Woolard suggests this was also the reason for his frequent use of the phrase "in turn"—everything relating to everything else at the same level. Others saw the "in turns" as a nervous stalling mechanism, like "uh . . ." Revlon personnel occasionally ran pools based on the number of "in turns" counted in a given speech.

Revson was not unaware that his mind worked better than his tongue. It caused him great frustration. In the midst of one of his lectures, having become hopelessly involved in—"a round lamp with an electric light in it

253

and I think the outside of it is chrome and you press the button and the light reflects on the base and, in turn, it reflects on her face, so that she, in turn, can then take some of the makeup off her face and, in turn . . ." . . . but trying actually to make a simple point about window displays versus counter displays (namely that women can't sample a product in the window, but they can at the counter) . . . he finally said: "Now, these things come out very childlike, and I know they do, but goddamn it, for anybody who wishes after this meeting is over, which will be on Thursday morning or Wednesday night, I will go with them into this city or any city that they want, and I will prove with the greatest conviction and positiveness that I have that that does not follow." (That *what* does not follow? Hello?)

Because his foibles contrasted so sharply with his position and success, they drew attention. But attention should be drawn, too, to the cold competence his success was based on. There was his much noted preoccupation with detail, but also the ability to see the big picture. He could ramble endlessly, but also cut through to the heart of a matter. He could choose an odd assortment of friends and confidants, but also frequently tell when he was being conned. The power behind this emperor's throne was his own inner strength. The brains behind his operation were, notwithstanding the hundreds of good minds in his organization, his own.

The following account shows the emperor at his efficient best; the boy from Manchester High School coping effectively, if undiplomatically, in a rarefied atmosphere.

Revlon's Man in Argentina

I was general manager of the branch in Argentina and he was making his first trip here, in 1971. He had been as far south as Caracas once, but he'd never been to Argentina or Brazil. He flew to Brazil, looked at Rio, looked at São Paulo, and then cruised to Argentina on the *Ultima II* just after New Year's.

Argentina is the most European of the South American countries and it's like the U.S. in both climate and habits, except that it's got the Latin temperament. We organized there in 1962 and I took over as manager in 1966.

He had been in Argentina maybe three or four days when he requested a meeting with prominent people who knew something about the Latin American common market and the general economy. The major Latin American countries years ago set up a common market to try to trade between each other, but it never really functioned because of too much acrimony and vested interest. Revson was interested because we weren't in Brazil at the time, or a lot of other countries, and he wanted to see if he could manufacture in Argentina and export from there. The company was always afraid of Latin America because of what they read in the papers . . . changes of government, devaluation of currency . . . so they were very cautious. I set up a meeting with bankers and industrialists and a man directly involved with the Common Market. They all spoke English.

Most Argentines have one hang-up: They are sometimes irrationally proud of their country. At that time, Argentina had gone through what was for them a relatively stable period. They had a military government which came in about 1963 and the currency was reasonably stable . . . there wasn't the terrorism you read about today, Peron was still in Spain with his wife, and there really weren't any thoughts of his coming back.

We went over to the bank around noon and discussed the economy of Argentina, the common market, and so on, and these people kept going back to one point: "If you want to invest in Latin America, the only place to put it is in Argentina. The currency is stable, the government is stable, even though it is a military government . . . The guys in Brazil haven't come down from the trees yet and the Chileans have got a Communist government coming in . . ." They were giving him half a story, not the true story. Finally they came down to this: "Charles, as long as the generals run the country we will never have any trouble. This is really the only place to go."

255

Up to that point he had just asked a few general questions, and I thought these people were giving him a snow job. And with two questions he just tore the meeting apart. His first was: "What happens when the colonels get pissed off at the generals?" That's how he put it. I had to translate it for them because they didn't understand what he had asked. They turned around in surprise and said: "Charles, this has never happened in Argentina. The generals run the army and the army runs the country."

His next question was: "Peron was a colonel, wasn't he?" This floored them because Peron *was* a colonel when he took over in the forties. But if you walked down the street in Buenos Aires and asked them, seven out of ten Argentines would get it wrong. But Charles knew. It totally tore apart their arguments and made them seem ridiculous. He got up and said: "Thank you, gentlemen. I have another engagement." They just sat there with sort of shock on their faces and then had to get up and smile and say good-bye.

After the meeting, all Charles said was, "I don't think I got a lot out of that meeting." He saw through these men.

The next evening, the president of the Argentine Yacht Club and his wife came on board for dinner and a movie. A pleasant elderly couple who had done a lot for Charles because they were so impressed with the size of his yacht. This was strictly a social occasion. As they were leaving the boat, just out of earshot, Charles turns to me and says, "How much would you spend against that woman?" I said, "What do you mean?" He said "I wouldn't spend a nickel against her promotionally." I said, "Charles, she's from a very wealthy family. Her husband is president of the yacht club, which is no small thing in Argentina." And he said, "She hasn't changed her lipstick shade in twenty years." She was well dressed, but he could pick that out in a person. She was not fashion conscious. And he proceeded to lecture me on the importance of spending your promotional dollars against those consumers who will buy.

When we launched Ultima in Argentina, at three times the U.S. price (because of a 200 percent customs duty), women in very humble dwellings were buying it. It had nothing to do with high society. He knew what he was talking about.

(XVIII)

Follow the Lauder

I don't think if the competition have got something
wonderful, whomever they may be, that there is anything wrong in looking at it, and copying it. You know,
great copyists or great experts in copying are those that
can create a copy, and for that you have to be smart.
On how to create a copy. Does everybody understand?
Is that too hard to understand? It means if you copy
something, that you copy it so well and so differently
that nobody recognizes the fact you copied it. That's
creative copy.

—Charles Revson

It was easy to forget, if you knew Charles Revson,
that Revlon was not the world's largest cosmetics company. In 1975, it trailed Avon, L'Oreal and Shiseido. But
Avon's sales were exclusively door-to-door and thus not
directly competitive. To Charles, Avon barely existed.
And neither L'Oreal nor Shiseido was important in the
U.S. market. His real competitors through the years
were companies and brands such as Blue Bird, Chen-Yu,

Contouré, Peggy Sage, Hazel Bishop, Helena Rubinstein, Elizabeth Arden, Max Factor and—his arch rival in the last decade of his life—Estée Lauder.

He felt the same inner rage toward competitors an apartment dweller feels toward a burglar. They were encroaching on *his space.* "If you come into my ball park," he warned Gulf & Western's Charlie Bluhdorn, "I'll kick your ass." He put tremendous pressure on suppliers not to deal with his competitors; on jobbers and retailers not to sell or feature their products; and on magazines never to give their ads a more prominent position than his own. "Of *course* the other guy has a right to make a living," he liked to say—"but let him make it in some other business."

He made a point of never mentioning his competitors by name. They did likewise. Arden, a poor Canadian truck driver's daughter made good, called him, simply, "that man." (To tweak her, he brought out a men's line by the same name.) Rubinstein, a Polish immigrant-via-Australia, called him "the nail man." He referred to them, and to Lauder, a social climber whose first rung varies from interview to interview, only as "competition." Or, if he wanted to become exceedingly specific, he would say, "she." When Love cosmetics were big, he banned the word "love" from all his advertising.

He had a CIA-like intelligence network and—because he assumed his competitors did, too—a fetish for closed doors. All his products were assigned code names prior to introduction—"Park Avenue" (Cerissa), "Cosmos" (Charlie), "Bruckner" (the CHR line). The Ciara fragrance was designated "March," its targeted launch date. It was seven months late. "If we don't get the engravings by July," people were saying, "March won't go out before November." It was enough to confuse the canniest competitor.

Ingredients at the lab were coded. Only a handful of department heads knew what "Ritex," "Bankit," "Neville," "Tylex," and hundreds of others really were. Even Lillian Dunn, a thirty-two-year veteran after whom "Dunnex," a wax, had been coded, didn't know. Suppliers were instructed to label their shipments by code name. As far

259

as the factory knew, they were mixing Dunnex with Neville to make Zarega—or whatever.

From his yacht, Revson was unusually cryptic for fear competitors might be tuned in to his radio frequency. Nail enamel was "n.e.," lipstick, "l.s."—pronounced fast, like "any" and "else." Projects and companies were referred to by code; people, as "what's his name." "Have what's his name call me about that other matter," he would tell Jay Bennett, fully expecting him to comply. (And because they had such a close working relationship, Bennett usually could.)

But if Estée Lauder did not have a cadre of ham radio operators scanning the Mediterranean for trade secrets, she could still find out a thing or two. When Etherea, Revlon's hypoallergenic line (code name: New Jersey), was being launched to compete with Lauder's Clinique, a memo was circulated to four trusted employees listing the names to be used for each item in the line. Top secret stuff. Lauder ran an ad for Clinique in *Women's Wear Daily* using every name in the memo as an adjective, and underlining each one lest there be any doubt in Revson's mind that he'd been stuffed. Etherea was to have an item called "B.C.O."—biologically correct oils; Lauder's ad said, "our night cream is *biologically correct*." And so on.

Revson had a conniption. But all manner of sleuthing by his FBI-trained security chief failed to reveal the leak. It was then that he instituted mandatory signing in and signing out, and had photo-I.D. cards issued to everyone. A Revlon marketing man ran into Lauder's sons, Leonard and Ronald, at a party sometime later. "You know," he said, "you guys are crazy to spend five thousand dollars just to aggravate us."

"It was worth it," one of the brothers replied, smiling.

At any given time in Revlon's history there was some one competitor in particular Revson felt he had to destroy. Blue Bird, the first, was easy: Revlon had a demonstrably better product. It was that simple. Revson was soon able to demand that jobbers drop Blue Bird—and all their other competitive lines—if they wanted to carry

Revlon. The jobbers didn't like it, or other tough policies that followed, but they had no choice. By the time the Federal Trade Commission ruled some of Revlon's exclusive agreements out of order, the company had acquired a lock on the beauty salon market.

When Contouré learned in the late thirties that Revson might launch a lipstick in competition with their own, they brought out a nail enamel. Revson's friend the jobber with a hernia the size of a baseball sent him a sample as soon as it came in. Revson was beside himself. The product was identical to his own. He was apoplectic when he found out it was being made by *his own supplier*.

"Why not?" was the supplier's attitude. "We can make nail enamel for anyone we want."

Reason having failed, Revson got hold of the man at the plant who actually compounded the lacquer and, according to an executive then, paid him $100 to slip an extra ingredient into Contouré's brew, with $400 to follow when the mission was accomplished. The extra ingredient, whatever it was, had an unsettling effect on the quality of the product. What's more, it caused a marked deterioration in the relationship between Contouré and the errant supplier, who thenceforth agreed to make Revlon nail enamel only for its biggest customer— Revlon.

During the war, Chen-Yu was the brand to beat. One quirk of wartime rationing was that glass allocations were issued to companies that made the bottles rather than to the companies, like Revlon or Chen-Yu, that used them. Charles wanted to know what Chen-Yu's Chicago-based bottler might require to steer Chen-Yu's allocation of bottles his way. Jack Price arranged to fly the co-owners of this bottling firm to New York. He says he watched as Charles settled with them for $15,000. Chen-Yu suddenly found itself scrambling for upwards of half a million bottles. After the war, Revlon offered to replace all the substandard inventory it had out, such as those cardboard lipstick cases, with new, quality merchandise. It took money to do that, and Chen-Yu hadn't the resources to match the offer. Then Revson lured away

Chen-Yu's all-important merchandise manager, Burt Reibel. It was the coup de grace.

Hazel Bishop—"stays on you, not on him"—was another dragon to be slain. This upstart had built a huge lipstick business overnight through the use of television. Merv Griffin, a young singer, started pitching the nonsmear brand on *The Kate Smith Show* in 1952. "People couldn't understand how with only three salesmen we managed to get such massive distribution," Raymond Spector, who owned the company, says.* "But Revson personally sent a memo around to his salesmen saying, 'Wherever you go, find out how Hazel Bishop is doing and send the information directly to me.' At that time we were still in only a few major markets. People started calling us from all over. They figured that if Revlon was interested, they should be too."

Charles got him in the end, though. The biggest marketing blow was *The $64,000 Question*. The biggest psychological blow was Spector's discovery that someone—he states categorically it was Revson—had been listening in on his most private conversations for more than a year. He first grew suspicious when information that could not possibly have leaked to the trade did. Revlon kept beating him to market with his own ideas, he says. He then tried planting false tidbits to see if they, too, would come back to him and *they* did. Alarmed, he retained the services of two eavesdropping experts, Charles Gris and Carl Ruh. Ruh was awaiting sentencing on some other wiretapping work he had done. These were the same two men, as it happened, Bill Heller had engaged to tap Revlon phones. In fact, Spector testified, while Ruh was off checking the phones for taps, Gris told him about the Revlon job and offered the same service to him.

Ruh found that several of Spector's phones were indeed tapped, and his office bugged as well. It may even be that Gris and Ruh had themselves done the tapping they

---

* Hazel Bishop herself founded the company in 1950, was forced out two years later, and in 1975 was working as a cosmetics analyst with the Wall Street firm of Evans & Company.

were now being paid to detect—a dicey way of having and eating one's own cake if ever there was one.

Revson's market timing was uncanny, Spector alleges, at least in part because he had advance knowledge of his competitors' plans. Winston Churchill had the same edge on the Germans. "I think Revson was a prick," he says simply. Among Revlon competitors, this was not an uncommon view.

Madame Rubinstein thought the nail man was "heartless." She was anguished by the way he would copy her products ("only better!"). But he fascinated her. She couldn't help admiring him. She even bought Revlon stock.

They were not so dissimilar, Madame and the nail man. She, too, was an earthy, idiosyncratic, impossible, tyrannical Jewish founder/one-man-show. She hired people, milked them, and fired them. She played one off the other. She burped unabashedly and blew her nose in her bed sheets. She felt surrounded by ingratitude. She complained bitterly about having to close the office after John Kennedy's assassination. *Un*like Revson, however, she was not out to prove herself to anyone, she did not live in fear of being embarrassed, and she was thoroughly—ludicrously—cheap. Yet far better liked than Charles, for all his lavish entertaining. Her quirks were seen as amusing rather than gauche or offensive. No one called her ruthless, although she had much the same obsession with her business that Charles did.

For many years it was not he but "the other one"—Arden—whose competition most irked Madame Rubinstein. Arden once raided virtually the entire Rubinstein sales staff. Madame retaliated by hiring Arden's ex-husband as her sales manager. At least the nail man and she were in largely separate fields. He had the lipstick and nail enamel markets, yes, but Madame was queen of the treatment creams. It was only in 1962, when Revson launched Eterna 27, the remarkable skin cream, that Madame felt really threatened. A Rubinstein executive walked into her office that day to find the window open wide and Madame leaning out, screaming and shaking her fist. Her third-floor office was directly opposite 666 Fifth

Avenue, where Revson ruled the twenty-seventh floor (hence the name—Eterna 27). This tiny ninety-year-old woman was screaming up at him in a very heavy Polish accent, "What are you *doing?* You're killing me, you rat! What's the matter with you?" It looked as though she might fall out of the window. "Don't worry about it, Madame," the Rubinstein executive said, pulling her back in and hoping to cheer her up, "it's not going to sell. In fact, I think they're going to change the name to *Returna.*" She looked at him blankly. Like Charles, she had very little sense of humor about her business. "Why would they want to do that?" she said. "It's a good name, Eterna."

Later that year Madame met Revson briefly at a fashion gathering. Her comment afterward: "He has an awful skin."

In 1965, she died. A year and a half later, Arden died as well. That left two: Revson and Lauder. Most of the other companies had been or soon were merged into conglomerates, with results that ranged from fair to poor.

Max Factor, swallowed by Norton Simon in 1973, had done better than most since the death of its founder/ namesake decades earlier in 1938. It was Factor that in 1967 challenged Revlon's privileged position in the fashion magazines. Revson had always demanded that his ads precede those of his competitors. (He would also demand —and receive—advance proofs of fashion stories that were to run, and sometimes have them changed. But that's another story.) Chet Firestein, then executive vice president of Factor, lodged a protest. Bill Fine, then in charge of three Hearst magazines, had to agree that the policy was unfair. With much apprehension, he told Revson he was sorry, but Revlon could no longer be first in every issue. "We made our stand," Fine says, "and Charles said, in simple terms: 'Fuck you. I'll pull my advertising out of all Hearst magazines.'" Which meant not only Fine's three, *Harper's Bazaar*, *Town & Country* and *House Beautiful*, but *Cosmopolitan* and *Good Housekeeping* as well. Revlon's annual outlay in these books approached seven figures. (Patty's abduction was thus in effect the *second* extortion attempt on the Hearst family.)

There was a period of two or three weeks' impasse. And as word of the confrontation spread, Fine found himself in a box. He had to win *some* concession lest other of his major advertisers revolt. It got so that Fine used to have a man come massage his neck and arm each time before he went over to see Revson, because he would start to get a tingle and an ache in his back.

Fine managed to emerge with at least this much: When Revlon had a black and white page, it would run first. When Revlon had a color page, it would be the first color page—but another cosmetics ad, in black and white, could come first. As Revlon was not running black and white ads at the time, it was what Fine calls "maybe a fifty-one percent victory—which is pretty good when you're dealing with Revlon."

The changed policy worked to the advantage of Estée Lauder. (Most people, wrongly, credited her with forcing the confrontation in the first place.) Lauder *was* running black and white ads. Revson soon followed. In fact, *whatever* Lauder did, Charles soon followed. She offered "gift with purchase"; he offered gift with purchase. She went to using a single model exclusively; he followed with Lauren Hutton for Ultima—and one-upped her by signing Richard Avedon as her exclusive photographer. She went to sepia ads; he went to sepia. She switched back from sepia; he switched back. She brought out a "stinky" fragrance (Charles's word); he brought out a stinky fragrance. She brought out Aramis; he brought out Braggi. She brought out Clinique; he brought out Etherea. She brought out a fragrance called Estée; he brought out Charlie. To add insult to unoriginality, he would put copied products in one of his less-than-Ultima lines, to cheapen the originals by association.

Charles was reviewing a new eye-shadow compact. Suzanne Grayson had brought along Lauder's version for comparison. In order not to lose the instruction sheet that came with it, she had scotch-taped it to the mirror inside. Charles picks up the Lauder compact and thinks: "Look how smart that ---- is. Why don't we think of

things like this? The customer can't miss seeing the instructions, so, in turn, she's going to learn how to use
the product and, in turn, she will like it better. Why the
---- can't *we* think of things like this?!" He got so wound
up in his grudging enthusiasm for the way Lauder was
taping her instruction sheet inside the compact, even
though she wasn't, that there was no interrupting him.
The Revlon compact was modified accordingly. It was
one of the few times Revson copied Lauder without her
knowing it.

Stan Kohlenberg, who no longer has a mole the size
of a dime (now it's on Michel Bergerac), runs the Ultima
line, Charles's department-store, carriage-trade answer
to Estée Lauder. He keeps Lauder's photograph on a
dart board in his office and says he sometimes thinks
she is just Charles in drag.

When Ultima was first put together (before Kohlenberg's time) it was a flop. One ad showed the most
obnoxious-looking, spoiled, chubby kid in shorts and
knee socks with his mother, who looked more uncomfortable than sexy, sitting on an over-stuffed ottoman in
an overdone living room . . . the idea apparently was to
reach into Park Avenue's poshest parlor—and it didn't
work. But Charles Revson, we all know by now, was not
a man to give up. The products, packaging, and approach
were all reworked, the line doggedly promoted, until
eight years after its initial introduction it finally turned
a profit.

In the meantime (September 1968), Lauder had
brought out Clinique, her hypoallergenic line. Kohlenberg provides a fascinating case study of the forces of
competition at work.

Stan Kohlenberg

Charles came back from his August cruise and had a
fit, because he had been talking for a long time in a vague
way about bringing out a hypoallergenic line, and now
she had beaten him to it. He called me in and he said:
"We have to create a line and I've been thinking about

it for three years and you have to do it. You can handle Ultima while you do this ... it's the same kind of line." Charles throws it to you as a challenge.

I started working on it in the beginning of October. He comes back two weeks later, before we even had a name for the line, and he says to me, "I just told Mildred Custin that we're introducing it April 28 in Bonwit Teller." I said, "How could you do that? We don't even have a line!" He says, "I told Mildred we would have it out April 28 and you can't disappoint her." So April 28 is the date.

To put out a full line in seven months—it is virtually impossible because you are dealing with the packaging, the names, new products and so on. Nobody tries it. But Charles didn't want Clinique to have a long time on the market without a strong competitor. The faster he could get out, the faster he could step on her toes. I made the first presentation to him in the middle of October. It was a concept for a brand-new line, to be manufactured under the same conditions as pharmaceuticals; the white room, everything surgically clean, everybody wearing masks, ultra-violet lights to kill bacteria ... we had a negative-pressure door, so that when you opened it the air blew out. They still use it. And this was going to be in the ads, how the products were made. Clinique doesn't go through all that trouble. And every item would have a tamper-proof seal to guarantee sterility. There was a profile created by Brauer [the staff dermatologist] so you could determine what skin you were. Originally we wanted all the liquids in vials.

We then came up with several names and none of them was acceptable. We didn't want a French name because it was an American line and Charles is very sensitive about our line being uniquely American. He doesn't want the phony chic of a French name. He liked the concept of the line and he agreed to a lot of things, but we had no name. It became a big problem because you couldn't do any packaging. We didn't come up with the name until February.

Charles came in one day and said: "Here's the name to go on: 'Etherea.' It's a good name because it has kind of a different meaning in it and yet it's not a meaning and you can pronounce it." We all hated it at first, but he said: "That's the name, no argument," and it grew on us.

So now we had the name and ninety days to do everything. We had to cut across every procedure in the company. Forget the paper work, the ordering, the purchasing—we ordered our own bottles and worked with the lab ourselves and alienated everybody in the company. Alec Faberman threatened to hit me with an ashtray one day. We worked seven days a week, twenty-four hours a day, from February through April. It was things like writing package copy for an entire line, 125 items with shades. We were going to come in with just a narrow treatment line. We'd go to Charles and he'd say: "You've got to have lipstick." So we added twenty shades of lipstick. Next time: "Where's the eye shadow?" I said, "I can't have eye shadow, Charles." He says, "How can you have a line without eye shadow?" Eye shadow goes in. By the time he finished with me I had a full line. It meant going back to the lab and getting more formulas. Meanwhile, the rest of the company had to keep running. We were always late with everything to begin with, and here I am sticking this whole new thing in.

We were sure we wouldn't make it—the bottles weren't ready, the dates we were getting for delivery were way beyond April 28, everything had to be tested, and we were living day by day on the premise that we were going to fail. Fortunately, we had formulas from other lines to establish a base, but we had to find a product difference for each one. It meant taking a product and putting a twist in it. If we already had a cleanser that tissued off, we had to find one that tissued and *washed* off, because this was a special line. This was all from October to the week before April 28, in some cases.

We get down to two weeks before the promotion and nothing is in. There are no bottles in the plant to fill, some of the boxes are just coming off the press. I asked them to change the date to September and they said they couldn't. So we set up a press party at Bonwit's to introduce the line and I have no product to show. Nothing is filled. I told Tom Dulick, my assistant: "Run out to the plant, get every dummy you can, everything that's come in and is unfilled. At least we can set it up; if the people just look and don't touch it will look nice."

The beauty editors of all the magazines and newspapers were invited, and we had it set up so we could do a profile of all the faces, tell them what kind of skin they had. We told them as soon as the line is complete, then we'll send a complete set. Charles walks in and I'm quaking. He's been approving things as we went along but he hasn't seen it in its finished form. He walks over to the alcove and stands there by himself looking at the line. He had seen the cartons in artwork, but he hadn't seen the finished product. We didn't have the time. He stood there quietly for a few minutes and then he looked around. I was watching him out of the corner of my eye and so was everybody else. He went over to Jessica Canne of *Vogue* and started talking about the line. She loved it. He knew the premise of the line, the story behind it, which was his with a few embellishments, so he was able to talk about the line and each of the beauty editors would tell him how nice it was. He was becoming visibly more assured about how well the line was going to do. Finally he got up and made a speech to everybody about how he had been working on this line for three years . . . which he had, he had had the concept for three years . . . and how this was the culmination of what he wanted to do and how pleased he was with it. And everybody applauded.

Charles walks over to me, away from everybody else, and he puts his hand on my cheek and starts giving me a clip as if he's saying "Nice boy." Everybody's watching. As he does this to me he says, "You know what?" I said, "What?" He says, "Schmuck, the cartons are fading."

I said: "I know, Charles, they're only dummies." We are smiling at each other as we are talking. He's having a fit because the cartons are fading under the lights. He's still holding my cheek and he turns to Dulick, who he knew had worked with me on the project, and he says to me, "Does he know the cartons are fading?" I said,

"Yes, Charles, he knows. But we fixed it, Charles." And he said, "You know, you guys are ruining my business." And he walks away. Somebody came over to me and asked what he said to me. I said, "He said, 'Schmuck, the cartons are fading.'"

In the meantime the stores had sent out their mailers, we had hired all the girls—but we had no merchandise. Components had just come into the plant. By Thursday we are hysterical because there is no product and we are supposed to break Monday at Bonwit's—Manhattan, Manhasset, Short Hills, Scarsdale, and Philadelphia. If it doesn't happen by Monday, we're all dead...the mailers are out, the women are coming into the store. I said to Tom: "I think we better go to the factory and see what's happening." They were just starting to set up all the lines. It was a disaster. They wanted to run all the powder, then all lipstick—which is efficient, but we couldn't do it that way and still make the order. We had to tailor-make Bonwit's order with tiny runs of each item.

By Saturday I'm starting to get emergency calls from Paul [Woolard]. "What the hell is happening?" Mildred Custin called me: "There's no merchandise in my stores." By Saturday afternoon we began to get representative portions of every part of the line. We got three station wagons. I had one kid make a run to Manhasset; Tom made a run to Short Hills. We sent a messenger truck to Philly. I live in Scarsdale, so Saturday night I put about sixty cartons in the wagon, driving blind.

Sunday at seven A.M. we drove back out to Edison and started loading trucks again. We finished all of the branches by Sunday afternoon. Not a piece had gone to the downtown store.

I called Mildred at home and said, "Don't worry, at seven o'clock Monday morning we will be at your receiving entrance with your whole order." I had eighty cartons in my wagon, Tom had seventy-five in his. Seven o'clock Monday morning, in suits and ties, we drive up. We had our own consultants waiting at the counters to set up. And we run the wagons through the store and as I go through the store the guard says: "You can't go

270

through the store without the order being checked." I said: "Get out of my way or I'll put wheel marks on you." I was so frantic at that point, he let us in. We set it up, and at nine-thirty, when the store opened, we put the last piece of goods on the counter.

It was done. And tremendously successful. So much so that we had to call the police at one point because the crowd was so big. We were giving away a gift free without any purchase. All you had to do was to have your profile done. Every woman will do that for nothing to get the gift.

Three years later I did the whole thing all over again with Ciara. The station wagons and the whole bit.

Thus does the nation's most successful cosmetics giant (Avon aside) develop and introduce a major new product line. Normally, there would have been vastly more interference from Charles and interminably greater delays. But the enemy had stormed the barricade and was already in the department stores. If it had been another competitor, he might not have put on quite the same pressure. But it was Estée Lauder.

Of all the women in his life, although he never spoke more than two words to her, it was probably she who had the greatest impact. She was the one competitor he set out to beat but couldn't. It had taken her a full fourteen years, from 1946 to 1960, to reach $1 million in sales—but a mere fourteen more to reach $100 million. Revlon was still much larger, but she had captured exactly the segment of the market that mattered to him most. As Revlon owned sex and fashion in the fifties and Arden owned pink, so Estée Lauder by the late sixties owned class. Suddenly she was beating him in all the best department stores, *she* had the houses in Palm Beach and the South of France, *she* was dining with the Duke and Duchess of Windsor (who had long since learned to live well by allowing a bit of royalty to rub off on eager commoners). The Park Avenue socialite he had always had his eye on had found a counter at Bloomingdale's she liked better than his. Never mind what a small segment of the market she represented. As a result,

271

Mandel says, "his priorities came all out of whack. The whole corporation was working on one percent of its business ninety percent of the time to satisfy this ego of his: Ultima, Borghese, and Braggi. He left a hole wide open in the marketplace for Factor to make a comeback and for others to get into the business as well."

Revson argued that the quality image of his top lines would enhance the image of basic Revlon. But pride, not profit, was his fundamental motivation in taking the course he did.

And so it was Lauder, not Lyn, who led Charles to be more "social." Lauder, not Lyn, who lured him to the black-tie affairs Ancky had always longed to go to. It was to combat Lauder, not to amuse Lyn, that he landed on the Breakers Hotel golf course in a helicopter, photographers and reporters lined up on the fairway, where he was to judge a very hotsy-totsy, uppercrust (read: Gentile) Palm Beach beauty contest. That Lyn was young, beautiful, vivacious, and extraordinary in bed were sources of genuine pleasure and great allure. That she helped him protect the glamorous image and generate the *Women's Wear* coverage he wanted to combat Lauder was perhaps even more important to him. And why not? Lyn's motive for marrying this notoriously difficult fifty-seven-year-old must have included an element of practicality, also.

(XIX)

The Bronx Nefertiti

My husband is twenty-six years older than I, and I am
running, literally on my knees, to keep up with him.
                                        —Lyn Revson (1972)

Finally Charles was marrying a nice Jewish girl. Lyn
Fisher Sheresky Revson, born in New York around the
time Revlon was, may not have had all of Ancky's European sophistication, but she was younger, she had been
around—and she, too, had an accent: thick New Yorkese.
She had splendid qualities, witness her popularity, her
three lovely children (by her first husband), and the fact
that of all the women he could have married, Charles
chose her. Except for her Liza-Doolittle-of-the-Grand-
Concourse speech, and her use of little rabbit punches as
exclamation marks, she had all the Park Avenue elegance
and earthy sexiness Charles could possibly have wanted
in a woman. What elegance she lacked initially he soon
built in. And, according to his son John, he was not
looking for a woman who would do a lot of talking,

anyway. "He thought he'd marry a 'Yes, Charles; sure, Charles' kind of woman, but it didn't work out that way. There's a marriage that should have ended after two months but didn't."

But almost did.

The wedding itself, in February of 1964, was a model of Revson efficiency cum eccentricity. Just as he preferred to design his own pedal-pusher pajamas, and made a point of sending Christmas gifts to arrive late (so they would be noticed), so he chose of all places to be married Windsor Locks, Connecticut. It was relatively central (John was at Brandeis and Charles, Jr., was at Deerfield), and it was out of the way. He thought if it were held in New York it would be in all the papers, and he didn't want that. (It would not have been like him to explain *why* he didn't want that—he just didn't.) He and his brother Joe, the Meresmans, Lyn, her mother, brother, and children flew up from New York in two small chartered planes. Limousines were sent for John and Charles, Jr., who met the party at the airport and accompanied them to the town hall for the ceremony. The reception, also small, was held in a railroad car in Springfield, Massachusetts. Charles's friend and neighbor at Premium Point, Al Perlman, head of the New York Central Railroad, had loaned them his private car for the occasion. It didn't go anywhere, but the food and champagne were delicious and it was all over "one-two-six," as Charles would have put it, with the limousines back to the airport and the planes back to New York all by five that same afternoon.

The next weeks were not pleasant ones for Charles. On the one hand, he had this gnawing suspicion that his young bride might not have terminated affairs she had been having prior to their wedding. There had, apparently, been some difficulty in this regard during the courtship, and Charles had made it very clear that it was to stop.

The other thing was the impending marriage of his son John, just turned twenty-one, to Ricki Brody, nineteen-year-old daughter of a prominent New York restaurateur. Remembering his own early mistake, Charles was dead set against it. "He was horrified that a man his age would get married," Irving Botwin says. "He felt that his son should complete school and come into the business as a man who is able to take care of his wife. And he wasn't wrong, because otherwise he's throwing himself at the father and saying, 'Here, we're married. Take care of her.' This is a lack of manliness."

John, however, had become quite used to getting what he wanted. So, apparently, had Lyn. While preparations were being made for the Brody-Revson wedding at the Plaza, Charles was working with George Beck to satisfy his suspicions. If he was suspicious by nature, in this case at least it was not without cause. At one point he arranged to be out of town solely for the purpose of leaving his wife to her own devices. It became clear to him that Lyn was still seeing two men—one, a matzoh monarch-by-marriage; the other, since deceased, head of a leading rent-a-car company. (It goes without saying that had he been cheating on *Lyn*, that would simply have been the male prerogative.)

It was touch-and-go for a while as to whether the fledgling marriage would come to an abrupt halt. Either way, Charles's pride had to suffer. It was handled this way: Lyn was given, in the words of one insider, "some very heavy papers" to sign as a supplement/amendment to the prenuptial agreement they had already drawn up. In these, allegedly, Lyn abrogated all rights to Charles's estate. There was even a termination clause, as one might find in an employment contract. Moreover, Lyn was moved out of the Revson suite at the Pierre and into one of her own at the Stanhope. She was on probation, in a sort of purgatory. It was like dating all over again. Charles would send the car for her in the evening, take her home at night, and spend weekends with her up at Premium Point. (The cover story was that the Pierre was simply too small for everyone.) He would even take back her jewelry at the end of each evening.

Meanwhile, John was getting married at the Plaza. Charles arrived late to the wedding, as he was late to everything. John, typically, was later still. "The tailor delivered my tails late," he explains. But what is forty-five minutes when you have a lifetime ahead of you? The tragedy was that the young Mrs. Revson did not. She and John were divorced five years later. Then, in April 1972, aged twenty-seven, she was found dead in her bathtub, an apparent suicide. During their years together, despite such savvy investments as a chunk of the musical *Hair* (with his mother and stepfather, John owned 20 percent, an investment which has to date multiplied forty-odd times over), John managed to go through much of his wife's substantial wealth. Like his father, he was always a big spender—Ancky thinks he went through $2 million in one year—but he lacked the personal fortune to back it up. Charles wound up bailing John out to the tune of several hundreds of thousands—at least. The marriage had turned out to be even worse than he had feared; in *this* case he took no pleasure in having been proved right. Jill, his granddaughter by this marriage, became the single most important person in the last years of his life. He was able to lavish on her the kind of pure love he had never been able to offer anyone else.

John was also late to his second wedding. This marriage, to Alexis Turpin, ended in divorce as well. Charles was not late, because, in John's words, "nobody invited him." The only people present were the judge, John, Jill, Charles, Jr., Alexis, and her maid of honor. Charles was invited to the Harmony Club reception about a week later, arriving about midway through the affair. "When Dad walked in," Charles, Jr., says, "the place got very quiet. He just walked in and sat down, but you could see that his presence had a strange effect on the people there."

Oddly, while John's marriages were crumbling in direct testimony to the difficulty of growing up Charles Revson's son, Charles and Lyn were managing to make a go of it, after all. They became, in fact, quite the loving couple. "I think he was really devoted to her," Suzanne Grayson says, echoed by others. "The only time I ever saw him soft in any kind of personal relationship was with her." He would be at his most bilious, lambasting an executive . . . his gold phone would ring—as it did a dozen times each day—and he would switch instantly to a tender, "*Yes*, my darling. Where are you *now*, my darling?

276

Of *course*, my darling." Without missing a beat, he would then return to the man's jugular. It had never been that way with Ancky. Time had turned the tables on him. He had never taken Ancky with him on business trips; he would never leave Lyn behind. His possessiveness came most openly into view at public affairs when the uninitiated would occasionally, and in all innocence, ask Lyn to dance. "Nobody dances with my wife other than myself," he would say icily for all to hear.

For her part, Lyn became "very attentive—maybe even too attentive," to Charles. When they traveled, her friend Jerry Zipkin says, she would do everything—"his pills, his arrangements, she would order his proper breakfast, sit right there as it was brought in to make sure it was right (because it was a very complicated breakfast) —she was unbelievable."

When it came to the larger matters, such as Lyn's wardrobe, Charles was in charge. "He ran the house, he ran the yacht, he ordered the meals, he decorated the apartment. Lyn very wisely stayed out of it," Zipkin explains, "because then he wouldn't have anything to criticize. He treated her more like one of his executives than his wife."

His first order of business was to make Lyn over. Out went the high heels, the wad of chewing gum (it's back now), and the heavy makeup. He took Lyn to *his* tailor for her slacks, to get them just right. Very man-tailored, very simple. Norell would send his latest offerings up to the office and Charles would choose Lyn's wardrobe. The "look" he gave her was austere. Always a high neckline. "She has the most beautiful bosom in the world," Kay Daly confided, "and it was never again seen after she married Charles."

(When Ancky had once had her portrait done, Revson called the artist back to raise the V of her neckline. Caesar's wife must be beyond reproach.)

Lyn had loads of life and vitality. Charles toned her down and took some of the life out of her. She became somewhat hostile and bitchy, people said. She was not beloved by the crew of the *Ultima II*. She did, however, become a great hit with the press. About a year after they were married, the Revsons went on what was, in effect, a national publicity tour.

Before Lyn's first interview, Charles kept coming in to ask, "Sweetie, are you nervous?" "I'd be a lot less nervous if you went away," she said. And the next day, where he got just a couple of paragraphs buried in the business section of the paper, there was a half page of Lyn on the women's page with quotes and pictures. It happened that way all over, and it was great for Revlon.

"I'm not sunburned," she told *Women's Wear* in a full-page interview a couple of years before Charles left her, "it's makeup. People are always stopping me to ask where I got my tan. But, actually, it's the result of at least six different transparent makeup products. As a matter of fact, Charles and I have this running battle about my getting sunburned. I love sitting on the sundeck of our yacht when it is parked in the Mediterranean and just soaking up the sun. I often have to arrange to wake up earlier than Charles to do this, because if he catches me, he begins to lecture me on the dangers." She admits that on their last trip he really got through to her. "There was a cool breeze one day and I wasn't really aware of how much sun I was getting. The next day my eyes and lips were swollen. Charles didn't say a word. He knew I had learned my lesson, and now I am more careful."

Charles taught Lyn to blend her makeup. "Now," she says, "people don't even think I wear any. Actually, my makeup list is a yard long."

His feeling about makeup was—ironically—that most women use too much. Older women try to cover their wrinkles and wind up looking terrible. He bemoaned the problems he had trying to get his mother-in-law to use less.

To achieve her natural look, Lyn merely scrubbed with Ultima II Skim Milk Liquid Facial Soap followed by Ultima II Astringent Toner followed by Etherea B.C.O. Face Oil followed by Ultima II Transparent Bronzing Tint, Ultima II Blushing Creme (in deep Sienna), and Ultima II Color Gel Stick in Bronzelit Copper to tint the chin, cheeks, and forehead. She listed twenty other Revlon products for the eyes, lips, scent, sun, and bath. *Women's Wear* faithfully recorded each one.

Charles, meanwhile, admitted to using Natural Wonder Clean-Up Lotion in the morning before his Remington Electric shave, and to deodorizing with Revlon's Mitchum Spray. ("Hi," says the Mitchum man woken up by the TV lights and camera crew in his bedroom, frankly: "I didn't use my antiperspirant yesterday, and I may not use it today . . ." Three-fifty a can.) Also: Braggi cologne, Bill Blass soap, and, nightly for ten years, Eterna 27.

Lyn went on to tell her interviewer how, when she finished making up, Charles would come over to her and pat her forehead and cheeks with a Kleenex. "It is his way of telling me, 'Now you look perfect,'" she said. "On the other hand, when I tell him I like his hair when it is longer, he gets a haircut. And that's his way of telling me that he is the authority."

"But," said Lyn, "he knows that I appreciate everything I have and that nothing would mean anything without my husband. For instance, I have this thing about bathing and perfume. I can take as many as three baths a day, and I use practically a bottle of bath oil a day. And I love perfume. I spray Ultima when I feel sexy and Norell when I feel elegant . . . Sometimes he watches me using the bath oil and the perfume, and he smiles and says, 'You know, it's a good thing I'm in the business.'"

It was probably most fun being Mrs. Charles Revson aboard the *Ultima II.* There were the cowboy movies under the stars . . . the Christmases in Acapulco . . . the excitement of not knowing where you would be going from one day to the next (in later years, Charles took to telling the captain only the night before which port to steam for—which meant frantic middle-of-the-night calls to groggy harbor masters, but gave him more of a feeling of control) . . . the crew lining up on deck, in uniform, with foghorn sounding, whenever the Revsons arrived or left for a cruise . . . the hot Mediterranean breezes, freezing staterooms, and warm-as-toast electric blankets . . . the fabulous service and unmatched cuisine . . . the Bingo and backgammon . . . the special television hookups for prizefights and presidential addresses (Charles was more interested in whether Nixon speeches would "sell" than in whether they were honest) . . . and, of course, the parties. Dinner guests aboard the yacht included the likes of Alec Guinness, Princess Grace and Prince Ranier, and the former president of Mexico. One party in Capri attracted such names as Faye Dunaway, the Earl of Litchfield, Valentino, Count and Countess Bismarck, Merle Oberon and Bruno Paglieri, and the Cornelius Vanderbilt Whitneys. Charles, et al, would sometimes dock at a port, go ashore and round up all the friends they met for a dinner that evening, radioing instructions back to the yacht on the walkie-talkie they always carried ashore.

How had he suddenly become so popular—and so *social?* Any suggestion that Earl Blackwell, owner of Celebrity Register, and gossip columnists Eugenia Sheppard and Aileen Mehle (Suzy Knickerbocker) were on the payroll for this purpose is outrageous. But they were regular guests on the yacht (flown to and fro) and good friends and so very helpful. Aileen Mehle was named Revlon's first female board member, at an annual compensation of $6,500, in 1972. Also, by happy coincidence, her column began appearing in the *Daily News* right around the time Revlon began advertising in that unlikely publication for the first time, to the tune of $50,000 or $100,000 a year.

Anyway, the Revsons began appearing in the columns with some regularity. And what people Earl and Eugenia and Aileen couldn't introduce them to, Jerry Zipkin ("The Duke and Duchess of Windsor are very good friends of mine") and Dennis and Ann Slater, always in the columns themselves, could. (Mrs. Slater *was* on the payroll for a while, "consultant to the chairman," arranging private luncheons with twelve or fourteen society ladies at a time—Ann Ford, Mary Lou Whitney . . .)

Eat your heart out, Estée Lauder: the Revsons had become international socialites, too . . . with a little help from their friends. At one costume gala in Venice (Charles wore a plain dinner jacket), Estée Lauder only barely made it in. Earl Blackwell had arranged the affair, which the London *Times* called the "ball of the century," for the flood relief of Venice. The *Ultima II* and Onassis's yacht were among the many anchored in the Grand Canal. Blackwell, staying aboard the Revson yacht, naturally had not invited his host's archenemy, Ms. Lauder. So, according to Zipkin she went to Paris, hired a press agent, and, with her husband, went in with him as "press." "I happened to be right there when they arrived," Zipkin says. "She made a sweeping good entrance off the barge, or whatever she came on . . . I can see her holding her husband's hand and the flashbulbs popping as they swept up the stairs . . . and Earl Blackwell fainted dead away." Charles arrived shortly thereafter. "It may fascinate you to know," Zipkin told him, "that just five minutes ago Estée Lauder made a sweeping entrance." Charles had a fit. Whenever their paths crossed, he always got very uptight, very panicked. He could manage, at best, a curt bow.

Revson's noncosmetic rival was William Levitt, the home builder. Levitt's yacht was a few feet shorter than Revson's and less well constructed, but it had a pool. And the Levitts could dive from their stateroom right into the ocean. Somehow a rivalry developed between these two not entirely dissimilar men. Perhaps Charles was irked simply because people did see it as a rivalry. At any rate Earl Blackwell, having transformed Charles from a social hermit into an international jet-setter, began taking on much the same assignment for Levitt. And naturally, many of Blackwell's friends followed him.

Not so! says Blackwell who finds the whole Revson/Levitt rivalry idea both fictitious and offensive. What happened, simply, was that one August 1st in Monaco, the day Charles and Lyn flew in to begin their summer cruise, the Levitt yacht was docked next door and the Levitts were giving a party. They sent over a nice note asking the Revsons to come, Blackwell says, but Charles, being tired from the flight, declined. (Eugenia Sheppard says he declined because he didn't like Levitt.) The revelers aboard Levitt's *Belle Simone* that night saw Charles, Lyn, and the doctor sitting alone, silhouetted in the moonlight, having dinner out on the deck. It might

281

have been less awkward, Blackwell admits, if they had had dinner inside that night.

Back in dreary old Manhattan, they would often have dinner in bed watching TV. *The Sonny and Cher Comedy Hour* was a favorite, not least because Revlon sponsored it. Lyn, however, preferred to go out. Sunday nights there was often an argument because Charles wanted to get something over at the Sixth Avenue Deli, while Lyn had in mind Elaine's or Pearl's. Charles had a low tolerance for New York social life. If it was for the business, it was one thing; but a lot of small talk at Elaine's . . .

He preferred to dine at home with a business-related guest. It seemed to one such guest, whom Charles was trying to hire, that at least eight people were waiting on them. The only thing he found offensive about the Revson library/dining room, he says, was "a really awful portrait of Charles staring down from over the fireplace." Over dinner, there was little discussion of the job he was being offered, much discussion between Charles and Lyn as to the crispness of the french fries—was it sufficient? After dinner they spent two or three hours showing him the apartment, "a symphony in beige." The foyer, he thought, looked like the lobby of the Squibb Building. Charles made a point of the fact that the ceiling in their bedroom was genuine gold leaf. As they left one room and walked into another, Charles would grab hold of Lyn and kiss her. In all, the evening went on until three A.M.

Saturday was the ritual silent movie at Premium Point. Silent, because nobody talked to anybody. Two features would be shown, with one in reserve in case Charles decided (unilaterally) to kill one in midrun. He wanted a good action plot, but he also watched with an eye for the appearance of the actors and actresses; the styles, clothes, houses, cars . . . At the end of one movie he turned to Irving Bottner and said: "If I were going to make an acquisition, it would be in sunglasses. From now on women are going to walk around in slacks, fur coats, flowing hair and sunglasses." According to a fashion maven who recalled the incident, his timing was perfect.

Sometimes Charles was amorous with his wife; other times, aggravated. There was a Sunday meeting up at Premium Point in the midst of a small blizzard. Lyn was quietly needlepointing in another room when Charles called her in and asked her to have the garage come put snow tires on the car. He wanted to be sure he could get in to work the next morning. She reported that the garage was closed—the men hadn't been able to make it in on account of the snow. Charles was annoyed. Paul Woolard asked whether the tires were on rims—if they were, he said, they could change them for him. Charles looked at Lyn, who asked, "What does that mean?" He got more annoyed and said something about women not knowing anything. He put her down in front of everyone. She turned around and walked out. Charles went back to his meeting. He was facing away from the window, but others could see Lyn with her coat on, trudging through the snow to the garage. A few minutes later, they saw her rolling a tire from the garage across the snow and slush, picking up all sorts of dirt along the way. She rolls it on into the house, across a very light carpet, and right into the meeting. Charles looks up and there's this ugly tire. Lyn does the dumb-blonde routine: "Does this tire have a rim on it, Charles?" He says: "Why the hell did you bring it into the house?" She says: "Well, I didn't know, and you were so angry I thought I should show it to you." She knew—or even if she didn't, this was her way of getting even with him. She walked away while he carried on for another ten minutes about how dumb women are. Then he let it drop. But the tire sat there through the rest of the meeting, annoying him, and not much was accomplished. Lyn and Charles, in other words, were not entirely without their moments.

Mildred Custin, former president of Bonwit Teller, is one of many who thought that all in all it was "a lovely marriage." "He treated her like a child," she says. "He babied her. He always wanted her to be happy and cheerful." When he was first romancing her and they had had a little spat, he went out to Cartier and bought what might easily have been a hundred grand in

283

gems. When he returned to their suite at the George V, in Paris, Lyn asked where he'd been. He said he'd been out working on some business. Then he said, "Here—I found a little candy store and bought you some candy." And he tossed her the jewels, which he had put in a little brown paper bag. She dumped them out on the bed —flabbergasted.

Later, Lyn became mad about a certain kind of little English terrier. Cables were going back and forth across the Atlantic to a Revlon International vice president. When he found just the right puppy, he was instructed to take it on board the plane with him in first class ("Don't put it in the hold; slip it under your arm"). And when he arrived in New York, Bill White, Charles's chauffeur (formerly Eleanor Roosevelt's; and jazz artist Josh White's brother), was at the airport with the Rolls to pick him up—the only time he had ever been so met.

Eight years into their marriage, Charles celebrated his sixty-fifth birthday in Las Vegas with Lyn, Eugenia Sheppard, and one other couple. As they were driving in from the airport he reached into his briefcase and took out—yes, another paper bag. "Here's something I forgot to give you," he said over his shoulder, from the front seat. He tossed it into her lap and Lyn pulled out a beautiful aquamarine and amethyst necklace.

But there was no telling with this man . . . you never knew what he was thinking. At their tenth anniversary party he presented her with a tin can containing a check for $30,000, plus five little Van Cleef & Arpels bracelets she had always wanted—and began divorce proceedings two days later. Eugenia Sheppard attended the intimate Saturday night affair up at Premium Point. She says that as well as she knew the Revsons, she couldn't detect anything amiss. In fact, when she presented the anniversary gift she had brought—an apple pie with an *Ultima II* replica frosting and "May Your Next Ten Years Be Apple Pie" written across the top—Charles was delighted. "He said, 'We must get a camera and photograph it—this is the most thoughtful gift we've had,' " Eugenia says. "Little did I think that would be the last time I would be in that house."

Yet Charles had been planning to leave Lyn for about a year, Irving Botwin says. ("When he told me, I was so surprised I dropped my cigarette on the floor.") Things had kept happening to delay him. There was his son's divorce, for example. He didn't want both to be going through divorce proceedings at the same time. It wouldn't look good.

He had gradually gotten fed up. "She was bugging him," Irving explains; "he didn't want to get dragged into her hysterics." And he was tired of being dragged to one affair after another. One executive overheard Charles's end of a phone conversation not long before he left her. They were having quite an argument, the gist of which was that she wanted him to go to a party with her that night, but he had already invited some of his marketing people over to the apartment for dinner and a meeting. He was telling her to go to the party herself, if she wanted to, because he was going to be busy all evening. She apparently didn't understand, because he then said, "Look, I've got *business* to do." And then it escalated to, "Look, I didn't want to go to France but I did what you wanted [they had just gone over for the Norton Simon/Max Factor gala, which he had managed to turn to Revlon's advantage] and I'm getting *tired* of this kind of thing." He sounded beleaguered, as though he were not winning. That evening, he had his meeting and she went to the party herself. About a month later, he left her.

He must have known at the time of his tenth anniversary party that he would have Judge Rifkind call Lyn the following Monday to break the news. (He never fired anyone himself.) But there was not even a hint of trouble at the party. The story goes that as he left for work that Monday morning he told the butler, "Take good care of Mrs. Revson today—she'll need it." Lyn told Eugenia Sheppard that he was wearing the tie she had given him for Valentine's day.

Like all his decisions, this one had been mulled and mulled. ("Charles would fire you in his mind a year before anyone else knew it," Mandel had said.) According to Botwin, by this time one of his closest confidants, he had decided to change his life-style and gradually withdraw from the business, spending more and more time on his yacht, dating beautiful women, having last flings. The tenth anniversary timing may have been revenge, retribution for the embarrassment she had caused him some ten years before—the kind of grudge it was by no means beyond him to bear. Or it may have been out of considerateness—waiting until after the event so as not to embarrass her and as if to say: "There. We've had a good ten years, all in all, but now it's time to end it." Or it may simply have been that the occasion itself triggered a final decision.

Whatever it was, he left Lyn to break the news as she wished. She waited a full three weeks to do so. When she finally did talk to friends, after the news had been leaked in Earl Wilson's column, she said she could offer no explanation for his leaving her, that it had come as a total surprise.

There may have been other reasons for Charles's unexpected action. Eugenia Sheppard admits Lyn may not have told her the whole truth about the divorce—"Her pride was at stake." But she is quite certain that the rumor of Lyn's having had another affair was untrue. "I'm sure of that. Lyn would not be that foolish. And whatever you say, she was really devoted to Charles in her own way."

After the breakup, friends of the couple had pretty well to join one camp or the other. Jack and Lorraine Friedman joined Charles's camp. "From the morning he left her," Mrs. Friedman says, "Jack and I were the only two people who knew about it for three weeks. And from that morning on I started calling her right away and she never answered the phone to me. I wrote her a note which I swear to you was the most beautiful note I've ever written in my life. I sat down and I cried over it. She never answered that. None of that bothered me until it was announced publicly and she told everybody, all our friends and everybody, that I had dropped her like a hot potato when Charles walked out on her. She said I had never tried to call her or do anything."

Supposedly, the prenuptial agreement, or its amendment, called for a settlement of $1 million on severance, but Charles gave her, according to John, "a lot more than she deserved on the basis of her prenuptial agreement" but "much less than $5 million." The most reliable rumor places Lyn's settlement at $2 million. One provision in the divorce agreement was that Lyn could not speak with anyone from the press about her marriage, nor write anything herself. To assure this, her settlement is paid out over a period of time. (She is, however, talking about doing a book on beauty and cosmetics.)

(XX)

Last Rites

Was he a good man or a bad man? He was both. He
was a very strange man.
                    —Sy Wassyng,
                        former Revlon package designer

The man from the temple had arrived promptly for
his appointment with Charles Revson, which meant that
he could have a long wait. He was sitting in Revson's
office with Irving Botwin.

"Revson always had me sit with people," Botwin
explains, "because he was always an hour late for any
meeting. Rather than have someone sit in the office all
by himself, he'd say, 'Irving, sit with the guy; I'll join
you shortly.'"

The man Irving was sitting with had come on behalf
of Temple Emanu-El, of which Revson was an inactive
member, to solicit money for a building fund. He was
new to this, Irving recalls his saying, had never approached

288

anyone for a contribution before . . . but, being a C.P.A. and active in the temple, they had made him chairman of the drive. He was understandably nervous about meeting Revson, and wanted to know what he was like.

"He's not going to bite you," said Irving. "The worst that can happen is that he says no."

Charles comes in, Irving introduces them, and Revson says, "I suppose you're here on behalf of the temple?" The man says, "Yes, we have a drive on for the building fund." Revson says, "I'm in between meetings and I know you're busy and I don't want to waste your time and you probably want to get home to your dinner . . ." It was by now around six-thirty. ". . . Irving, give him twenty-five thousand dollars." And he shook the man's hand and walked out.

"The guy started to tremble," says Irving. "He probably would have been happy to get two thousand. I started to walk him back to the elevator and I could see he couldn't put his coat on; he couldn't find the sleeves. He said: "That's the most remarkable guy I've ever met in my life."

The man from the temple, Alfred Bachrach, remembers the incident a little differently, though with much the same result. He wasn't chairman of the building drive, he was president of the temple. He wasn't new to the fund-raising business, he had already received $25,000 and $50,000 donations from several prime donors. It's true he was a bit leery of his meeting with Revson, but as no one on the fund-raising committee had really known him, it fell to Bachrach to make the approach. Charles came in, Bachrach described the new school the temple was trying to build. Charles said he was interested in the temple even though he wasn't able to attend as often as he would have liked, and asked what "they" were giving, meaning the other prominent members. They were giving $25,000 or $50,000, Bachrach said, using some names he'd been given permission to use, and Charles generously offered $25,000, the amount for which a classroom would be named in his honor. Appreciative as he was, it is unlikely that Bachrach trembled unduly.

289

But the essence of the story—Charles's generosity—holds. Over the years he gave many millions of dollars to Jewish, medical, and educational causes. Roughly fifty million more—half his estate—was placed in a charitable foundation upon his death.

The block-long "Revson Plaza" that spans Amsterdam Avenue and connects Columbia Law School with the rest of the campus was his $1-million-plus gift, as was the $750,000 black marble computerized (to compensate for shifts in the wind) fountain at Lincoln Center: "Estée Lauder builds a little park on Sixty-sixth Street," sniffs a senior Revlon marketing man, "and she makes a big deal about it. All the rich people in the world live there —they don't need a park. They need it in Harlem. But she built it there because that's where she'd get some publicity. And here Charles gives three-quarters of a million dollars for a fountain at Lincoln Center, which everybody can enjoy—and nobody knows about it." (Except that it isn't in Harlem, either, and the inscription, cut across four feet of black marble, reads: FROM THE CHARLES H. REVSON FOUNDATION IN HONOR OF CHARLES H. REVSON.)

Many of his most touching gifts—$1,000 to the Cuban refugee brother of a manicurist at The House of Revlon, for example—were purely spontaneous, in no way publicized and, for that matter, not even tax deductible.

Like most donors, Charles was both embarrassed by, and eager for, recognition of his generosity. Those who spoke of his "buying his way into heaven" were simply unfair. If he was no more purely altruistic than the next guy, he was also no less. He believed, as he stated often, that "we who take have got to give." He felt particularly strongly about supporting the state of Israel. Why should he build a factory there when it looked as though it would be more economical to ship goods in from other markets? "Because we're Jews, that's why," he told his financial vice president. He was not one for prayers, and he knew little of the history of his people—but he knew who his people were.

And now, August 26, 1975, after a year-long struggle

with pancreatic cancer,* he was being credited by the rabbi at Temple Emanu-El with having been "a giant" among those people. Nearly a thousand of them—many current and former employees—had come to his funeral. ("I wouldn't have missed this one for the world," said Bill Mandel on the way in.) And when former judge Simon Rifkind, who delivered the eulogy, characterized Charles's unbending perfectionism as having been "both his greatest strength and his greatest failing," nearly a thousand heads nodded imperceptibly.

Lyn's among them. She had arrived at the temple in a white, low-cut dress, her hair disheveled—looking exactly as her former husband would not have wanted her to look. No seat had been reserved for her. Unlike Ancky, she was not considered a member of the immediate family.

In other respects, everything was just as Charles would have wished. Quietly impressive. (Well, he would have had something to say about the lack of air conditioning, numerous of those assembled remarked, but other than that . . .) The casket was smothered in red carnations. At Ferncliffe, the nonsectarian cemetery where he was laid to rest beside his parents and his brother Joseph, each of the 150 onlookers was given a red carnation to place on the casket upon leaving, by way of farewell. Charles had arranged the same farewell for the Major years before, only with white carnations.

It was widely assumed that Charles had divorced Lyn (and hired Bergerac) only after he had learned of his terminal illness, thereby to assure that she would be cut out of the estate. This was not the case. He may have sensed that he was entering the last phase of his life, but he did not know how short that phase would prove to be. "He wasn't sick at all when he divorced Lyn," Dr. Steiner states flatly.

By his sixty-eighth birthday, however—October 11,

* An unusual variety of cancer—of which, through some morbid coincidence, Kay Daly passed away just months after her former boss.

1974—he had already been in the hospital for an operation on "an obstructive jaundice due to a gallstone"—they thought he had hepatitis at first—and he knew he would soon be going back for more treatment. The ritual surprise party held for him in the office each year thus took on a special significance. "All his birthday parties were moving," Paul Woolard, head of Revlon domestic, reflects, "because he had an ambivalent attitude toward them. He didn't want anything to be done, yet I think he really was touched that his people would remember him and respect him and thank him."

Before this last party, Woolard acted as decoy while everyone gathered in the executive dining room. Charles was trying on a new fedora—he loved hats—with a broad band and a snap-down brim. "He kept trying it on and asking me how I liked it," says Woolard, "and he looked good. He always looked good." Meanwhile, Revson's secretary kept coming in with messages for Woolard about the people who were gathering. When everyone had assembled, Woolard told him he had a very private matter to discuss with him—would he mind coming into the next room? "You shit," said Revson, "you did it—didn't you?" Woolard played dumb, but the jig was up. So they went into the adjoining dining room amidst the applause of everyone from Mickey Soroko to John and Charles Revson, Jr. (but not a woman in the crowd).

There was champagne and low-cholesterol cake, and some gag telegrams the advertising people had come up with, as well as a handsome oriental chest for which they had all chipped in. Charles began to say something, but his voice was quivering. "I didn't think I was going to make it this year," he started to say—and he began to cry. He actually began to cry. He quickly left the room. Woolard started to say something—and he too choked up. "Well, that proves he's human," someone said, to break the uncomfortable silence. Once Charles had regained control, he returned to the room and said something about it's having been a tough year, but that he was feeling better and was looking forward to more parties like this one. Then they had lunch and got back to business.

"It was very touching," says Charles, Jr. "Although people respected and feared him, they could feel sympatico towards him. The telegrams and the gift were not what choked him up, because he'd seen this for thirty-five years. It was his having just had the operation, and the fact that he would never hold the same position in the company that he had had. Bergerac would be coming in, and it was going to be a new era for him."

It was the beginning of the end of what had been a lifelong, all-consuming love affair. But it was also a measure of his remarkable self-discipline and clear thinking that he *had* decided to begin a process of orderly succession. Other founder/chief-executives run their companies halfway into senility and halfway into the ground rather than relinquish the reins to an able successor—Elizabeth Arden was a case in point.

In Revson's judgment, no one man within the company stood out sufficiently to be certain of commanding unquestioned respect and unchallenged authority. With Mandel's departure, Paul Woolard had become the frontrunner. Victor Barnett had high hopes, as well. But talented as Woolard was, efficient as Barnett was, Revson shrewdly decided to go after a man head and shoulders above the rest.

He hadn't been much interested in his first three presidents. Indeed, when the board of directors chose Revlon's first, George Murphy, they did so knowing he would never last. It was, in one director's words, just a way to get Charles used to the idea of having someone between himself and the rest of the company. But now that *he* wanted Revlon to have a president—a post that had been vacant for five years—he wanted the best that money could buy. After considering a number of possibilities, including John Delorean, the General Motors maverick, he decided on Michel Bergerac.

Bergerac was then head of ITT/Europe, with $5 billion in sales. His brother, Jacques, had been known primarily as Ginger Rogers' handsome husband until, at the age of forty, he met Charles Revson at a party on Earl Blackwell's terrace and decided to give up his mediocre career in grade-B movies (*Les Girls, Gigi, Taffy and the Jungle Hunter*) for a role in the cosmetics business. He spent a year learning the business behind the cosmetic counters at Abraham & Straus and Bambergers, in training classes, and at the lab, and soon after rose to head Revlon/France. Supposedly, the negotiations between Revson and his brother Michel were kept so secret that Jacques learned of them only when the deal was announced.

To initiate contact, Charles had called Bergerac at ITT/Europe headquarters in Brussels. "This is Charles Revson," he said. "I guess you know who I am." Of course. "I understand that you come to New York once a month, and I wonder whether you could have dinner with me on your next trip." Certainly.

After a dinner at the Revson apartment during which nothing of substance was discussed, Charles asked Bergerac if he could guess why he had been asked to come. Bergerac, model of the efficient, well-organized, modern global executive, answered that it would be one of three things: "You could be having trouble with one of your companies in Europe and need my assistance, which I would naturally be delighted to give; you could be interested in selling your company for estate purposes; or you could want to hire me." Charles was so incensed at the idea that he might want to sell Revlon that he flew into a (controlled) rage. "This company will never be sold out to anyone! *No* one is going to take over Revlon, now or ever." And so on. It was only after he had established that point beyond any conceivable doubt that he returned to the third of Bergerac's alternatives. Yes, he wanted Bergerac to become president of Revlon.

"It was an interesting romance," Bergerac admits, and it led to one of the most remarkable compensation packages in corporate American history. (And presaged, some believe, more such big-money deals for corporate heads in the future.) The $1.5 million bonus he received just for signing won him the sobriquet "Catfish" Bergerac, after pitcher millionaire Catfish Hunter. And a key point in the deal, leaked to the press so that Revlon's veterans would know where their bread would in future be buttered, was that Bergerac would become chief executive officer of the company within one year—failing which he could quit and receive his full five years' pay (at $325,000 a year). The signal was very clear: this was not just another president for Charles to practice on. This was the future of Revlon.

A result of Bergerac's leadership skill, and of some enormous financial incentives, was that none of Revlon's veterans left the company. Not even Woolard, despite his disappointment. (Barnett was soon moved into a staff position, where his dedication and acumen could be put to good use, but where he would be less apt to antagonize his colleagues. This move alone was enough to win Bergerac considerable loyalty among the other veterans. Shortly thereafter, he resigned.)

Revlon won't fall apart without Revson, in part because of Bergerac, but also because—despite all the turnover—he built an organization with depth. He reproduced himself. It wasn't always the most pleasant training, but it pervades the entire cosmetics industry. When Suzanne Grayson, who left Revlon to build her own company, examines a product, her question is always: "Would Charles approve this?" As one observer put it, he carved his initials into everyone he ever worked with.

Little more than a month after leaving Lyn, in March 1974, and a few weeks before going into the hospital for his gallstone operation, Charles was aboard the *Ultima II*, cruising in the Caribbean. (Martin had disembarked in Nassau a day or two earlier.) On one of his innumerable routine calls to the office, he received the chilling word that hours later would be blasted across the front page of the *Daily News:* PLAYBOY RACER KILLED IN CRASH. Peter Revson, thirty-five years old, had been making a test run in preparation for the South African Grand Prix when his racer crashed into a iron railing and burst into flames. The *News* credited "the handsome, dark-haired Revson" with having had "money [self-made], style, and the adulation of beautiful women all over the world. His well-publicized liaisons," they said, "sometimes overshadowed his record as the best road racing

295

driver in America and one of the best in the world." His last "liaison" had been with twenty-year-old Marjorie Wallace, the first American ever to have been crowned Miss World—who then had to relinquish the title because of unfavorable publicity over their affair.

Peter's parents and uncle had never approved of his career, opposing it most vehemently after his younger brother, Douglas, also a race-car driver, died in a crash in Denmark in 1967. Whatever strain Peter's career must have placed on his father, his uncle dealt with it by adopting a sort of fatalistic attitude. When Lyn called to tell him that Peter, racing in 1971 at Indianapolis, had hit the wall and was being rushed to the hospital (unscathed as it turned out, but Charles didn't know that), he turned to the men he was meeting with, told them what had happened and, although visibly upset, said simply: "You're in that business, you take that chance."

Now Peter had been killed, and his uncle, tears in his eyes, flew up to New York for the funeral.

As children, Peter, Doug, Johnny, and Boochie had all grown up together. Peter saw his uncle fairly often. Later, their contact was very limited. Peter was one Revson who never worked for Revlon. Indeed, he lent his name to Yardley, a competitor. But they were close in spirit. The Revson toughness, pride, and drive for excellence was every bit as clear in Peter as it was in Charles and Martin. In an autobiography he coauthored shortly before his death, Peter sounded much like an articulate version of Charles Revson himself*: "The ability to concentrate is the most important thing you can have . . ." "From turn to turn around a race course you are dealing with perfection . . ." "Understand this: Losing really hurts. To fail in the race is the most painful thing imaginable."

His own two sons were alive and well, fortunately, but had faced the awesome challenge of growing up just that —his sons—and, for that matter, in Peter Revson's

*Speed With Style, The Autobiography of Peter Revson (Doubleday, 1974).

shadow. John was basically his father's son; Charles, Jr., his mother's. Where Charles, Jr., is punctual and returns phone calls, John is notoriously late and unreliable. Where Charles, Jr. (like neither parent), might convert a first-class ticket to coach and pocket the difference, John would never dream of flying anything but first class. John went to school where his father wanted him to, Brandeis ("That's where I could get in," he admits—his father's millions helped); Charles, Jr., refused his father's help or advice and chose Penn. But John—like his father, who never went at all, and his cousin Peter, who tried three —never graduated from college. Charles, Jr., did. John is outgoing and a great womanizer; his brother is more reserved. John is short and lean; Charles, Jr., taller and heftier.

Charles, Jr., does have *some* of his father's characteristics. I could see him staring in amazement at my brown shoes (scuffed at that), wondering how someone otherwise presentable could be so gauche and he had the captain move us to what was apparently "a better table." But he is much easier going than his father was or his brother is. At least this much can be said for John: once you *do* manage to get him on the phone, you get straight answers. If, as his father was, he is no diplomat, neither does he mince words or "beat around the rosary bush." And if he does not have all of his father's shrewdness and drive, he does have some of it.

Demanding as much from his sons as from his other executives—or more—Charles, much as he loved them, was not satisfied. Charles, Jr., was responsible but he just didn't seem to grasp the overwhelming, all-consuming importance of the business. John had the spark—but not the same sense of responsibility. "I saw John and his father get on the elevator one day four or five years ago, when John was between wives and living at home." says a former colleague, "and it's a long ride up forty-nine flights. John looked bad. He always looked like he'd been out all night. His hair was always a mess . . . Charles is in one corner of the elevator and John is at the opposite end, and I'm in there with about seven other people. 'What time did you get in last night?' Charles asks him in that whine of his. 'About three-thirty,' John says. 'Goddamn it, I was down in your room at twelve and you weren't there, and at one, looking for you—I had some great ideas and you're not there. Where were you, the Hippopotamus with some broad? Three-fifty, four bucks a drink —what happens if you weren't a vice president? What if I made you a goddamned clerk—would that keep you home? Here I'm paying you whatever it is and when I come to talk to you, you're not home...'"

Most men derive satisfaction and a shot at immortality of sorts by leaving the world offspring. Whatever reservations Charles felt about his own (they were not perfect, so he felt reservations), he had Revlon to leave as a monument to his memory. In later years he had, increasingly—and under the guise of its having been necessary for business—become more and more to Revlon what Colonel Sanders is to Kentucky Fried Chicken. A constant struggle went on within him between his shyness (insecurities) and his ego, with the latter winning more and more of the battles as he got older. He had always resented the fact that his company was not called Charles Revson, the way Arden was Arden; Factor, Factor; Rubinstein, Rubinstein; and Lauder, Lauder. But he couldn't come right out and *say* that—he wanted others to goad him into stardom for the good of the company. A woman who worked for Revlon first in the late fifties and then again in the early seventies noticed a huge change in Charles: his ego had inflated tremendously. She recalls a package designer presenting a new carton, with the product name in large type above CHARLES REVSON, smaller. Charles didn't like the package. The elements were not in balance, he said. The designer, who knew all about elements, begged to differ. Charles said the design looked top-heavy. The designer said he thought it was just right. Charles tried every way to say it without saying it: *screw the design; he wanted his name bigger*.

A few years earlier, Revlon had got a terrific write-up in *Women's Wear*—it was all "Revlon says this" and "Revlon is bringing out that"—a very positive piece—

and Charles called his PR man, Warren Leslie, livid. Furious. Why? "It should be personalized! I want it personalized!" Mandel had been trying to convey just the opposite image—that Revlon was an ongoing corporation, not a one-man show—so that Wall Street would have more confidence. But Charles wanted to be portrayed as the last word in fashion and marketing. Wall Street would keep buying the stock, he said, as long as they kept showing the earnings. And he was right.

And so it was that month by month the CHARLES REVSON grew into Charles Revson into *Charles Revson* into CHARLES REVSON, in ads and package designs. By the time of his death, there was a CHR line, a Charles Revson Inc., a wildly successful perfume called Charlie (which blossomed into a full cosmetics line), and a men's line that would be introduced called Chaz. No one will say whether Jontue, a fragrance that followed Charlie, was a coy bow in the direction of "John, too."

Probably not, but the question of John's future role in the company is often raised. And that, in turn, raises the question of Charles's will—a curious document. Neither John nor Charles was given a seat on the board of the Revson Foundation, into which half Revson's estate was placed. Nor were they given control over much of the other half, even though a good deal of it is being held in trust for them. Thus neither son has a significant block of Revlon stock to vote. Instead the foundation, as well as the various trusts set up in the will, are directed by Charles's executors, Harry Meresman and Simon Rifkind with Victor Barnett named as an alternate.

The executors receive $1 million to execute the estate —a far cry from the $15 a month Harry Meresman pulled down when Revson first put him on retainer. There is no love lost between the irrepressible, and at times irresponsible, John and Harry Meresman, who is professionalism personified (and who, when I saw him a few days before Christmas 1975, was wearing a plain black suit, black socks and shoes, a white shirt, and, for contrast, a solid black tie). Even Charles had begun to consider Harry a little "square" as he himself was exposed to the limelight, and so dropped him from his list of social regulars. But he trusted him implicitly, and presumably was depending on him to provide the kind of discipline he felt John lacked. (What discipline Meresman does not provide, the Securities and Exchange Commission might: Months after his father's death, John was charged by the S.E.C. with stock market manipulation in concert with, among others, ex-embezzler Eddie Gilbert.)

Others named in Charles's will were his stepchildren, Steven, Jeffrey and Susan Sheresky; his granddaughter, Jill; Katie Lowery, to whom he was always grateful for having in large measure brought up his children—and who, accordingly, will receive $10,000 a year tax-free for the rest of her life; and Irving Botwin, his friend and executive assistant, to whom he left $250,000 in cash.

Had he wanted to, with a mere 2 percent of his estate he could have bestowed $10,000 on each of 200 people toward whom he felt kindly, or by whom he particularly wished to be remembered—but that was not what he had in mind. There were not a great many people toward whom he felt special fondness, nor many whom he would admit had had a hand in his success. He had paid them well, and he would not stand for being taken advantage of in death any more than he would in life. So to his chauffeur of eighteen years, Bill White (who in the last year had had to be on call twenty-four hours a day, because Charles refused to go back and forth from his apartment to the hospital in an ambulance), and to the crew of his yacht and to his butler and servants and secretaries, and to Dr. Mac, *et al*—not a dime.

Beyond pointing out that Bill White had been on the corporate payroll all those years, not on Charles's personal staff, neither Irving Botwin—dumbfounded by his good fortune—nor Harry Meresman, who helped prepare the will, could offer any explanation or rationale for the seeming omissions. "You never knew what that man was thinking," Botwin says of his departed friend and benefactor.

Far from bringing on a rush of vituperative revelations, Charles's death elicited an outpouring of fond and respectful remembrances—some hypocritical, to be sure, but many genuine. One of the nicest came from Marlene Beck, George Beck's fourth wife. She had not been a key figure in his life, of course, but in a way her impression is all the more significant for that. "Charles was the most fantastic man I ever met," she told me quietly. "It's just sad he allowed so few people to know him. He expected you to understand the feelings he couldn't express, and if you didn't, that was just too bad. You never had to ask people whether he was in the office or not—you just knew from the electricity. Now people don't run any more. The urgency is gone."

So are the fear and chaos.

THE BEST OF BESTSELLERS
FROM WARNER BOOKS!